Kant's Aesthetic Theory

Continuum Studies in Philosophy
Series Editor: James Fieser, University of Tennessee at Martin, USA

Continuum Studies in Philosophy is a major monograph series from Continuum. The series features first-class scholarly research monographs across the whole field of philosophy. Each work makes a major contribution to the field of philosophical research.

Kant's Aesthetic Theory

The Beautiful and Agreeable

David Berger

continuum

Continuum International Publishing Group

The Tower Building   80 Maiden Lane
11 York Road   Suite 704
London SE1 7NX   New York NY 10038

www.continuumbooks.com

British Library Cataloguing-in-Publication Data
A catalogue record for this book is available from the British Library.

ISBN: HB: 978-0-8264-3580-4

Library of Congress Cataloging-in-Publication Data
Berger, David, 1974-
Kant's aesthetic theory : the beautiful and agreeable / David Berger.
    p. cm. – (Continuum studies in philosophy)
Includes bibliographical references and index.
ISBN: 978-0-8264-3580-4 (hb)
1. Kant, Immanuel, 1724-1804–Aesthetics. 2. Aesthetics, Modern–18th century.
I. Title. II. series.
B2799.A4B474 2009
111'.85092–dc22   2008048860

Typeset by Newgen Imaging Systems Pvt Ltd, Chennai, India
Printed in Great Britain by the MPG Books Group, Bodmin and King's Lynn

In Loving Memory of My Grandparents,

Sidney and Naomi Olshein

Contents

Preface and Acknowledgments

Kant's distinction between the beautiful and the agreeable may seem a rather narrow topic for a book-length study. Or perhaps not. After all, extreme specialization—some, myself included, would say overspecialization—abounds in contemporary philosophy and in the contemporary academy at large. All too familiar nowadays (whether intended or not) is a model of philosophy as a series of narrow, isolated intellectual inquiries, each interesting and accessible only to a small community of academic specialists. Kant scholarship is by no means immune to these destructive trends, even though the idea of a 'specialist' in one or another area of philosophy would have been utterly foreign, even bewildering, to Kant. Indeed, the critical philosophy is as striking a model of a wide-ranging and unified inquiry as philosophical history has ever produced.

Let me begin, then, by disavowing any commitment to philosophical specialization, and by denying that Kant's distinction between the beautiful and the agreeable is the narrowly focused topic it might appear to be. Quite the contrary: it is, in one sense, an unruly distinction, crosscutting a vast terrain of aesthetics, epistemology, metaphysics, philosophy of mind, and perhaps many other 'areas' as well—if one goes in for this familiar compartmentalization of philosophical inquiry. Part of the interest of Kant's distinction, to my mind anyway, is precisely the richness of its philosophical texture and the complexity of its philosophical grain. It resists easy classification, beyond the jejune: just to reiterate the obvious, it is one of the most basic building blocks of Kant's aesthetic theory in the third *Critique*.

Hence my surprise upon discovering that there is hardly any literature on Kant's distinction between the beautiful and the agreeable. This was all the more surprising in light of the recent deluge of scholarly and philosophical writing on Kant's aesthetic theory. But few have been concerned to understand Kant's aesthetic theory for the sake of aesthetics, or even for the sake of tracing out a fuller picture of what Kant was up to in the critical philosophy. Recent work on Kant's aesthetic theory, for the most part, has been in hot pursuit of the alleged epistemological lessons—lessons about the possibility of cognition—that Kant promises to reveal by means of a careful and sustained study of judgments of the *beautiful.* In a rush to claim these lessons, commentators have simply taken for granted that they know what the beautiful is—which is to say, in part, how Kant distinguishes it from the agreeable.

I take issue with this quick and easy assurance. And I reject the unspoken assumption that a resolute focus on one half of Kant's foundational distinction will yield a proper understanding even of the epistemological lessons Kant promises on behalf of his aesthetic theory. When we stop to ask in earnest how this distinction is framed, and how it is properly applied to some simple but well-described cases of aesthetic appraisal, we quickly discover that its contours are anything but obvious—so far from obvious, in fact, that tracking them down is material enough for a book. An interesting book I hope, but certainly one whose terrain is surprisingly wide for having such an ostensibly narrow focus.

I write from a conviction that the philosophical questions worth pursuing are questions from ordinary life. Accordingly, I attempt to locate Kant's distinction between the beautiful and the agreeable within a range of recognizable, theoretically unburdened concerns about matters of taste, which I identify with something I call the 'twofold conception of taste.' Kant's distinction, roughly speaking, is an attempt to locate this ordinary conception of taste within the terms of his overarching philosophical system. Tracing the contours of this distinction, then, turns out to be a matter of discovering how a transcendental idealist is constrained to think about matters of taste.

Some will already balk, given the disfavor into which transcendental idealism has fallen in our post-Strawsonian world. I have no intention of resuscitating transcendental idealism as a philosophical position (or rather, nest of philosophical positions), but I have long wondered how commentators can claim to make sense of *Kant* without it. I confess that I cannot, and I hope that the following pages bear out my claim that Kant's distinction—thus, the basic terms in which he frames his aesthetic theory—cannot be understood apart from transcendental idealism.

Let me forestall a potential misunderstanding. I applaud Kant's sense of the intrinsic interconnectedness of philosophical questions. Now, conceiving of philosophy as a unified discipline is one thing; conceiving of it as architectonic is quite another. Of course, there is nothing new in a skepticism about Kantian architectonic, but such skepticism needs to be backed up with detailed inquiry into precisely *which* distortions in a philosophical account it can be held responsible for. By asking how a transcendental idealist is constrained to think about matters of taste, I hope to put some meat onto the often bare bones of this familiar criticism. Otherwise put, I make no claim that the rich and varied philosophical texture of Kant's distinction is not without its attendant perils. I claim only that the lessons of Kant's aesthetic theory cannot be grasped apart from them.

However unruly Kant's distinction between the beautiful and the agreeable may be, the overall text of the third *Critique* is surely more so. At times, it appears to be a morass of hesitant claims or, worse yet, contradictory ones. I have no interest in tidy history or interpretation where the facts do not warrant it. I have no interest in wringing a stable position from a text that does not espouse one. These simple points are often lost, regrettably, in much work in the history of philosophy. But I embrace them, and seek to explain—rather than explain away—the unruliness of the third *Critique*. Truth be told, there is much in Kant's aesthetic theory that he did *not* settle; nor did he pretend otherwise. The third *Critique*, or so I will argue, is not built upon a settled distinction between the beautiful and the agreeable; it is an attempt to work out a distinction between the beautiful and the agreeable—it is a theory's attempt to work out its basic terms in response to its own internal difficulties. The third *Critique* is much less a *result* of a philosophical inquiry than a *record* of a philosophical inquiry. It is philosophy in motion—a motion that, by Kant's own lights, does not, even cannot, manage to reach its intended destination. I hope this study will reveal how and why the inquiry of the third *Critique* unfolds and unravels as it does.

A sampling of the issues that will arise along the way includes the usefulness of so-called ordinary language philosophy in explicating the basic terms of Kant's aesthetic theory; the viability of subjectivist or eliminativist conceptions of secondary qualities; the perils of theory cut loose from simple, concrete examples; the limits of the systematicity that Kantian theory can achieve; transcendental idealism's characterization of the sensible conditions on cognitive representation; the theory of synthesis and the role of the imagination in the construction of intuitions; the content of and problems with Kant's substantive aesthetic theory, known as 'formalism'; the differences between cognitive, linguistic, and aesthetic norms in everyday human discourse; the relevance of Kant's category of the agreeable to contemporary debates about so-called nonconceptual content.

Thus, I am modestly hopeful that this study will appeal to a wide range of scholars and philosophers. In part, that's due to the unruly nature of Kant's distinction and the vast range of issues it implicates. In part, it's due to a purposeful eschewal of methodological or doctrinal dogma. I am generally less interested in taking sides than in understanding what Kant was up to in the third *Critique,* or for that matter, in understanding how serious reflection on matters of taste can crisscross with other philosophical inquiries, even though some of the areas Kant trundles into would have been better left undisturbed, at least for these purposes.

This study seeks to bear out some philosophical and interpretive ideas that I began exploring as a graduate student at UC Berkeley. I am grateful to Continuum Books for giving me the occasion to revisit and to publish them. And special thanks to Tom Crick at Continuum for his unfailingly gracious and prompt assistance with every last detail of the publication process.

My debts are numerous, and at the risk of offending the many with rightful claims to my gratitude, I here acknowledge only the few whose claims are beyond the ordinary. The ideas from which this book eventually grew simply would not have come to fruition without the personal friendship and philosophical companionship of Berislav Marušić. Beri's sympathetic yet searching engagement with nearly every philosophical thought in these pages improved them at every turn, and his confidence in the project often restored my own when it faltered. Steve Sergo's friendship, support, and intellectual stimulation has made all the difference over the years. Similarly for the support and sympathetic understanding of the vicissitudes of philosophy I have long relied on from Trent Teti. In more recent years, Heidi Manschreck's supportive and loving partnership has meant the world, and has seen me through the strains of completing this book while simultaneously coping with the rigors of law school, the demands of teaching, and a long weekly commute between Ann Arbor and Chicago. I am also grateful for her comments on an earlier version of Chapter 1; her keen and sharply critical linguistic sensibilities undoubtedly saved me from a number of obscurities.

Some years ago, during graduate school, I had the great fortune to spend several months frequently discussing the third *Critique* with David Hills. I simply cannot estimate how much I learned from David, or how many of my own thoughts about Kantian taste theory (and much else) he deserves credit for provoking. Of course, he bears no responsibility for any of the shortcomings of this book.

I have been fortunate my whole life to have the unconditional love and support of a wonderful family. To my parents, I have racked up more than the usual unpayable filial debt. Both of my maternal grandparents passed away between the time I submitted my dissertation and the time I completed this book. I fondly recall how happy they were to learn I had completed my dissertation; it is a source of sadness for me that I can only imagine how happy they would be to see this book in print. Not that they would have much interest in its particular contents, although my love of music—a priceless inheritance from my grandfather—is undoubtedly one root of my interest in aesthetics. But the sheer fact of this book's existence would have delighted them. The best and the least I can do is dedicate it to them, in loving memory.

Note on Translations and Citations

Throughout, I have consulted both Kant's original German and, where available, the leading English translation(s). In most instances, I have followed what I consider to be the best available translation, although at times—duly recorded in the notes—I have provided my own translation. Unless otherwise indicated, translated passages from Kant's works are from the English editions found in the bibliography. In the case of the third *Critique*, I have consulted both the translation by Werner Pluhar, *Critique of Judgment*, and the translation by Paul Guyer and Eric Matthews, *Critique of the Power of Judgment*. With a few noted exceptions, translated passages from the third *Critique* are from the Guyer-Matthews translation. I thank Cambridge University Press, and Professors Guyer and Matthews, for permission to quote extensively from their fine edition.

References to Kant's works are provided in the notes. I use the canonical citation form: usually, the volume and page number(s) of the passage in the standard scholarly edition, *Kants Gesammelte Schriften*. This is for the convenience of readers who wish to consult Kant's original German, and for readers who use alternative English editions; the *Akademie*-edition pagination is reproduced in the margins of any decent English volume. References to the third *Critique* include the relevant section number, and references to the first *Critique* include the usual A- and/or B-edition pagination. When the title of a work does not make patent which corresponding English volume to consult, assuming there is one, I indicate the relevant volume parenthetically.

Chapter 1

The Twofold Conception of Taste

Everyone has his own taste. This we all know to be true even with little or no serious reflection. Our tastes diverge; we do not all find pleasure, or delight, or beauty in the same things, or in the same ways, or on the same occasions. The ubiquity of disagreement is a striking and stubborn fact of life in matters of taste. While there is universal or near-universal agreement about the pleasures to be found in certain *kinds* of things—the existence of beautiful human faces is an obvious example; the seemingly universal human need to make and listen to music is perhaps another—there is conspicuously scant agreement about *which* faces or compositions are the beautiful ones. It becomes all the more conspicuous as one reflects on both the fact and the extent of the agreement we achieve in our ordinary claims of knowledge. In general, the extent of our agreement about which things are beautiful, or where any of the varieties of aesthetic delight are to be found, is nowhere near the extent of our agreement about which things are pens, or cats, or blue, or which inferences are valid.

One natural reaction to this asymmetry is to say, 'Of course. That's just what it is for something to be a matter of taste. Everyone has his own taste, and there is no problem about that. There are no standards, and no such thing as being right or wrong. To each his own.' Now, that is one strand in our thinking about taste. 'To each his own' in matters of taste is indeed a time-honored maxim of common sense. Matters of taste, we sometimes think, are purely personal affairs, about which there can be no genuine dispute. But we do not always follow common sense's advice to humbly allow each to have his own taste. Sometimes, even in the face of stubborn, irresolvable disagreement, we persist in criticizing one another, accusing one another of having poor or unrefined taste, and insisting that others are wrong to be of a different mind—even if we are none too clear about what this charge comes to. Taste, we sometimes think, is not a purely personal affair, immune to the criticism of others, but an interpersonal standard of appraisal, in accordance with which the preferences of others are to be, or at least rightfully can be, assessed, criticized, and judged. In our ordinary lives, we find ourselves thinking in terms of two very different idioms of taste, and any philosophical reflection on our aesthetic lives had best register and account for this fact.[1]

This twofold conception of taste, as I shall continue to call it, is familiar from our everyday role as seekers and judges of aesthetic pleasures. Much to Kant's credit, this ordinary, pretheoretical conception of taste is one of the basic data from which his philosophical aesthetics begins. In particular, his distinction between 'the beautiful' [*das Schöne*] and 'the agreeable' [*das Angenehme*] articulates this ordinary conception of taste within the terms of a general and systematic philosophical theory—but not without some substantial distortions of our ordinary aesthetic attitudes. Or so I will argue. Its commonsense origins notwithstanding, Kant's developed, theory-laden distinction between the beautiful and the agreeable fails to adequately express the contours of the personal and the interpersonal—the nonnormative and the normative—dimensions of our everyday aesthetic discourse.

Here is the plan for the present chapter. In Section 1, I present Kant's distinction between the beautiful and the agreeable—to the extent possible—free from the technical paraphernalia of his philosophical system, and I examine Stanley Cavell's attempt to do the same.[2] In Section 2, I examine Paul Guyer's claim that Kant correctly believes that his distinction captures the ordinary language standards for the use of the terms 'beautiful' and 'agreeable.'[3] This view distorts a range of perfectly ordinary and legitimate uses of these terms in ways that helpfully point to the theoretical bases of Kant's distinction within the terms of his overarching philosophical system. In Sections 3–4, I take a very cursory look at these theoretical bases, and how they color Kant's initial starting points, by trying to sort out the various things Kant might mean when he applies his indeterminate and multiply ambiguous label 'judgment about the tone of a (musical) instrument.' This will set the stage for a detailed inquiry into the role of Kant's transcendental idealism in shaping his foundational distinction between the beautiful and the agreeable. In Section 5, I provide a brief sketch of that inquiry, to be pursued in subsequent chapters. So now to the text.

Section 1: Commonsense Roots

In the first two 'Moments of the judgment of taste,'[4] Kant attempts to draw a sharp distinction between two varieties of aesthetic appraisal, which he calls judgments of the agreeable and of the beautiful, the pronouncements of the 'taste of the senses' [*Sinnengeschmack*] and the 'taste of reflection' [*Reflexionsgeschmack*] respectively.[5] They are alike in being entirely subjectively grounded, that is, in being made on a wholly subjective basis. Roughly put, in judging that something is either agreeable or beautiful, I have nothing but my own felt pleasure in the object to go on.[6] The most salient difference between the two types of judgment is that while a judgment of the agreeable restricts itself to a subjective or personal claim—what I judge to be agreeable I judge to be agreeable for me—a judgment of beauty makes a sweepingly intersubjective claim. What I judge to be beautiful, in Kant's sense of the word, I judge to be beautiful for everyone, everywhere, always.[7] Kant seems to be saying that we do, and ought to, insist upon the agreement of others in some matters of taste, and that we are, and ought to be, content to let disagreement stand without further ado in others. Why should this be so?

Concerning judgments of the agreeable, Kant says, 'everyone is content that his judgment, which he grounds on a private feeling, and in which he says of an object that it pleases him, be restricted merely to his own person.'[8] He offers an example of two diners, one of whom is pleased by the taste of the wine, the other of whom is not. The pleased diner will be 'perfectly happy' if someone reminds him that he should, strictly speaking, express his pleasure by saying 'it is agreeable **to me**.'[9] Concerning judgments of the agreeable, Kant accepts common sense's time-honored advice to humbly allow each to have his own taste.

In taking the qualification 'to me' as implicit in a judgment of the agreeable, Kant maintains that the judgments of the two diners are not rationally opposed.[10] Suppose I enjoy the wine, and you do not. I could just as well express myself (in lieu of saying something) with a relaxed, contented smile, or an easy sigh, or any one of a number of gestures recognizable as bodily expressions of delight or satisfaction. The same goes for you: a moan, or a wince, will serve me just as well if I want to ascertain whether or not you are enjoying the wine. My smile and your wince are not rationally opposed; there is no genuine disagreement between my expression of delight and your expression of disgust. In fact, our respective announcements 'about the wine' only appear on the surface to be announcements about the wine. They are really expressions of how the wine affects each of us, whether it brings about in each of us delight, or disgust, or anything in-between.[11]

That sounds plausible enough. We don't even anticipate, much less demand, that we all find sensuous satisfaction or delight in the same things; concerning such satisfactions we normally just speak for ourselves, and ask what others *do* enjoy, rather than dictate what they *should* enjoy. Judgments of the agreeable are simply expressions of the bodily, sensuous, animalistic side of our nature. That side of our nature is not determined in precisely the same way in all of us. Nor does it make sense to demand that it ought to be. Nor does it bother us that it isn't. That is why we are content to speak for ourselves, which means here, to speak for our own bodies.

But compared to the modest announcement that the wine is pleasing to me, my declaration that something is beautiful sounds like a rather high-minded affair:

> It would be ridiculous if someone who prided himself on his taste thought to justify himself thus: 'This object . . . is beautiful **for me**.' For he must not call it beautiful if it pleases merely him. Many things have charm and agreeableness for him, no one will be bothered about that; but if he pronounces that something is beautiful, then he expects the very same satisfaction of others: he judges not merely for himself, but for everyone, and speaks of beauty as if it were a property of things. Hence he says that the **thing** is beautiful and does not count on the agreement of others . . . but rather **demands** it from them. He rebukes them if they judge otherwise, and denies that they have taste.[12]

I quote at such length here to let the high-mindedness of the Kantian judgment of beauty come through. Although Kant expresses something quite correct in this passage, his attitude toward the judgment of beauty seems way out of proportion. First, if I claim that something is beautiful, Kant says it is 'ridiculous' [*lächerlich*] of me not to 'demand' [*fordern*] that others be of like mind. Second, another's failure to be of like mind is immediate cause for me to 'rebuke' [*tadeln*] him. That is excessively strong language. But that is not all: I demand that others be of like mind 'as if' my judgment were about some definite, ascertainable matter of fact about the object I am judging, while knowing that it is not and cannot be.

One may well grow nervous that Kantian judges of beauty are in too much of a hurry to brand others as tasteless and in violation of some not-yet-specified and none-too-clear normative requirement. At least part of the unclarity is due to the 'as-if' force of the requirement: the judgment of beauty demands the concurrence of others even as it is made in full consciousness of the fact that beauty is not a genuine property of things, that there is no set of determinate criteria for ascertaining that something is beautiful, by ascertaining whether or not it possesses the features indicated by the criteria. That is the point of saying that a judgment of beauty has a wholly subjective basis or 'determining ground' [*Bestimmungsgrund*]: I ascertain whether or not something is beautiful on the basis of my own felt pleasure or displeasure in it. But that means that a judgment of beauty cannot be either true or false. Upon encountering disparity in taste concerning the beautiful, I am entitled to maintain that the dissenter's claim is in some sense wrong, but I cannot say that the claim is false. Nor, obviously, can I say it is somehow morally wrong. Why, then—if it is in the service of neither standing human cognitive nor practical aims—does common sense grant itself a limited exemption from its own time-honored maxim to humbly allow each to have his own taste? In connection with this question, Stanley Cavell's views are worth thinking through.

Cavell attempts to mark the difference between judgments of the beautiful and the agreeable by following out Kant's idea that we speak of beauty 'as if' it were a property of things. We don't speak that way when making a judgment of the agreeable; we simply speak for ourselves, and construe our judgments as expressions of personal likes and dislikes, rather than as claims about objects with correlative demands for the agreement of others. But a judgment of beauty expresses a more complicated attitude. Like a judgment of the agreeable, a judgment of beauty is an expression of likes or dislikes, of pleasure or pain. But it also 'demands' [*fordern*] or 'imputes' [*zumuten*] or 'requires' [*ansinnen*] like-mindedness on the part of others.[13] In making a judgment of beauty, we do not *just* speak for ourselves.

Now, if there were legitimate reasons to think that beauty were a property of objects, there would be nothing particularly troublesome about a judgment of beauty. If finding something to be beautiful were a matter of ascertaining some definite matter of fact about it, my conviction that my assessment of the object has been competent and sincere would allow me to pass without further ado to a demand for the like-mindedness of others. If I could ascertain that an object is beautiful in anything like the ways I ascertain that it is 2.5 x 4 x 8 inches in size, or is made of hardened clay, or is used to build the façades of buildings, or is a brick, the claims of taste would be no more or less troublesome than the claims of knowledge.

But Kant vigorously contends that beauty is not a property of objects whose presence or absence can be produced or detected on the basis of criteria. The attitude encapsulated in the judgment of beauty is not that beauty is a property of objects but rather that it is 'as if' it were. Cavell writes:

Only 'as if' because it cannot be an ordinary property of things: its presence or absence cannot be established in the way ordinary properties are; that is, they cannot be established publicly, and we don't know (there aren't any) causal conditions, or usable rules, for producing, or altering, or erasing, or increasing this 'property.' Then why not just say it *isn't* a property of an object? I suppose there would be no reason not to say this, if we could find another way of recording our conviction that it is one, anyway that what we are pointing to is *there*, in the object; and our knowledge that men make objects that create this response in us, and make them exactly with the idea that they will create it; and the fact that, while we know not everyone will agree with us when we say it is present, we think they are *missing something* if they don't.[14]

According to Cavell, the judgment of beauty expresses my conviction that there is something about an allegedly beautiful object that elicits and demands a certain response from me, and that this response—the experience of aesthetic delight[15]—is the correct or appropriate response. A failure to respond *this* way is a failure to respond to something that seems to be there in the object, something the object makes accessible to everyone, whether or not they avail themselves of it. And when I feel that others are missing something about the object, an insistence that *this* disparity in taste be allowed to stand unchallenged and unresolved will come off as 'a feeble rejoinder, a *retreat* to personal taste.'[16]

Cavell, then, seems to be saying that we call something beautiful rather than agreeable when we wish to register our sense that some feature of the object demands a particular response from us, and we demand that same response from others because we feel that the object itself demands it from us—even though we know this isn't true, and that our demands are all too likely to meet with frustration. Disparity in taste sometimes presents itself as a simple divergence of personal preferences. But it sometimes presents itself as a genuine disagreement, complete with a shared sense that the other is missing something about the object of our dispute, something he ought to be responsive to, something I should help him see, or see in the right light, so he can bring his judgment into attunement with mine, and with the object itself, and with what it demands from us both. In the latter case, it will be appropriate for me to try to orient his attention toward the object in the right way—as *my* attention is oriented toward it—and make available for him the experience that I have. It is as though he has failed to hear what the beautiful thing has to say, so I undertake to teach him how to listen to it properly. Though my best efforts may and often do fail, it will strike me as a 'retreat' to personal taste if he stops up his ears and shuts his eyes in the face of my best efforts to make available to him the experience that the object has provided for me, to explain to him what it is about the object that makes my response to it feel appropriate, or fitting, and his not.

Of course, if beauty is not a property of objects, the procedures of aesthetic criticism cannot be the same as the procedures for investigating the truth of knowledge claims. But that does not mean we have any more right to shrug our shoulders and dismiss the claims they purport to make on us by 'retreating' to personal taste, with all the invulnerability to criticism it provides. Where we feel there is something *there*, in the object, for others to miss, we call it beautiful rather than agreeable, and we undertake a rational commitment to criticism: to procedures for investigating, challenging, elaborating, and defending our claims of taste.

Cavell's account provides a helpful vantage point from which to illuminate our twofold conception of taste and the commonsense roots of Kant's distinction. But how well does it square with that distinction as Kant applies it to particular cases? To help bring out the limitations of Cavell's view as an interpretation of Kant, I want to examine Paul Guyer's account, which attempts to locate Cavell's guiding thoughts more explicitly in the text of §§ 7–8.

Section 2: Ordinary Language Roots?

Guyer claims that Kant's distinction between the beautiful and the agreeable—and more specifically, that the 'criterial role of the claim to universality' of the judgment of beauty—is supported by 'a broader appeal to linguistic usage.'[17] Guyer is correct that Kant attempts, in §§ 7–8, to set forth his distinction by appealing to (what he claims to be) the correct usage of the terms 'agreeable' and 'beautiful.' As we've seen, Kant claims that someone who says the wine is agreeable will be 'perfectly happy if . . . another corrects the expression and reminds him that he ought to say: It is agreeable **to** *me*.'[18] In other words, Kant claims that the term 'agreeable' is indexed to particular speakers, and functions merely to report the occurrence of pleasure in a particular person on a particular occasion, even though we generally do not make the indexical element of the term explicit in common speech. Insofar as the term is properly indexed to particular speakers on particular occasions, the correct usage of 'agreeable' expresses no expectation and no demand that others agree.

The correct usage of 'beautiful,' on Kant's view, is very different. As we've also seen, Kant says it would be 'ridiculous' [*lächerlich*] to index the term 'beautiful' to particular speakers on particular occasions; the correct usage of 'beautiful' mandates that it be used to make a claim to the assent of everyone. Kant maintains that 'this claim to universality so essentially belongs to a judgment by which we declare something to be **beautiful** that without thinking this it would never occur to anyone to use this expression.'[19] Following Kant, Guyer concludes that the 'criterial significance' of universality for the judgment of beauty and the indexical nature of the judgment of the agreeable are both implicit in the correct linguistic usage of the terms 'agreeable' and 'beautiful.'[20] Guyer is careful to note that Kant does not attempt to justify the claim to universality made by a judgment of beauty by appealing to what we ordinarily say; that remains the task of his 'Deduction of Taste.'[21] The role of Kant's appeal to ordinary linguistic usage is rather to set forth the distinction between two dimensions of the notion of taste and to remind us that ordinary language recognizes the distinction as a matter of course. I have claimed that common sense recognizes a two-fold conception of taste, a distinction between taste as a purely personal affair and taste as an intersubjective standard of appraisal. Guyer seems to be adding that Kant's theoretical articulation of this commonsense distinction is a straightforward and accurate reflection of ordinary language.

Guyer is correct to find this view expressed in the text of the First Moment. However, this view is wrong. Kant's strictures about the correct usage of 'beautiful' and 'agreeable,' or *schön* and *angenehm*, are not accurate reflections of ordinary language. They are, at best, philosophical idealizations of ordinary language, which impose substantial revisions on the way we ordinarily speak about matters of taste.

In fairness to Kant, one can see how he might have been misled, for these strictures have an air of plausibility in German that derives from the surface-grammatical features of the adjectives *angenehm* and *schön*. While 'Es ist mir angenehm' is perfectly proper German, 'Es ist mir schön' is not. Nor would a native speaker say 'Es ist schön zu mir' or 'Es ist schön für mich.' But these are just surface-grammatical features of German, and we should not rest any heavy conceptual weight on them. In particular, they do not establish that a demand for universal agreement is 'criterial' for, or essential to, the concept *beauty* or *Schönheit*. That much can be seen from the way in which Yiddish, German's closest linguistic relative, provides for surface-grammatical forms that Hochdeutsch doesn't. In Yiddish, 'Bei mir bist du schön' is perfectly normal and appropriate speech, and means, just as one expects, 'To me, you are beautiful.' Moreover, it is especially worth noting in this connection that the famous song 'Bei Mir Bist Du Schön' (originally from the ill-fated Yiddish musical *I Would If I Could*) was a smash hit in Germany, at least until the Nazis discovered it was originally written in Yiddish. They had mistaken the Yiddish construction in the title for one in a Bavarian dialect which also tolerates this usage of *schön* with the preposition *bei*.[22]

This grammatical form, whether in Yiddish or a south-German dialect, makes patent the possibility of calling something *schön* without making any demand on the like-mindedness of others, even if more standard forms of German preclude the constructions that would make such usage transparent. One *can* simply voice one's own responsiveness to an object of delight with the word *schön*, or for that matter, with the word 'beautiful.' Kant's strictures about linguistic usage are not accurate descriptions of ordinary language.

Consider a brief list of judgments that Kant counts among his judgments of the agreeable: the taste of the palate, colors, and the tones of instruments. Insofar as they are judgments of the agreeable, it should be inappropriate to express them with the word 'beautiful,' yet all three provide contexts for perfectly legitimate uses of the term. There is nothing wrong with the sentence 'The 1995 La Vicalanda Rioja has a beautiful bouquet,' or with the exclamation 'What a beautiful shade of purple!' or with the expression of delight 'Paco de Lucia's guitar has the most beautiful tone, the most richly textured sound, I've ever heard. I wonder what kind of wood it's made of.' Nevertheless, Kant appears to count all of these as judgments of the agreeable. The crucial point is that they can be expressed using the word 'beautiful' without any violation or distortion of ordinary language. Wherever the roots of Kant's distinction are to be found, they are not in the standards for correct usage of the terms 'beautiful' and 'agreeable.'

Now, one might object that the general terms of Kant's distinction, including his strictures about the correct usage of 'beautiful' and 'agreeable,' are fine as they stand. It's Kant's application of the distinction to particular cases that goes awry; he should just count judgments about colors and tones as judgments of the beautiful rather than the agreeable.[23] I think he should, though that still does not account for the legitimate expression of delight in the wine's bouquet with 'beautiful.' On nobody's view, as far as I can tell, does the taste of the palate fail to count as an instance of the to-each-his-own conception of taste. More importantly, the objection flatly assumes that the terms of Kant's distinction allow him to describe judgments about colors or tones as judgments of the beautiful. For reasons I explore in detail in Chapters 2 and 3, it is not clear that they do. To begin this line of investigation, I want to look briefly at some of the difficulties that arise in trying to apply the general terms of Kant's distinction to particular examples. We will begin to see how Kant's characteristic examples are theory-laden right from the start.

Section 3: Theoretical Roots: A Preliminary Glance

A fruitful source of difficulty is Kant's tendency to underdescribe examples, or rather, to describe them at too high a level of generality and abstraction. His various discussions of judgments about the tone of an instrument are exemplary in this regard and repay further scrutiny. I begin with a dispute over the tone of an instrument that does not fit Kant's model of judgments of the agreeable. It can be made to fit his model of judgments of 'dependent beauty,' and I will come to that topic in Section 4. The kind of dispute I have in mind is whether the tone of an instrument is appropriate for playing a particular piece of music. Imagine a disagreement about the appropriateness of playing Jobim's 'The Girl From Ipanema' on a steel-string banjo:

A: 'This is atrocious. That bright, metallic sound of the banjo is altogether too glib for this music. This song is about longing, about the frailty of the human heart in its susceptibility to beauty. It's supposed to be tender, sensual, nostalgic. That bright twangy tone makes it sound like a hoedown. This guy's got no feel for Jobim's music at all, no idea what it tries to express.'

B: But I like it played on the banjo.

If A's judgment about the appropriateness of the steel-string banjo's tone for playing bossanova were a judgment of the agreeable, that should be the end of the matter. A should, as Kant says, be 'content' to have B bring to light a brute disparity in taste. But it is far more natural to think, with Cavell, that A will see B's expression of brute disagreement—with no attempt to respond to the grounds A has offered—as a *retreat* to personal taste.[24] Imagine two rejoinders that A might offer to B:

A_1: Good, I'm glad you like it;

A_2: Well, you don't have any feel for Jobim's music either.

Only the second is appropriate, given the grounds that A has offered for his judgment. Were A to offer the first rejoinder, we would have to conclude that his statement of grounds was insincere, that he didn't really mean what he said, since he has retracted it willy-nilly, with no reason for doing so having been brought to light.

The tone of an instrument can count as beautiful, or as anything but, according to its suitability for achieving some particular musical end. In such contexts of appraisal, 'One person loves the tone of the steel-string banjo, another that of the acoustic guitar' expresses a genuine disagreement which can be articulated and pursued by adducing grounds. When Kant speaks of the tone of an instrument, though, he often seems to have in mind an immediate and passive responsiveness to an instrument's sound that makes no reference to musical context. Perhaps that's why he often says that 'a *mere* tone' [*ein bloßer Ton*] is the subject of a judgment of the agreeable. If so, a disparity in taste like 'One person loves the tone of wind instruments, another that of string instruments'[25] does not involve two rationally opposed judgments, since each judgment expresses nothing but one's enjoyment of a sensory feeling. But this is complicated by Kant's claim that 'mere tone' is to be distinguished from 'sound and noise' [*zum Unterschied vom Schalle und Geräusch*].[26]

Whatever distinction Kant has in mind here is (at best) badly expressed.[27] It's clear enough how to make a judgment about the tone of an instrument by reference to standards derived from the music that the instrument is being used to play: bossanova really should not be played on a steel-string banjo. Similarly, one might think that the English horn has just the right kind of slightly haunting tone to introduce the 'Adagio' of the *Concierto de Aranjuez*, that the tone of the flute would have been too light, too delicate, to introduce a movement so rhapsodic and introspective. Our willingness to speak freely and critically of a composer's talent for instrumentation makes patent that we do not consider these to be judgments of the agreeable, with the immunity to criticism that would provide.

Now, people sometimes judge—which means here, express preferences about—the tones of instruments without reference to standards derived from a musical context, either because they lack sufficient appreciation of those standards or simply don't (care to) take them into account at the present moment. Some people are not so interested in, or even capable of, *listening to music* as they are in finding a place to sit down where a wave of pleasant sounds can wash over them. In this sense, one person might enjoy being awash in the sound or tone of the violin, while another finds the clarinet more pleasant. One would have thought this provides the needed context to make sense of Kant's example as a judgment of the agreeable. But if Kant wants to distinguish 'mere tone' from 'sound,' it's hopelessly unclear what kind of judgment he's trying to describe. Charitable interpretation, then, counsels dropping this distinction and understanding a judgment about '*mere* tone' as I have here.

More importantly, though, it should now be clear that the label 'judgment about the tone of an instrument' does not suffice for characterizing a judgment as a judgment of the agreeable. On the contrary, this label obscures the salient differences between very different kinds of judgments about the tone of an instrument and further encourages examples that are too indeterminate, too thinly described, too divorced from concrete context. Kant's paltry examples, I believe, are largely the result of substituting an abstract and general metaphysical theory about sensations for a close and careful examination of actual aesthetic judgments and disputes on their own terms.

A judgment of the agreeable is supposed to be an announcement of an essentially mindless pleasure, a purely bodily or sensory form of satisfaction or enjoyment. Preferring the sound of the clarinet over the violin can sometimes, as in the case above, be fairly described that way. But sometimes it cannot. Judgments about instrumentation draw on one's grasp of the features and expressive purposes of the music being played; in that context, one's delight in an instrument's tone is not in the least mindless. Not being one for attention to concrete examples, Kant blithely assimilates all judgments about musical tone to a single general model couched in the terms provided by his overarching philosophical system. Describing the judgments about the pleasantness of the tone of the violin versus that of the clarinet, Kant says that each person's judgment '[has as its] ground merely the matter of the representation, namely mere sensation.'[28] This captures the mindless or purely bodily character of the judgment of the agreeable—and imports a massive edifice of theoretical claims about the nature of sensations and mental representations more generally.

For instance, notice that Kant's examples of judgments of the agreeable are always examples of judgments about so-called secondary qualities: tastes, colors, smells, sounds. I suspect Kant believes that the alleged subjectivity—or in his phrase, the 'empirical ideality'—of secondary qualities disqualifies judgments of the agreeable from making any rightful normative claims on the assent of others. In the first *Critique*'s 'Transcendental Aesthetic,' Kant construes secondary qualities as nothing but the effects that objects have upon our senses. They are 'mere sensations and not intuitions,'[29] which are thus 'correctly considered not as qualities of things but as mere alterations of our subject, which can even be different in different people.'[30] In § 14 of the third *Critique*, Kant reiterates these claims when he says that 'the quality of the sensations themselves cannot be assumed to be in accord in all subjects,' and hence cannot be 'universally communicated with certainty.'[31] The fullest statement of Kant's view comes in § 39:

If sensation, as the real in perception, is related to cognition, it is called sensory sensation; and its specific quality can be represented as completely communicable in the same way only if one assumes that everyone has a sense that is the same as our own—but this absolutely cannot be presupposed in the case of a sensory sensation. Thus, to someone who lacks the sense of smell, this kind of sensation cannot be communicated; and, even if he does not lack this sense, one still cannot be sure that he has exactly the same sensation from a flower that we have from it. Still more, however, we must represent people as differing with regard to the **agreeableness** or **disagreeableness** of the sensation of one and the same object of the sensations; and it is absolutely not to be demanded that pleasure in the same objects be conceded to everyone.[32]

The legitimacy of my demand that others take pleasure in the same things I do requires (among other things) that those pleasures are available to others on the same terms on which they are available to me. If the taste of the wine is nothing but the effect of the wine on my palate—a 'mere sensation' or 'mere alteration of [my] subject'—I cannot demand that you find the taste of the wine agreeable as I do, since I am not entitled to presume that the wine causes a sensation in you that is at all similar, much less qualitatively identical, to the sensation it causes in me, and this sensation is the 'ground' of my judgment of the agreeable.[33] For all we know, the taste of the wine is very different for each of us; any one person's satisfaction with it is therefore not 'communicable.' Aesthetic judgments based on a 'mere sensation' (including, for instance, a 'mere tone') necessarily fall within the to-each-his-own conception of taste and thus within Kant's category of the agreeable.

Kant's view that judgments about taste, smell, color, or tone cannot justifiably demand the assent of others appears to be rooted in his conception of secondary qualities as nothing but sensations, nothing but the ways objects causally affect us. That is an essentially mindless affair, for which it doesn't seem to make any sense to hold each other accountable, as though we might violate some normative demand in being causally affected by an object in one way rather than another.[34] In the context of a typical eighteenth-century eliminativist ontology, it seems reasonable to claim that judgments of the agreeable, grounded as they are on 'mere sensation,' are one and all nonnormative. To my eye, then, Kant's ontological and epistemological commitments systematically shape his philosophical articulation of our twofold conception of taste and frame his examples of aesthetic judgments right from the start.

Section 4: A Problematic Example

With that in mind, I want to return to an example I mentioned above but did not discuss: the example of judging the tone of one guitar, for instance, the exquisite instrument that Paco de Lucia plays, as better or more beautiful than the tone of another guitar, say, a cheap student model. Here it is natural to say that de Lucia's guitar has a *better* tone than the student model. That might incline Kant's readers to assume that the example is of a judgment of so-called dependent or adherent beauty, rather than a judgment of the agreeable. But it's neither. It should be counted as a pure judgment of taste.

A judgment that an object possesses dependent beauty is a finding that one is pleased with an object insofar as the object is a good or exemplary specimen of its kind. It is, in other words, both a judgment that a thing is beautiful and that it is well suited to perform its natural or humanly intended function or purpose. Of course, beauty and perfection do not always, and usually do not, come to the same thing: a beautiful watch may be quite inaccurate and unreliable, hence not very perfect as a watch, and a very accurate and reliable watch may indeed be rather ugly. Sometimes, though, the question of a thing's beauty cannot be prized apart from the question of its perfection. A thing's imperfection as a member of its kind may automatically detract from its beauty; as Kant says, 'One would be able to add much to a building that would be pleasing in the intuition of it if only it were not supposed to be a church.'[35] Or, in stronger cases, a thing's perfection may automatically render it beautiful. One might, in this connection, think of one of Kant's paradigmatic examples of dependent beauty, namely, the beauty of a human body.[36] In matters of dependent beauty, a thing's beauty (or ugliness, or anything in-between) is dependent upon standards of perfection that we associate with some functional characterization of what an object is or is supposed to be. The direction of dependence here is crucial: beauty depends upon perfection. In the judgment about Paco de Lucia's guitar, as opposed to some second-rate instrument, the order of dependence is reversed.

The dispute about the tone of the steel-string banjo is a clear case of a judgment of dependent beauty: A's disgust over the tone of the banjo is grounded in his assessment of it as ill-equipped to serve the expressive purposes of Jobim's music. It is precisely the imperfection of the banjo's tone for these purposes that leads A to find it ugly, at least in this context. (A might find the tone of the banjo beautiful in some other musical context, which would be perfectly consistent with his finding here.) The crucial point is simply that in A's assessment, the (lack of) beauty of the banjo's tone depends upon its (lack of) perfection.

In contrast, there is no standard of perfection for a guitar that can provide a basis for the judgment that the tone of Paco de Lucia's guitar is better or more 'perfect' than the tone of a cheap student-model guitar. More precisely, there is no standard of perfection that we can specify independently of what we find immediately pleasing or beautiful about the tone, and so there is no standard of perfection that can provide noncircular or nonempty grounds for a finding of beauty. As always, further specification of what is meant by 'judging the tone of a guitar' is needed.

Compared to that of the student-model guitar, the tone, the sound, of Paco de Lucia's instrument has a far richer and deeper texture (largely due to the resonance that the physical composition and aging of the wood produces). That is an immediate and sensory response to the sound of the guitar(s), and does not presuppose a concept of what a guitar ought to be, or how a guitar ought to sound. It has nothing to do with de Lucia's guitar being more suitable for expressing a particular piece of music; one can hear the difference between the two instruments even if one is only strumming them, and not playing any piece of music at all. Nor does it have anything to do with the technical sense of 'tone' as a regularity of vibration that produces an identifiable pitch, which can stand in harmonic relations with other such sounds. That sense of 'tone' might be taken to establish a (minimal) standard for what a guitar is supposed to be: it is, speaking way too generally, supposed to be a device that one can use to produce a certain range of (whole- and semi-) tones within a certain range of octaves. But the student model is not deficient in that regard; you can play whatever notes you like on it. The difference is that playing them on de Lucia's guitar will still produce a richer, deeper, more beautiful sound than one could ever achieve with the student model. *That* difference does not presuppose any independent standard for how a guitar ought to sound; on the contrary, it *sets* the standard for how a guitar ought to sound. The sound of de Lucia's guitar is not more beautiful than the sound of the student model because it is more perfect; it is more perfect precisely because it is more beautiful. We have no standard of perfection for the sound of a guitar that we can articulate here independently of our immediate responsiveness to its beauty. Of course it is true that a guitar, or any musical instrument, 'ought to sound beautiful.' In the present context, however, that is every bit as empty as it is true: offering beauty as a standard of perfection will not provide a standard of perfection that one can use to ground a judgment that something is beautiful (or more beautiful than another) because it is perfect (or more perfect than another).

The finding of beauty here is not 'mediated' by any concept of the relevant object, of what it is or is intended to be. The finding of beauty is direct, immediate, and sensory. For that reason, it cannot count as a judgment of dependent beauty. In Kant's taxonomy, a judgment based on an immediate sensory pleasure is classified as a judgment of the agreeable, and that appears, in any event, to be Kant's official classification for the entire (multiply ambiguous) category of judgments about the tone of an instrument. Applied to the present example, that is a mistake.

It is wrong to count this judgment as falling within the scope of the to-each-his-own conception of taste, which Kant aligns with his judgments of the agreeable. I would not let it stand as a purely personal matter of taste if someone preferred the tone of the student model to that of de Lucia's guitar or was indifferent between the two. Rather, I would think that someone who was nonresponsive to the difference between the guitars, or whose responsiveness was different than mine, was missing something that was there to be heard. Differences like these will inevitably lead us to say that de Lucia's guitar is better than the student model: we assess musical instruments as (among other things) better or worse in terms of the richness, the texture, the beauty, of the sound they produce, and will feel these differences to be real, to set standards of perfection for instruments to measure up to. When people cannot appreciate these standards—when they cannot hear the difference between better and worse instruments—we do not say that they have 'different taste' in musical instruments. We say that they are 'poor judges' of musical instruments. Here, then, is another example of a judgment about the tone of instrument that cannot be a judgment of the agreeable; nor can this one be a judgment of dependent beauty. In Kant's taxonomy, it must be a pure judgment of taste. But can it be?

Section 5: The Inquiry to Come

It sounds like a simple question: can Kant make what looks like a minor adjustment to the application of his aesthetic categories? Yet, we'll see that this simple example wreaks far-flung havoc with Kant's philosophical system. In § 14, Kant acknowledges that the epistemological and metaphysical apparatus of transcendental idealism appears to preclude characterizing *any* judgments about tone or about color as judgments of beauty. He also acknowledges that this result flies in the face of our ordinary thought and talk in matters of taste, and he embarks on a protracted and wide-ranging inquiry into his theory's prospects for reconciliation with the more plausible ordinary view. Ultimately, Kant throws up his hands in defeat and admits that his theory cannot yield a determinate result.[37] I hope that a serious study of this inquiry offers some useful lessons about the hazards of philosophical system building. I also hope it serves as a reminder—much needed in philosophy—not to slough over simple concrete examples in the race to high theory.

In Chapter 2, I begin my interpretation of Kant's aesthetic formalism. This doctrine maintains that only formal, or spatiotemporal, features of objects contribute to their beauty, as opposed to agreeableness. Taken in its most literal—and strictest—sense, formalism disqualifies colors and tones from contributing to the beauty of objects. Kant is well aware that this view conflicts with our ordinary aesthetic discourse, which routinely counts colors and tones as features that contribute to the beauty of beautiful things. Kant therefore searches for a way to relax the restrictions of formalism, to accommodate a more expansive conception of form, on which colors and tones are themselves formal features of objects. In the end, Kant concedes that he cannot decisively determine the aesthetic status of colors and tones.

Thus, it will not suffice to say that the problem with Kant's distinction between the beautiful and the agreeable lies in a faulty *application*, since it is not at all clear that Kant has the resources to characterize judgments about colors and tones as pure judgments of taste. By Kant's own assessment, this line of reply to the problem raised in Section 4 cannot be sustained. Or at the very least, nobody—including Kant—has made clear how to do so.

Chapter 2 examines, in some detail, the issues on which Kant takes the outcome of his investigation to depend. The details of this investigation confirm my interpretation of Kant's distinction between the beautiful and the agreeable as a theoretical articulation of our ordinary twofold conception of taste, in at least three significant ways. First, and most generally, Kant perceives a conflict between the principles of his overly restrictive formalism and the ordinary starting points of his aesthetic theory, and feels a need to bring the mandates of his theory into line with the more plausible views of ordinary aesthetic discourse. Kant thus correctly senses that the theoretical pressures of his philosophical system have knocked his aesthetic theory off of its original moorings. These theoretical pressures, I argue, derive principally from transcendental idealism and its characterization of our cognitive representations. That leads to two more specific points.

Second, Kant's investigation of the aesthetic status of colors and tones stands or falls with his broader investigation of the metaphysical status of these qualities and the epistemological status of our representations of them. More precisely, Kant discovers that he can only count colors and tones as contributing to an object's beauty if he can characterize colors and tones as real or objective features of spatiotemporal objects, and our representations of colors and tones as part of objective intuitions rather than mere sensations. Ultimately, these are the questions that Kant admits transcendental philosophy cannot adjudicate once and for all.

Third, Kant's investigation reveals the pervasive role of transcendental idealism in shaping his aesthetic theory, in particular, his distinction between the beautiful and the agreeable. This role has not been adequately appreciated or explored in the contemporary literature on Kant's aesthetics. Yet it *shouldn't* be surprising that a transcendental idealist takes the fundamental constraints on cognitive representation—space and time—to provide the norms that constrain judgments of taste. An interpretation that anchors Kant's aesthetic formalism in doctrines as fundamental to his thought as those of transcendental idealism has a natural explanation of why Kant remains committed to some variety of formalism, through thick and thin, even in the face of its implausibility as an aesthetic doctrine and the convoluted inquiries that implausibility provokes. Indeed, Kant never entertains the possibility of abandoning formalism altogether. Thus, my interpretation explains why Kant feels that he must find a way to argue that colors and tones *are* part of an object's spatiotemporal form.

Kant's investigation of colors and tones raises vast, varied, and extremely intricate questions. I cannot pretend to provide decisive answers to all of them. But I hope to reorient current approaches to Kant's aesthetic formalism along what I think are more promising interpretive lines, notwithstanding that formalism is unappealing as an aesthetic theory. In a sense, then, my investigation is largely diagnostic: I seek a more detailed and nuanced understanding than I believe we have of how and why Kant's aesthetic theory goes awry in the ways it does, and what lessons this might offer about the potential hazards of constructing comprehensive philosophical systems.

In Chapter 3, I provide an account of the notion of an *interest* that Kant uses to characterize judgments of the agreeable. I build on Chapter 2's account of the systematic relation between the *formality* of the pure judgment of taste and the conditions of its *universal communicability* by exploring how the *disinterestedness* of the pure judgment of taste can be systematically related to these two other central features. I argue that Kant runs together two distinct conceptions of an interest, which I call the *desire conception* and the *existence conception.*

Kant needs the desire conception to argue that the universal communicability of the judgment of taste entails its disinterestedness. He can further argue that its universal communicability entails its formality—an argument I reconstruct in Chapter 2—but this leaves the intended systematic relation between disinterestedness and formality unexplained. Worse yet, on the desire conception, the claim that only formal features of an object can ground a disinterested pleasure in the object is false.

In contrast, the existence conception allows Kant to argue that the disinterestedness of the pure judgment of taste entails its formality, but only because the existence conception smuggles in transcendental idealism's conceptions of pure intuition and sensation. On the existence conception, moreover, Kant cannot argue that an interested aesthetic judgment, and therefore a judgment of the agreeable,[38] is necessarily incommunicable—an inference he clearly thinks we are entitled to make.

Hence, these three core components of the pure judgment of taste—disinterestedness, universal communicability, and formality—cannot all be systematically related unless Kant equivocates on the notion of an interest. The argument of Chapter 3 thereby exposes the limits of the systematicity that Kant's aesthetic theory can achieve. And it further confirms my claim that Kant's aesthetic formalism is fundamentally motivated and shaped by the overarching doctrines of transcendental idealism: on the existence conception, the argument for the formality of the pure judgment of taste requires transcendental idealism's characterization of our cognitive representations. But once that characterization is in place, a transcendental idealist doesn't even need the notion of disinterestedness to have an argument for aesthetic formalism. This shows that the existence conception is superfluous. It merely adds the claim that *only* a pleasure taken in spatiotemporal features of an object could be disinterested, a claim that Kant is better off without. The separability of these two conceptions of an interest thus emerges as a positive result for his aesthetic theory.

Standing back from the nitty-gritty, one might ask what philosophical interest such an interpretation holds for contemporary readers. I offer some suggestions at the end of Chapter 3. My interpretation offers a fresh perspective from which to ask after the scope of Kant's sympathies toward a broadly empiricist conception of sense experience, assess the specific ways in which he attempts to set himself against it in the third *Critique*, and appreciate the difficulties he encounters in doing so. In contemporary parlance, my interpretation sheds new light on the question whether Kant endorsed the presence of any so-called nonconceptual content in our representations.

On my view, Kant's investigation of the aesthetic status of colors and tones is most profitably read as part of an investigation into the question, made prominent in recent years by the work of John McDowell, whether aspects of our mental states that are due to sheer receptivity—independent of any discursive activity of the mind—can be subject to norms at all, and hence whether they are genuinely part of the 'content of experience.'[39] I hope that my interpretation, despite its warnings about the hazards of constructing philosophical systems, reminds philosophers engaged in these contemporary debates of the potential relevance of philosophical aesthetics, which, unfortunately, seems to have largely fallen out of fashion in recent times.

Transcendental idealism, which my interpretation views as an essential component of Kant's aesthetic theory, is—for better or worse—also largely out of philosophical fashion, if not in downright ill-repute. Indeed, post-Strawsonian interpretations of Kant have principally been geared toward (re)casting Kantian philosophical lessons in forms that can be deployed without any commitment to transcendental idealism.[40] Thus, a post-Strawsonian might seek a conception of the pure judgment of taste that offers philosophically interesting and fruitful lessons—perhaps for an aesthetic theory; perhaps for an account of the possibility of cognition—without any such commitment. One might even object that my interpretation focuses on distortions in what might be called Kant's *substantive* aesthetic theory—his attempt to answer what I will call the *traditional aesthetic question*: which features of objects contribute to their beauty, and so to their being objects about which judgments of taste are appropriately made? After all, my interpretation depicts transcendental idealism as the basis for Kant's commitment to aesthetic formalism, and formalism is Kant's answer to the traditional aesthetic question. Perhaps if we distinguish a substantive aesthetic theory from what I will call a *purely transcendental* aesthetic theory—one which offers an account of the conditions for the possibility of (a judgment of) taste, while remaining neutral about the traditional aesthetic question—we can steer clear of any commitment to or need for transcendental idealism.

Such an interpretation would have to bear out Kant's conviction that the judgment of taste manifests a condition for the possibility of cognition without relying on transcendental idealism to explain what such a 'condition' could possibly be. Without endorsing transcendental idealism as a philosophical position, I freely confess that I do not understand how an interpretation that detaches this 'condition' from transcendental idealism will be recognizable as an interpretation of *Kant*. Yet, it might still be worth its philosophical salt, much as the leading figure in the *Bounds of Sense* is worth his, even if, on my view, he is much less like the historical Kant than he is often taken, and perhaps intended, to be.

Of the available interpretations of Kant's aesthetics that are both purely transcendental and resolutely opposed to any commitment to transcendental idealism, I take Hannah Ginsborg's to be the most philosophically trenchant and rigorously defended.[41] Accordingly, I take aim at Ginsborg's interpretation in Chapter 4. I ask whether we can detach the notion of a 'condition for the possibility of cognition' from transcendental idealism and still extract a useful interpretation of the Kantian thought that an analysis of the judgment of taste reveals some such condition. More specifically, Ginsborg's application—both to empirical cognition and to aesthetic judgment—of Kant's so-called principle of reflective judgment provides a helpful context for asking whether there could be a single overarching model of normativity that characterizes our mental states in both of these cases. I conclude there cannot be.

The connection Kant seeks to forge between the conditions for the possibility of *cognition* and the conditions for the possibility of *taste* faces a completely general difficulty, with or without a commitment to transcendental idealism: cognitive and aesthetic norms serve crucially different roles in our lives, and this difference vitiates any attempt to subsume them under a univocal model of normativity.

Briefly: cognitive norms, like linguistic norms, operate within a shared social context of training, instruction, authority, and general patterns of human agreement. Within—but only within—that context, the idea of a universally valid cognitive norm makes the kind of sense it makes for us. Human agreement, as Wittgenstein's later work has taught us, is *part of* our conception of a 'rule,' or 'norm,' as it applies to cognition (or to language). But this is not true of the normativity that applies to matters of taste. Taste, I argue, manifests a robust individualism and autonomy that cognitive and linguistic norms lack.

Thus, any interpretation that seeks to forge a fundamental connection between cognitive and aesthetic normativity faces a dilemma: either it loses its grip on the role that cognitive norms play in the everyday activities of human beings, or it is forced to take an analogous conception of general human agreement as part of the very idea of taste. Not only do I think this distorts the facts; more importantly, it also distorts our conception of taste. It fails to take into account the individualism that genuine exercises of taste manifest and indeed require; general patterns of human agreement are in no way a part of or required for the exercise of taste. Nor can there be literal instruction in matters of taste, as there is in the cognitive and linguistic domains, through which people are *trained* to perform a uniform activity in the way that others, by and large, perform it. Indeed, this is not *cultivation* of an individual's taste; it is a *suppression* of her taste.[42]

This dilemma, therefore, is no artifact of Ginsborg's interpretation; it is a standing feature of any attempt to construct a single general conception of normativity that applies in both the cognitive and aesthetic domains. It is to Ginsborg's credit that her interpretation captures this dilemma so sharply, in the form of a tension in her view that will be the main focus of examination.

Subsuming taste and cognition under a general univocal model of normativity will inevitably distort either our conception of taste or our conception of cognition. Transcendental idealism, in other words, isn't the *only* culprit here: something else may well be amiss in epistemologically laden approaches to matters of taste, whether the epistemology comes from transcendental idealism or elsewhere. It is difficult, however, to gauge the appropriate measure of skepticism. Whether there is a coherent conception of taste that retains some looser form of connection to cognition, and whether that conception of taste can provide a more satisfactory articulation of our twofold conception of taste than Kant provides, are questions about which I remain open minded, even modestly hopeful. But they will have to be left for another occasion.

Chapter 2

The Beautiful and the Agreeable

In Chapter 1, I argued that on the whole, Kant takes his aesthetic theory to be respectful of and responsive to much of our ordinary conception of taste. Nevertheless, Kant appears to claim that colors and tones cannot be beautiful.[1] To this extent, he seems willing to depart from ordinary aesthetic discourse, since 'most people,' as he correctly notes, call colors and tones beautiful as a matter of course.[2] Kant's attitude toward this fact is hesitant and uncertain, as is his formalist restriction against counting colors and tones as beautiful, or as contributing to an object's beauty. His attitude, as revealed in § 14 of the third *Critique*, is best expressed by what I shall call the *disjunctive claim*: either ordinary people are wrong to count colors and tones as beautiful, or they are correct, at least in a limited way, but for the wrong reasons.[3]

Unless Kant can provide the resources for choosing between the two alternatives offered by the disjunctive claim, the strictures of his substantive aesthetic theory will remain indeterminate. His distinction between the beautiful and the agreeable will thereby fail to provide a plausible and determinate answer to the traditional aesthetic question: what features of objects contribute to their beauty, and so to their being objects about which judgments of taste are appropriately made? Indeed, in the rarely discussed § 51 of the third *Critique*, Kant declares the traditional aesthetic question, as it applies to colors and tones, to be intractable within the terms of his philosophical theory. Otherwise put, he abandons the hope of finding grounds adequate to the needs of transcendental philosophy for choosing between the two options offered by the disjunctive claim. For those who share in the aspirations of substantive philosophical aesthetics, this will surely be a disappointment.

In this chapter, I investigate how and why Kant lands in this predicament. This investigation will take us to the heart of the metaphysics and epistemology of the first *Critique*, for aesthetic formalism, in Kant's hands, is an application of some of the core tenets of transcendental idealism. In Section 1,

I survey the issues on which, from Kant's perspective, our prospects for choosing between the two options offered by the disjunctive claim depend. In Sections 2–3, I explore two of these issues—the variability of sensations hypothesis (Section 2) and Kant's distinction between objective and subjective sensation (Section 3)—in greater detail. Each provides essential clues to the theoretical basis of Kant's distinction between the beautiful and the agreeable. In Section 4, I begin to sketch an interpretation of that distinction by considering the role of the imagination in establishing norms for judgment. In Section 5, I consider some of the core features of Guyer's interpretation of Kant's aesthetic formalism. Responding to Guyer allows me to expand and defend the interpretation sketched in Section 4 by revealing the theoretical roots of Kant's attraction to aesthetic formalism and the specific ways in which he tries to attenuate its unacceptable conclusions. In Section 6, I conclude with some reminders about the centrality of transcendental idealism to Kant's aesthetic theory, especially his aesthetic formalism.

Section 1: The Disjunctive Claim

The key to understanding how and why the disjunctive claim arises in § 14 lies in Kant's distinction between 'matter' and 'form.' Kant remarks in § 13:

> And yet charms are not only often included with beauty (which should properly concern merely form) as a contribution to the aesthetic universal satisfaction, but are even passed off as beauties in themselves, hence the matter of satisfaction is passed off for the form: a misunderstanding which, like many others that yet always have something true as their ground, can be eliminated by careful determination of these concepts.[4]

Only an object's form—whatever that turns out to include—contributes to its beauty. Ordinary aesthetic discourse, Kant says, goes astray in its application of this distinction, but a precise specification of the notion of form can remedy the error.

Accordingly, the title of § 14 announces a clarification of the distinction between matter and form by means of examples. A 'mere color, e.g., the green of a lawn,' or 'a mere tone . . . say that of a violin' are presented as putative examples of matter, or more specifically, the matter of a representation. Kant immediately tells us that the matter of a representation is sensation, or as he puts it, 'mere sensation'; on account of this, judgments based on the matter of a representation are judgments of the agreeable rather than the beautiful.[5] Kant thus swiftly reaches his formalist restrictions: colors and tones are not features which can contribute to the beauty, as opposed to the agreeableness, of objects.

Unfortunately, Kant does not explain in any concrete detail what the relevant conception of form comprises in § 14, but he implicitly comes to the conclusion that the relevant notion of form is *spatiotemporal form*—the spatiotemporal organization of the matter provided by sensation. In the terms of Kant's system, the form that one judges to be beautiful is a 'formal determination of the unity of a manifold'[6]—the spatiotemporal organization of a manifold of sensations ('matter') into unified and connected representations of objects existing in space and time. The latter paragraphs of § 14 draw out the implications of this way of framing the distinction between the beautiful and the agreeable:

> [I]n all the pictorial arts . . . the **drawing** is what is essential, in which what constitutes the ground of all arrangements for taste is not what gratifies in sensation but merely what pleases through its form . . . All form of the objects of the senses (of the outer as well as, mediately, the inner) is either **shape** or **play**: in the latter case, either play of shapes (in space, mime, and dance), or mere play of sensations (in time). The **charm** of colors or of the agreeable tones of instruments can be added, but **drawing** in the former and composition in the latter constitute the proper objects of the pure judgment of taste.[7]

Here we arrive at the formalist restrictions on art. In the pictorial arts, the shape or drawing alone contributes to the artwork's beauty. In music, the analogous feature of composition alone contributes to the music's beauty.

Chapter 1 revealed that these restrictions are implausible as an aesthetic view and in conflict with ordinary aesthetic discourse. In objecting to Kant's formalist strictures, I am by no means alone. Guyer, for instance, asks us to consider Josef Albers's series of paintings *Homage to the Square*, in which the geometrical form is identical in all of the paintings, but the juxtaposition of colors varies from painting to painting.[8] Typically, our responsiveness also varies from painting to painting; we find some of them beautiful but not others. According to Guyer, that is because we feel that some of the selections of colors belong together and are pleasing in juxtaposition; others are not. And it would not be plausible to stipulate flatly that these differences in responsiveness are merely differences in agreeableness.[9] In the same vein as my examples of the banjo rendition of the 'Girl From Ipanema' and Rodrigo's use of the English horn, Guyer approvingly quotes Barrows Dunham's suggestion that we 'imagine the performance of a symphony in which the violin parts are played by the horns and horn parts by the violins,' along with Dunham's (obvious) conclusion that 'the finest music in the world will not survive ill-treatment of its tonal qualities.'[10] But there is no need to belabor the point. A set of aesthetic strictures is unacceptable if it disqualifies color or tone, or some confluence of colors or tones, from contributing to beauty. Ordinary usage, not Kantian aesthetic formalism, is in the right.

The disjunctive claim, however, offers another alternative. Perhaps ordinary language is correct to count colors and tones as contributing to beauty after all. If it is correct, though, it is correct in spite of itself, and for the wrong reasons. Colors and tones do not contribute to beauty by providing us with pleasing sensations—the view with which Kant saddles the thought and speech of ordinary folks, with little or no argument—because they can properly be considered part of an object's form.[11]

A broader canvass of the third *Critique* bears out the suspicion that Kant never settles the question whether colors and tones are part of an object's form and hence potentially part of its beauty. Put differently, one must suspect that Kant at least feels the pull of the ordinary view that colors and tones can be beautiful in themselves. Exotic parrots from South America (like the macaw and the toucan) and the islands of the South Pacific (in particular, the so-called bird of paradise) are always high on Kant's list of his 'free beauties of nature,' although these birds are all known precisely for the beautiful coloration of their plumage. And Kant speaks freely of 'beautifully colored birds' feathers' [*schönfarbige Vogelfedern*].[12] If the strictures of formalism are correct, *schönfarbige* is a vulgar error, which Kant's specification of the notion of form should root out. Furthermore, along with its reference to beautifully colored birds feathers, § 41 lists flowers and the shells of mussels, thereby replicating § 16's list of flowers, birds, and marine crustaceans as things that are 'beauties in themselves,' and judged to be beautiful 'according to mere form.'[13] But § 41 describes precisely these things as 'charms' [*Reize*], explicitly contrasting them to 'beautiful forms.' Here Kant inverts the application of his distinction between the charms of the agreeable and the beauty of form.

To put the point generally, if one surveys Kant's examples throughout the third *Critique*, one must wonder whether he ever settles on a clear and determinate conception of the relevant notion of form. Kant's examples are of little use in determining the content of the notion of form, or in particular, whether it includes colors or tones. There is ample evidence that Kant suspects his formalist strictures to run afoul of perfectly reasonable ordinary views, and he struggles to come to some resolution of this conflict. This uncertainty helps to explain the presence of the disjunctive claim. Recall the second disjunct: if ordinary thought and speech are correct to count colors and tones among the elements of beauty, it must be because such features can be considered elements of an object's form in the relevant sense. It is therefore crucial to determine which aspects of Kant's broader philosophical system he draws on in his attempt to articulate the content of his conception of form.

Kant frames the question as whether colors and tones are mere sensations. From the perspective of the 'Transcendental Aesthetic,' this is equivalent to asking whether colors and tones are secondary qualities. As I noted in Chapter 1, Kant's examples of the agreeable are all examples that the 'Transcendental Aesthetic' reckons among secondary qualities. There Kant construes secondary qualities as nothing but the effects that objects have on our sense organs, that is, 'mere sensations and not intuitions,'[14] which are therefore 'correctly considered not as qualities of things but as mere alterations of our subject, which can even be different in different people.'[15]

This reveals another way to formulate the issue from the perspective of Kant's epistemology and metaphysics, namely, whether we have unified representations of colors and tones as real qualities of objects that exist in space and time. That is to ask whether a representation of a color or tone involves a manifold of sensations ordered in accordance with a spatiotemporal form, or in other words, whether the representation of a color or tone includes the form of an intuition in contrast to mere sensation. An intuition, for Kant, is composed of both form and matter, where the matter is sensation. If colors and tones are mere sensations, they exhibit no form; nor do we represent them as existing independently of us (in the 'empirical' sense) in space and time. That is Kant's view in the 'Transcendental Aesthetic.' If the relevant notion of form in the third *Critique* is identified with this notion of 'perceptual form'[16] from the 'Transcendental Aesthetic,' it will turn out that colors, tones, or anything else counted as a secondary quality cannot contribute to beauty in Kant's sense.

So far, then, we have three formulations of the question: (1) whether colors and tones are *mere sensations*, (2) whether colors and tones are *secondary qualities*, (3) whether the representations of colors and tones involve a manifold of sensations ordered by a spatiotemporal form. (1) and (3) are equivalent, since matter (mere sensation) and form (a spatiotemporal ordering of a manifold of sensation) are the only possible candidates. (2) is equivalent to the other formulations, provided that one accepts the characterization of secondary qualities from the 'Transcendental Aesthetic.' The main thrust of these three formulations can be expressed by the question: (4) whether colors and tones are *empirically real*—whether they are spatiotemporal entities or genuine properties of such entities, or merely the phenomenal effects of other such entities or properties.[17]

It is not at all clear why the aesthetic status of colors and tones (or of anything else) should be thought to turn on the resolution of these questions. Suppose I just happen to like a particular shape (for instance, a highly elongated ellipse), and a particular color (say, hunter green). It does not seem that the status of the pleasures I take in these features of things—and in particular, whether I have any basis for requiring others to take pleasure in them as well—has anything to do with differences in their ontological or epistemological status. Kant, however, distinguishes pleasures in the beautiful from pleasures in the agreeable according to constraints on the notion of communicability that derive from his general ontological and epistemological views. In the next two sections, I will examine two lines of thought about communicability that—often for the worse—shape Kant's distinction between the beautiful and the agreeable.

Section 2: The Variability Hypothesis

Kant appears to endorse what I will call the *variability (of sensations) hypothesis*: for all we know, sensations, or secondary qualities construed as sensations, may not exhibit a constant and uniform qualitative character across different individuals. For all we know, my experience of redness, for instance, may be very different from some other observer's experience of redness.[18] If that is the case, Kant thinks, we cannot presume that even if you receive sensations that are pleasurable from some object, I will also receive sensations that are pleasurable from the same object; after all, the sensations each one of us receives may be very different. Thus, the requirement that a universally communicable pleasure must be available to everyone on the same terms precludes judgments about sensations from rightfully making any normative demands. Judgments about sensations or secondary qualities—including judgments about colors and tones, if that is what they in fact are—must be nonnormative judgments of the agreeable.

At first blush, it is difficult to understand why Kant would endorse the variability hypothesis. Consider again the claim about secondary qualities from the 'Transcendental Aesthetic': secondary qualities are 'mere sensations and not intuitions,' which are 'correctly considered not as qualities of things but as mere alterations of our subject, which can even be different in different people.'[19] These typical formulations at least intimate that the variability hypothesis is taken to follow from the characterization of secondary qualities as empirically ideal. If secondary qualities are 'mere alterations of our subject' rather than real entities or real properties of spatiotemporal objects that exist independently of us, then—for all we know—they might arise in each subject in a different way, resulting in a different character.

That is not a convincing argument. It isn't clear why anything Kant has said so far would disallow adherence to what I will call the systematic correlation view of secondary qualities, attributed by many to Locke.[20] On this view, secondary qualities like redness are said to be purely phenomenal or experiential, and so fail to be real properties of spatiotemporal objects. But objects—in virtue of their specific configurations of primary qualities— systematically cause us to represent them as having these properties. Objects do not have any property that resembles, for instance, our experience of redness, but our experience of redness is systematically correlated with, and caused by, a property or configuration of properties that real objects have. If there are causal laws that govern the human sensory system and its interactions with the surrounding physical environment, then it is not clear why one shouldn't presume that these causal mechanisms produce the same kinds of experiences of redness and the like in all of us.

I put this forward not as a proposal for a theory of secondary qualities but rather as a question for Kant's readers. Given that Kant construes our receptivity to sensation as a matter of causal interaction between the human sensory system and its physical environment, and given that Kant certainly believes in constant and unchanging causal laws governing the world of appearances, why does Kant not accept something like the systematic correlation view? Given the general thrust of Kant's views about causality within the world of appearances, the variability hypothesis seems gratuitous and poorly motivated. His basic characterizations of sensation and his views on causal laws exert pressure away from a commitment to the variability hypothesis, not toward it. At the very least, there is the appearance of a real tension in Kant's thought here.

The answer lies in the hidden assumption of the systematic correlation view. If this view is to provide us with good reason to reject the variability hypothesis, it must assume that the physiology of our sensory systems works the same way in all of us, that individual human eyes or human ears are instances of general types of causal mechanisms to be found in human beings quite generally, rather than idiosyncratic hunks of matter that obey their own special principles. Now that sounds like a fairly innocuous assumption; in the blink of an eye, even the most brilliant ophthalmologist would be reduced to tears if it were false. Or, more precisely, there wouldn't even be such subjects as ophthalmology or neurology if it were false. Yet this is precisely the assumption that Kant rejects, claiming quite firmly in § 39 that this 'absolutely cannot be presupposed.'[21] The question then becomes why we are not entitled to this presupposition, especially in light of its overall coherence with a view of nature as governed by discoverable causal laws and regularities.

In short, the answer is: the presupposition is an empirical claim, hence one that cannot be known *a priori*. Kant's remark in § 39 should be read as saying: cannot be presupposed *from the standpoint of transcendental philosophy*. Similarly, his statements of the variability hypothesis should be read as saying: sensations may vary from subject to subject, *for all that transcendental philosophy is capable of knowing*. Transcendental philosophy cannot help itself to empirical claims; the only claims it is entitled to are those which can be known *a priori*.

Consider the difference, from Kant's perspective, between the assumption that we all have the same sensory constitution, qua a set of physical causal mechanisms, and the assumption that we all share the same forms of sensibility. Whatever its status, this central claim of the 'Transcendental Aesthetic' is resolutely not meant to be empirical. I'll restrict my remarks to the form of outer sense, the *a priori* intuition of space. Kant's argument for postulating this *a priori* intuition, or 'form of sensibility,' takes as its starting point a commitment to the possibility of synthetic *a priori* knowledge of space. The postulation of a form of sensibility is meant to explain how such synthetic *a priori* knowledge is possible: only if the representation of space is in some (transcendental) sense due to us, as part of our cognitive constitution, will it be possible for us to know anything *a priori* about space, either in the general sense that any object of sensory experience will be located in space, or in the more specific sense of the laws governing spatial properties and relations as articulated by the synthetic *a priori* science of Euclidean geometry. The claim that space is an *a priori* form of sensibility is not and cannot be supported by any empirical investigation. Rather, it is offered as the only possible explanation of how we could ever arrive at synthetic *a priori* knowledge of space.

To be very brief: if one takes a commitment to the possibility of a body of synthetic *a priori* knowledge as a datum, which Kant unquestionably does, and proceeds to argue that a certain characterization of our cognitive faculties is the only possible way to explain how we could have such knowledge, one will have argued for the necessity of that characterization of our cognitive faculties.[22] Anyone capable of synthetic *a priori* knowledge of space, which for Kant is all of us, must have this *a priori* form of sensibility, for synthetic *a priori* knowledge is possible in no other way. The presumption that our sensible constitutions all share the same form is utterly unlike the presumption that they are all causally affected in the same ways, so that they all give rise to representations with the same qualitative or sensory features of color, smell, sound, taste, and the like. The former presumption cannot be supported by empirical evidence, whereas the latter must be, if it can be supported at all. Put differently, the former presumption can be known *a priori*, and therefore with absolute necessity. The latter presumption can make no claim to absolute necessity. No matter how much evidence we gather for the claim that our senses deliver to us representations with the same qualitative features in the same circumstances—however we would do that—we could never assert the contrary of the variability hypothesis with necessity; we could never rule out the possibility of a counterexample, someone whose representations do not have the same qualitative or sensory features as our own.

This is a very brief sketch of the route into the so-called transcendental perspective, from which we can make claims about the necessary features of our cognitive faculties. In this context, Kant points out that there is no body of synthetic *a priori* knowledge of colors, tones, smells, and the like—all the secondary qualities—analogous to our synthetic *a priori* knowledge of space.[23] Accordingly, there can be no transcendental characterization of our cognitive faculties in terms of these sensible features of our representations, since there is no corresponding commitment to a body of synthetic *a priori* knowledge in which they figure. Transcendental philosophy must therefore remain neutral about the similarities or differences that might obtain in these features of our representations; from this perspective, *for all we know* the variability hypothesis is correct. Kant does not assert that the variability hypothesis is true; rather, he leaves it as an empirical matter on which transcendental philosophy is neither equipped to take a stand nor entitled to base any conclusions.[24] This, in turn, means that transcendental philosophy cannot know *a priori* that pleasures grounded on these features of sensations (color, smell, sound, taste) are equally available to everyone on the same occasions and on the same terms. A judgment based on such qualities cannot legitimately demand universal agreement. It must, therefore, be a judgment of the agreeable.[25]

Thus, the variability hypothesis rules out the possibility of a communicable pleasure in mere qualitative features of a sensation. If pleasures taken in colors or tones are to be communicable—hence, if judgments about colors and tones are to count as judgments of beauty—Kant must show that our representations of colors and tones are not mere sensations. In the next section, I consider a line of thought in Kant which, though it ultimately establishes nothing on its own, points the way to the crucial considerations for determining both the epistemic and aesthetic status of our representations of colors and tones.

Section 3: Objective and Subjective Sensation

In the third *Critique*, Kant employs a distinction between 'objective' and 'subjective' sensation, which appears to be absent from the 'Transcendental Aesthetic.' Kant's claim in the 'Transcendental Aesthetic' is in fact more radical than just a denial that there is any body of synthetic *a priori* knowledge of secondary qualities that corresponds to geometrical knowledge of space. He denies that our experiences of colors, tones, and the like furnish us with *any* knowledge of objects. About secondary qualities—and here Kant mentions colors, sounds, and warmth—he says that 'since they are merely sensations and not intuitions, [they] do not in themselves allow any object to be cognized, least of all *a priori*.'[26] Kant's marginalia in his own copy of the first *Critique* put the point tersely: 'Intuition is related to the object, sensation merely to the subject.'[27] Kant relies on an eliminativist conception of secondary qualities, according to which they are not real features of spatiotemporal objects: if redness is not a real feature of objects, having an experience of redness does not furnish me with any knowledge of what objects are like.

That is difficult to square with the distinction between objective and subjective sensation. In his initial attempts to set forth the distinction between the beautiful and the agreeable, and to clarify the sense in which the agreeable 'pleases the senses in sensation,' Kant writes:

If a determination of the feeling of pleasure or displeasure is called sensation, then this expression means something entirely different than if I call the representation of a thing (through sense, as a receptivity belonging to the faculty of cognition) sensation. For in the latter case the representation *is related to the object*, but in the first case it is related solely to the subject, and does not serve for any cognition at all, not even that by which the subject **cognizes** itself.[28]

In particular, the claim that a sensation 'is related to the object' [*wird die Vorstellung auf das Objekt . . . bezogen*] does not square well with the earlier claim that sensations 'do not in themselves allow any object to be cognized.' This passage depends on the distinction between objective and subjective sensation, which Kant immediately proceeds to explain:

> In the above explanation, however, we understand by the word 'sensa-tion' an objective representation of the senses, and in order not always to run the risk of being misinterpreted, we will call that which must always remain merely subjective and absolutely cannot constitute a representa-tion of an object by the otherwise customary name of 'feeling.' The green color of the meadows belongs to **objective** sensation, as perception of an object of sense; but its agreeableness belongs to **subjective** sensation, through which no object is represented, i.e., to feeling, through which the object is considered as an object of satisfaction (which is not a cogni-tion of it).[29]

Recall Kant's definition of 'sensory sensation' [*Sinnenempfindung*] in § 39: 'If sensation, as the real in perception, is related to cognition, it is called sensory sensation.'[30] 'Sensory sensation' thus means the same as 'objective sensation.'[31] These formulations seem to be in even more obvious tension with the 'Transcendental Aesthetic.' One might conjecture that the 'Tran-scendental Aesthetic' confuses the distinction between objective and sub-jective sensation. Perhaps Kant had not yet clearly established the distinction, which may then provide a way out of the drastic eliminativist and subjectiv-ist view Kant had put forth in the first *Critique*.

That hypothesis is incorrect. The distinction between objective and subjective sensation appears in at least two independent sets of notes from two of Kant's lecture courses on metaphysics, both given well before the appearance of the B-edition of the first *Critique* in 1787. It is instructive to look at the relevant passages from *Metaphysik L₁* (dating from somewhere in the mid to late 1770s) and *Metaphysik Mongrovius* (from 1782–3).[32] In *Metaphysik L₁*, commenting on the five bodily senses, Kant explains:

> Some of these senses are objective, others subjective. The objective senses are at the same time connected with the subjective; thus the objective senses are not only objective but also subjective. Either the objective is greater in the senses than the subjective, or the subjective is greater than the objective . . . seeing, hearing, and feeling [NB: 'feeling' here refers to

the sense of touch] are senses more objective than subjective, but smell-
ing and tasting are more subjective than objective. The subjective senses
are senses of enjoyment, the objective senses, on the other hand, are
instructive senses.[33]

Here, Kant says that all five senses contain both objective and subjective
elements; this distinction divides the sense modalities as a matter of degree.
In particular, sight, hearing, and touch are said to be more objective, while
smell and taste are said to be more subjective. The objective senses are
predominantly oriented toward providing information about objects,
whereas the subjective senses are predominantly oriented toward providing pleasure or displeasure (in the sense of the agreeable): 'Some senses
are more concerned with sensation without producing cognition, others
belong more to cognition than to sensation.'[34] *Metaphysik Mongrovius* confirms that '[s]mell and taste are more subjective,' and adds the stronger
(and implausible) claim that 'if one merely smells or tastes, one can not yet
distinguish one thing from another.'[35] Similarly implausible, and incon-
gruous with the overall thrust of the metaphysics lectures, are remarks like
'[s]ight and touch are completely objective representations.'[36]

Three textual points are worth noting. First, while Kant's distinction
between objective and subjective sensation generally divides the sense
modalities by degree, some of Kant's formulations hint at a distinction in
kind. Second, the allegedly (more) objective senses provide the examples in
the passage from the B-edition's version of the 'Transcendental Aesthetic,'
in which Kant denies that sensation affords us any cognition of objects.
Third, color and tone are both perceived by allegedly (more) objective
sense modalities, and these are precisely the candidates that Kant considers
for promotion from the agreeable to the beautiful in the third *Critique*.

The thrust of the relevant passages from the metaphysics lectures is that,
on the whole, sight and touch provide us with more information about
objects than taste and smell. That is probably true, but it will not fund a
distinction between the beautiful and the agreeable that makes distinctions
in kind, rather than degree, between the different sense modalities. Kant
never contemplates the possibility that taste and smell could offer any
candidates for the beautiful; nor do the representations of taste and smell
ever come under the same kinds of (defeasible) considerations that the
representations of the (more) objective modalities do. By their nature, they
are modalities of the agreeable only.

The issue of the cognitive prioritization of some sensory modalities over
others is a pivotal part of the basis for Kant's distinction between the beautiful

and the agreeable. In particular, his thought that sight and hearing have a *cognitive* priority over smell and taste provides a theoretical impetus for claiming an *aesthetic* priority of sight and hearing over smell and taste. But for this strategy to succeed, it is necessary to provide a cognitive distinction in kind or category, rather than degree, which the distinction between objective and subjective sensation has obliquely gestured toward but has not clearly yielded. It will not suffice to say that the sensations afforded by different sense modalities are, in some way or other, more or less 'related to cognition.'

Moreover, Kant denies that specific qualitative features of a *Sinnenempfindung*—a 'sensory sensation' or 'objective sensation'—can be universally communicable. Here again is the crucial passage from § 39:

> If sensation [*Empfindung*] as the real in perception, is related to cognition, it is called sensory sensation [*Sinnenempfindung*]; and its specific quality can be represented as completely communicable in the same way only if one assumes that everyone has a sense [*Sinn*] that is the same as our own—but this absolutely cannot be presupposed in the case of a sensory sensation [*von einer Sinnesempfindung*].[37]

Once again, transcendental philosophy is constrained to proceed as if the variability hypothesis is correct. Consequently, no pleasure—hence no aesthetic judgment which takes as its ground the features of a sensation like color or tone—can be regarded as universally communicable, even if that sensation is thought of as 'sensory' or 'objective' or 'related to cognition.' The distinction between objective and subjective sensation affords no basis for declaring colors and tones beautiful, since it affords no basis for declaring pleasures based on them, or judgments about them, universally communicable. This conclusion can be seen in a number of passages, for instance:

> The universal communicability of a pleasure already includes in its concept that this must not be a pleasure of enjoyment, from mere sensation [*aus bloßer Empfindung*], but one of reflection; and thus aesthetic art, as beautiful art, is one that has the reflecting power of judgment and not sensory sensation [*Sinnenempfindung*] as its standard.[38]

Judgments of beauty cannot be grounded on mere sensation, even when sensation is construed in the objective or cognition-oriented sense of *Sinnenempfindung*. Something further is needed to secure their universal communicability.

At first blush, Kant's denial that the specific qualities of a *Sinnenempfind-ung* are universally communicable renders it unclear how much stock we are to put in the characterization of *Sinnenempfindung* as 'objective' or 'related to cognition.' For Kant, cognition is universally communicable, and he takes a denial of this point to be tantamount to wholesale skepticism.[39] Now, if a universally communicable aesthetic judgment (e.g., 'this is beautiful') cannot be based on a *Sinnenempfindung*, neither can a universally communicable cognitive judgment (e.g., 'this is red'). The universal communicability of such a cognitive judgment would, from Kant's perspective, require the same presupposition of similarity in the qualitative or sensible aspects of our representations that he has claimed we are not entitled to make. If having a representation of redness is a matter of having a mere sensation—if redness is just something given through sheer receptivity—then the judgment 'this is red' will not, according to the standard articulated in § 39, meet the criteria for being intersubjectively valid. Thus it will fail to qualify as cognition; for Kant, a judgment which fails to be intersubjectively valid also fails to be objectively valid or, more plainly, objective.[40]

The notion of objective sensation, then, is not sufficient to ground a judgment that claims intersubjective validity or universal communicability. It is thereby insufficient to establish the communicability either of a judgment of the form 'this is beautiful' or of the form 'this is red.' So it is insufficient to establish that judgments made about such things as colors or tones can be intersubjectively valid judgments, whether cognitive or aesthetic. Most importantly, it cannot establish that such judgments are judgments of the beautiful rather than the agreeable.

Nevertheless, the investigation of Kant's distinction between objective and subjective sensation has yielded an important clue to the ultimate basis of the distinction between the beautiful and the agreeable: it is founded on a distinction in the epistemic or cognitive role of the representations upon which judgments of either variety are made. Correlatively, it is based on an epistemic or cognitive privileging of certain sense modalities over others. But without further supplementation, the notions of objective and subjective sensation cannot provide the needed distinctions in kind between different sense modalities and their corresponding representations.

Now, I do believe that Kant takes there to be categorial differences in the cognitive status or role of different sense modalities. Like most contemporary philosophers who believe in the primacy of vision (and touch), Kant takes vision (and touch) to play a privileged role in representing objects as determinately located in space and time, a role that sense modalities like taste and smell cannot play. Indeed, the very term *Anschauung* intimates as much.[41] Thus, the distinction between representations that can ground a judgment of beauty and those that cannot turns on the following question: is the representation of some (putative) feature of an object mere sensation, or does having a representation of that feature require a manifold of sensation ordered in accordance with the spatiotemporal form of an *Anschauung*?

More generally, the spatiotemporal form of an intuition must be an essential aspect of the representation if a judgment made about it—be it cognitive or aesthetic—is to be capable of intersubjective validity (or, by implication, objective validity). The representation cannot be given through sheer receptivity. The notions of *Sinnenempfindung*, or 'objective sensation,' or 'sensation which is related to cognition,' must be understood in the specific sense of sensation that is presented to the imagination for the purposes of synthesis—the production of spatiotemporally unified intuitions. Not all sense modalities contribute sensations that the imagination can synthesize into intuitions, since not all sense modalities allow us to determinately locate objects in space and time; this is the cognitive province of sight and touch (specifically, visual or tactile perceptions of size, shape, motion, and place) rather than of smell and taste. Sense modalities that cannot contribute to the production of spatiotemporally unified intuitions cannot contribute to our overall fund of judgments of the beautiful, for reasons that will emerge more fully in Section 4.

The epistemological or cognitive prioritization of some sense modalities (and their corresponding representations) over others readily finds ontological correlates. Philosophers who take issue with eliminativist or subjectivist views of secondary qualities virtually always fasten on color, arguing either that colors are genuine features of objects or that we cannot find compelling grounds for concluding that they aren't.[42] Many think of sounds as ontologically self-subsistent entities.[43] In other words, many philosophers think of colors and sounds (hence, tones) as empirically real properties or entities, whereas nobody, as far as I can tell, is tempted to think of smells or tastes in the same way. And Kant certainly shares these common tendencies.

The thought that such epistemological or ontological claims provide grounds for privileging some sensory modalities and their corresponding representations in *matters of taste* is unconvincing. Helping oneself to an epistemologically or ontologically motivated privileging right from the start will prevent one from commanding a clear view of matters of taste on their own terms.[44] For better or worse, though, the question of the scope of Kant's aesthetic formalism is inextricably linked to more general questions about Kant's continued commitment to the first *Critique*'s eliminativist and subjectivist ontology of secondary qualities. In the third *Critique*, Kant revisits the question whether our representations of colors and tones are mere sensations or aspects of objective intuitions with a spatiotemporal form. Only if the latter is the case can aesthetic judgments based on these representations count as judgments of the beautiful. Thus we arrive at the question posed in § 14, which Kant ultimately finds he cannot answer with the certainty required by transcendental philosophy.

Section 4: Imaginative Activity and Norms

In § 14, Kant reiterates that 'the quality of the sensations themselves cannot be assumed to be in accord in all subjects,' and thus concludes that 'the only thing that can be universally communicated about these representations [of color and tone]' is 'a determination that already concerns form.'[45] By 'form,' Kant clearly means the perceptual form (as opposed to the matter) of an intuition. To be universally communicable, an aesthetic judgment must have as its ground not a mere sensation but rather a spatiotemporally organized manifold of sensation. Kant immediately turns to Euler's theory of light and sound for assistance. If Euler's theory is correct, colors and tones are not 'mere sensation[s]' but rather 'formal determination[s] of the unity of the manifold of [sensations], and in that case could also be counted as beauties in themselves.'[46]

Euler's theory has two parts. The first part is a claim about the ontology of colors and tones: 'colors are vibrations of the aether in uniform temporal sequence, just as tones are vibrations of the air disturbed by sound.'[47] Euler's theory describes colors and tones as (empirically) real spatiotemporal entities and so avoids any eliminativist or subjectivist claims. The second part, which Kant says is 'most important,' is a perceptual correlate of the ontological claim: 'the mind does not merely perceive, by sense, their effect on the animation of the organ, but also, through reflection, perceives the regular play of the impressions (hence the form in the connection [*Verbindung*] of different representations).'[48] Having a representation of a color or tone is more than just a function of sheer receptivity, of the sense organs being causally affected in one way or another. The causal effects of sheer receptivity are precisely what Kant has ruled out from being universally communicable. Having a representation of a color or tone, on Euler's theory, involves the perception of form—the unification or connectedness of a manifold of sensation into a representation or set of representations.

Only representations that have this sort of unity or connectedness—which Kant calls 'synthetic unity,' to indicate that it is the result of an active process of synthesis—are fit to be objective intuitions representing things in space and time. In sum, on Euler's theory, the representation of a color or tone is part of an objective intuition rather than a subjective sensation.

Kant's discussion in § 14 turns on exceptionally intricate questions at the heart of the first *Critique,* so a bird's eye view will have to suffice. Kant believes that unity or connectedness in our representations is something that we can never take as given; it is always made.[49] The process by which representations with this character are generated is synthesis. Synthesis is performed by the faculty called imagination, whose activity is governed by a set of conditions on representation. These are conditions for the possibility of the resulting representations figuring in intersubjectively (and, in the case of cognitive judgments, objectively) valid judgments, that is, communicable or normative claims.

The involvement of the imagination is the ultimate ground of Kant's distinction between the beautiful and the agreeable, and thus the key to the question whether judgments about colors or tones can have the universal communicability required for them to count as judgments of beauty. Recall that the imagination operates upon the manifold of sensation given to it by receptivity, which provides the matter of representations. (We can now, if we like, call a manifold that is taken up by the imagination 'objective sensation,' though that obscures more than it clarifies.) Out of the manifold of sensation, the imagination constructs unified or connected representations of objects. The activity of the imagination, though a natural psychological process, is not a brute psychological process. It is governed by the conditions on representation established by the concepts of the understanding and the forms of intuition (or sensibility), namely, spatiotemporality—the sensible condition on representation, which is required if these concepts are to be applicable to objects (have 'objective validity'). The activity of the imagination is thus exemplary of cognitive or representational norms.

Everything that we have seen so far can now be recapitulated in terms of the activity of the imagination. Only if the representation of a color or tone has a form generated by the representational activity of the imagination will it qualify as being related to objects or to cognition. Without a place for the unifying activity of the imagination, no conception of sensation can explain how we have representations that are related to objects and hence to cognition. More generally, it will never explain the possibility of intersubjectively valid judgments. We've seen why transcendental philosophy is not entitled to assume that the matter of our representations is universally communicable. But this argument does not apply to their form, to that which is generated through the synthesis performed by the imagination.

Synthesis is a necessary condition for the possibility of cognition, which is always the result of a cooperative undertaking of our active and receptive faculties. The receptive faculty (sensation) provides the matter of representations; the active faculty (understanding) provides the form by establishing conditions on representation that govern the synthesis performed by the imagination. In no other way, according to Kant, is cognition possible.[50] For this reason, we can and must assume that we all share common sensible and intellectual constitutions, conceived in terms of the most general or formal features of our representations. Necessarily, these features of our representations are universally communicable, for cognition would not be possible without them. Thus, the form of a representation is universally communicable, whereas its matter is not, because this form is produced by a synthesis of the imagination and therefore exemplifies the necessary conditions for the possibility of cognition. Representational form is the basis of intersubjective validity, and, in turn, of objective validity. Of course, this will not convince a skeptic, but Kant's explanation of the possibility of cognition is not designed to; his explanation takes for granted that cognition is possible.

We can now reformulate the requirements for a judgment about color or tone to count as a judgment of beauty in terms of the activity of the imagination. As we've seen, all cognition results from the interplay between sensibility, understanding, and imagination. The importance of the imagination lies in its production of representations that can ground intersubjectively and objectively valid judgments through synthesis of the manifold of intuition. In a judgment of beauty, the understanding and the imagination stand in a special relation called the *free play*, in which the activity of the imagination exemplifies, or is governed by, the understanding's conditions on representation in an indeterminate way.[51] This relation, Kant thinks, must be possible if the understanding and imagination are to be able to stand in the relation required for cognition, even though the free play is not the relation in which the understanding and imagination stand in any actual act of cognition, since the application of no specific concept is either presupposed by or produced by the free play.[52] But it is crucial that there be some kind of imaginative activity if a judgment is to be universally communicable (and hence count as a judgment of beauty), and this activity must exemplify conditions that are also required for cognition. Only then can a judgment be intersubjectively valid, and only then can a 'common sense' [*Gemeinsinn*] be presupposed 'as the necessary condition of the universal communicability of our cognition.'[53]

A judgment of beauty, in other words, must comprise more than just an exercise of sheer receptivity. If judgments concerning color or tone are to count as judgments of beauty, the representation of a color or tone must be produced by a synthetic and rule-governed activity of the imagination: our representations of colors and tones must be representations organized in accordance with the spatiotemporal form of an intuition. Of course, further argument is needed to establish that the pleasure that attends to a representation produced by the imagination is also universally communicable. But I am concerned here with just one necessary condition for this to be the case.

Thus, from Kant's perspective, Euler's theory of light and sound addresses the central epistemological and metaphysical questions that determine whether judgments about colors or tones can count as judgments of beauty. On Euler's theory, as Kant understands it, perceptions of colors and tones have intuitive form, which allows them to be the basis of universally communicable judgments. Moreover, the theory credits us with the capacity to locate and individuate objects spatiotemporally on the basis of additional visual representations (colors) and auditory representations (tones). So the question is whether we have good reason to accept Euler's theory.

Clearly, Kant does not accept Euler's theory straightaway. In § 14, he lays down his formalist strictures against counting colors or tones as elements of beauty immediately after introducing the theory; in subsequent sections, he continues to draw on these strictures, as if this foray into Euler's theory had proven to be at best inconclusive and at worst a failure. And Kant never fully settles the question whether he thinks Euler is correct anywhere in his writings: sometimes, he endorses Euler's theory; sometimes, he indicates a preference for alternative theories.[54] This uncertainty raises an important textual question. Given that Kant seriously entertains alternative theories of the ontology and perception of color and sound, why does he discuss *only* Euler's theory in § 14? Why does he not specify the consequences for the aesthetics of colors and tones of each of the competing theories he is willing to entertain, especially if he is not certain which one is correct?

I offer an hypothesis that I believe makes sense of the conflicting morass of textual evidence, building on some useful observations from Henry Allison.[55] Allison rightly observes a sudden shift in attitude and tone in the 'Third Moment.' In the first two moments, Kant speaks as though he is presenting generally accepted views—that he is, as I have put it, generally respectful of and responsive to the features of our ordinary aesthetic discourse. One feature of that discourse, I have claimed, is that colors and tones are routinely counted as beautiful in themselves, or as contributing to the beauty, rather than the agreeableness, of objects. But in the

'Third Moment,' as Allison points out, Kant suddenly shifts to a view that he acknowledges to be sharply at odds with ordinary discourse. That shift is accompanied by the introduction of the disjunctive claim in § 14: either ordinary discourse is wrong to count colors and tones as potentially beautiful, or it is correct but for the wrong reasons. Kant immediately looks for a way to reconcile his theory with ordinary aesthetic discourse, not simply because of the fact of conflict—Kant never takes ordinary usage to be authoritative, rather than a useful starting point—but, I propose, because he recognizes that the strict version of his formalist doctrine, on which colors and tones do not contribute to beauty, is deeply problematic. Hardly anyone thinks that it isn't, and everyone looks for a way to absolve Kant of responsibility for this doctrine, or at least to temper the strength of its conclusions.

I believe Kant does much the same thing. He looks for a way to show that his formalism is not *as* deeply at odds with the plausible views of ordinary thought and speech as it appears to be, that his distinction between 'beauty' and 'charm' needn't be taken in such a strict and revisionary sense—which is not to say that he is ever willing to give up the distinction. In § 14, when first introducing the doctrine of formalism, Kant realizes that it appears to have unacceptable consequences. He immediately hedges his position by saying that ordinary thought and speech may be correct after all, but if it is, we will need to find a way to bring that thought and speech into line with the demands of his philosophical theory.

Euler's theory, in particular, offers hope for doing so. From Kant's perspective, it provides evidence that our representations of colors and tones exemplify a spatiotemporal ordering or form that could only be the result of an activity of the imagination and therefore could not be mere sensations. If Euler's theory is correct, ordinary thought and speech would have misunderstood the *basis* for its claims, but its claims would be allowed to stand. Ordinary thought and speech would receive grounding from philosophical theory, and philosophical theory would not be in stark conflict with the claims of ordinary thought and speech, which do, after all, seem to make good sense. And as Kant's usage of words like *schönfarbig* indicates, he too felt the pull of ordinary thought and speech's conception of the aesthetic status of colors and tones. In short, Euler's theory provides a potential way out of the unacceptable consequences that seem to follow from Kant's general epistemological positions. If correct, it would show that ordinary aesthetic discourse isn't wrong in its assessment, but only in the (alleged) basis for its assessment, which transcendental philosophy could revise, thereby grounding ordinary discourse without completely running roughshod over some of its eminently plausible contentions.

I believe that is the best way to make sense of the morass of hesitant, uncertain, and sometimes conflicting claims about colors and tones spread throughout the third *Critique*. Kant thinks that if Euler is correct, the consequences of his epistemological doctrines for his aesthetic theory are not as extreme and counterintuitive as they first appear to be. That is why he immediately fastens on Euler's theory in particular: nothing else promises a way out of aesthetic formalism's unacceptable conclusions. But in the end, Kant does not know whether Euler's theory can be accepted, or precisely how to characterize our representations of colors and tones.

Kant's final expression of defeat comes in § 51: 'one cannot say with certainty whether a color or tone (sound) is merely agreeable sensations or is in itself already a beautiful play of sensations, which as such involves a satisfaction in the form of aesthetic judging.'[56] This remark is intended to sum up the following (badly put) passage:

It is remarkable that these two senses [sight and hearing], besides the susceptibility to sensations to the extent that that is required in order to arrive by their means at concepts of external objects, are also capable of a special sensation connected with that, about which it cannot be rightly made out whether it has as its ground sense or reflection; and that this affectability can yet sometimes be lacking, although as far as its use for the cognition of objects of sense is concerned the sense is not at all defective otherwise, but is rather exceptionally acute.[57]

The latter parts of § 51 reveal that Kant is referring to people who are either color blind or tone deaf yet have otherwise perfectly fine sight or hearing, whom he considers to be 'admittedly rare examples of human beings.' I'll restrict my remarks to the case of tone-deaf people. Kant takes their alleged rarity to speak in favor of counting tones 'not as mere sensory impressions, but as the effect of a judging of the form in the play of many sensations';[58] in other words, tone perception must involve a manifold of sensation that the imagination has synthesized into an intuition with a spatiotemporal form.

This is a very strange argument, but its point can be gleaned from the interpretation I have offered. If tone-deaf people truly are rare—if nearly everybody agrees about the discrimination of pitch—there is general uniformity in this aspect of our perceptions. Given transcendental philosophy's inability to reject the variability hypothesis, it cannot explain this agreement as the result of similarities in the quality of our sensations; rather, it must postulate an imaginative activity of synthesis that introduces an inter-subjectively valid form to a manifold of sensations. From the perspective of transcendental philosophy, the presumption that hardly anyone whose hearing is not otherwise impaired lacks the ability to discriminate tones puts pressure in the direction of explaining tone perception as a perception of the form of a manifold of sensations rather than as the causal effect of sensations.

This is all terribly unconvincing, and for a variety of reasons, Kant does not find this argument conclusive. One such reason is explicit in the text of § 51. Euler's theory describes sounds as vibrations of air, but Kant thinks these vibrations are 'probably' way too fast for us to notice or to be able to judge. Considering the speed of these vibrations, 'which probably far exceeds all our capacity for judging immediately in perception the proportion of the division of time,' one seems compelled to conclude that 'it is only the **effect** of these vibrations on the elastic parts of our body that is sensed, but that the **division of time** by means of them is not noticed and drawn into the judging.'[59] Given that the frequency of musically useful pitches extends to upwards of 5,000 Hz, and that normal unimpaired human ears can detect pitches to upwards of 20,000 Hz, it is indeed unlikely that the temporal divisions—say, 5,000 or even 20,000 vibrations per second—could be noticed, much less 'drawn into the judging.' From Kant's perspective, this would relegate judgments about tone to judgments of the agreeable, as they would be based on mere sensation ('the effects of these vibrations on the elastic parts of our body') rather than on any apprehended temporal form of a manifold, which an intuition requires.[60]

Kant thus adduces a morass of conflicting considerations and unpersuasive arguments both for and against the perceptual claim made by Euler's theory. These are also arguments for and against counting judgments about tone as judgments of beauty.

In the final sentence of § 51, Kant abandons hope of decisively resolving the issue and offers his 'definition' of music on each alternative, noting the differing extents to which it could be considered either a beautiful or an agreeable art, depending on which set of considerations one accepts.[61] But Kant is plainly unwilling and unable to commit. Even at the very end of the 'Deduction of Pure Aesthetic Judgments,' neither a resolution of the questions raised by aesthetic formalism nor a precise statement of the scope of the 'Deduction'—a precise answer to the traditional aesthetic question—is thought possible.

By now, Kant's investigation of the aesthetic status of colors and tones has wandered very far afield. It is not at all clear why the aesthetic status of colors and tones should be thought to depend on the truth of Euler's, or anyone's, scientific theory. But my purpose is to understand why Kant's investigation shapes up—and fails—as it does. The reason, again, is that judgments about colors or tones can count as communicable judgments of beauty, rather than private judgments of agreeableness, only if our representations of colors and tones exemplify the spatiotemporal form of an intuition. That is the foundational commitment of Kant's aesthetic formalism. Kant never wavers in that commitment, even as he discovers that he cannot determine the scope of its claims. In Sections 5–6, I will argue that the foundational commitment of aesthetic formalism is too deeply rooted in the epistemology and metaphysics of transcendental idealism for Kant to seriously consider abandoning it.

Section 5: Reply to Guyer

Kant's admission of defeat in § 51 notwithstanding, Guyer believes that Kant's aesthetic theory can be saved from itself, since there is nothing in the foundational commitments of the theory that entails restrictive formalism—the doctrine that only an object's perceptual form, in the strict sense of spatiotemporal form, can contribute to its beauty.[62] On Guyer's view, then, I may have posed an irrelevant inquiry: since none of Kant's arguments commit him to restrictive formalism, it does not matter whether Kant thought that it followed from his general epistemological and metaphysical doctrines or not; Kant's arguments on behalf of restrictive formalism are simply bad. This recognition should allow us to see that the core of Kant's aesthetic theory can be salvaged. In particular, the doctrine of the free play can be upheld independently of Kant's apparent commitment to an implausible restrictive formalism.[63]

Guyer claims that Kant illicitly identifies form with the strict sense of perceptual form. This identification does not follow from anything internal to Kant's analysis of aesthetic response, as set forth by the doctrine of the free play; Kant has simply imported epistemological and metaphysical doctrines from the 'Transcendental Aesthetic' without warrant.[64] Guyer proffers an explanation for this non sequitur: the doctrine of the free play provides no constraints on an answer to the traditional aesthetic question. It establishes constraints on 'what kinds of approval can found judgments of taste,' but does not restrict 'what sorts of properties of objects may contribute to their beauty.'[65] All that the free play requires, according to Guyer, is the presentation of some manifold to the imagination; nothing in the conception of the free play determines what features of a manifold allow it to be grasped and unified in the free and pleasurable play of the faculties characteristic of aesthetic response.[66] It's one thing to say that '**Beauty** is the form of the **purposiveness** of an object,'[67] but without some determinate specification of the notion of form—of what particular features can be purposive for the cognitive faculties, insofar as they can occasion the free play—such definitions provide no constraints on what features of objects may contribute to their beauty.

Searching for a way to provide some determinate linkage between his analysis of aesthetic response and an answer to the traditional aesthetic question, Kant illicitly slides from this general conception of the form of purposiveness to a particular and overly restrictive conception of perceptual form, imported from the 'Transcendental Aesthetic,' in a failed, last-ditch effort to bung the hole left open by his theory. While Guyer alleges that Kant cannot provide a determinate answer to the traditional aesthetic question, he also holds open the prospect that a responsiveness to (at least a manifold or array of) colors or tones can be seen as a responsiveness to beauty, rather than mere agreeableness. Guyer thereby hopes to exonerate Kant from some of the most implausible of the apparent implications of his formalism.[68]

Now, it is uncontroversial that a judgment of beauty must be based on an imaginative activity of unifying a manifold; anything else would be no more than mere physiological gratification and therefore a pleasure of the agreeable. It is equally uncontroversial that spatiotemporal form can occasion the free play; the question is why Kant believes that *only* spatiotemporal form can occasion it. Put differently, Guyer presses the question, why *must* the pleasurable imaginative activity of the free play involve only a unification of the manifold in terms of spatiotemporal form? Why *can't* the imagination and understanding be in free play when the imagination unifies the manifold in terms of some other feature or set of features? Guyer, of course, thinks they can.[69]

Kant, however, does not. That is why his search for a way to count colors and tones as beautiful takes the particular form it does: find a way to show that our perception of color and tone requires a synthesis of a manifold into spatiotemporally organized intuitions. In the face of Guyer's objection, however, Kant needs to defend his claim that no other form of unification of a manifold can occasion the free play. On my view, Kant's defense is that no other form of unification of a manifold can license the claim to strict universal communicability, or intersubjective validity, that is essential to the judgment of beauty.

The most central contention of Kant's theory of taste is that the judgment of beauty manifests a necessary condition for the possibility of cognition. For this to be so, the imagination and understanding must stand in the relation that is required for a 'cognition in general' [*ein Erkenntnis überhaupt*], even though this is not the relation in which they stand in any particular, determinate, act of cognition. The activity of the imagination exemplifies the necessary conditions for the understanding to be able to unify the manifold in terms of concepts, though a judgment of beauty cannot take as its ground or presuppose the application of any particular concept. In either a cognitive or an aesthetic judgment, the imagination and understanding are in 'harmony' [*die Harmonie der Erkenntnisvermögen*], or 'agree' [*zusammenstimmen*] with one another. Rather than resulting in a 'determining judgment'—the application of some particular concept—the cognitive faculties, in the free play, result in an experience of pleasure (in the beautiful). This pleasure is universally communicable precisely because it attends to a state of the cognitive faculties that is a necessary condition for the possibility of a 'cognition in general.'

Kant expresses this line of thought thus:

> If, then, the form of a given object in empirical intuition is so constituted that the **apprehension** of its manifold in the imagination agrees with the **presentation** of a concept of the understanding (undetermined which concept) [*unbestimmt welches Begriffs*], then in the mere reflection understanding and imagination mutually agree for the advancement of their business. . . . Such a judgment is called an **aesthetic judgment of reflection**.[70]

The 'business' of the imagination and understanding's cooperative endeavors is the application of concepts to the manifold for the purposes of cognition. The question, then, is what we are to make of the claim that, in a judgment of beauty, the imagination's apprehension of the manifold exemplifies a necessary condition for the understanding to be able to apply concepts *in general*—that is, to apply not this-or-that particular concept, but any old concept whatsoever, no matter which one. Our choice of concept is, in that sense, *unbestimmt.*

My claim is that the necessary condition for the application of concepts to the manifold is that the manifold have a spatiotemporal form.[71] Indeed, a central tenet of transcendental idealism is that the possibility of a synthesis of apprehension requires the forms of space and time.[72] Put differently, spatiotemporality is the necessary condition for the possibility of cognition that Kant has been obliquely gesturing toward. That is perhaps the most familiar Kantian thought of all, and much the point of the first *Critique*'s 'Transcendental Deduction.' Kant takes his central result in the first *Critique* to be that the concepts of the understanding have objective validity only in relation to possible objects of experience—objects that are subject to the human forms of sensibility, space and time. Our cognition is restricted to spatiotemporal objects, or appearances, because we cannot apply concepts to anything that is not subject to the forms of sensibility.

Here we have a necessary condition for the applicability of concepts in general to the manifold. In a judgment of beauty, the imagination apprehends the manifold in the way required for the understanding to be able to unify the manifold in terms of concepts in general, although a judgment of beauty does not (and cannot) take the applicability of any particular concept as a ground. That condition, again, is that the manifold be subject to the representational constraints imposed by the forms of sensibility. The necessary condition for the possibility of cognition that Kant discovered in the first *Critique* is the same necessary condition for the possibility of 'cognition in general' that forms the heart of Kant's analysis of aesthetic judgment in the third *Critique*. Thus, the imagination's apprehension of the manifold in a judgment of beauty must be an apprehension in terms of the manifold's spatiotemporal features.

The form of a manifold that is produced by a subject's imaginative activity for the purposes of cognition is the same form that is produced when the subject judges an object by taste. The difference is that, in an aesthetic judgment, the mere spatiotemporal unification of the manifold—irrespective of whatever particular concept applications may be achieved as well—is the object of reflection. On certain occasions—when the form is right, so to speak—this reflection is pleasurable and thereby grounds a judgment of beauty. None of this should be surprising. After all, it is the very same cognitive faculties, performing fundamentally the same activities, according to the same representational conditions, that are responsible for both cognitive judgments and judgments of beauty. That is Kant's point.[73]

On the view I have sketched, restrictive formalism is a natural development of Kant's underlying epistemology and metaphysics. The theoretical depths at which restrictive formalism is anchored explain Kant's continued commitment to it, even in the face of its highly implausible and counterintuitive conclusions. It also explains why Kant's attempt to escape these counterintuitive conclusions proceeds as it does, with no other possible route ever canvassed: if colors and tones are to be counted as elements of beauty rather than agreeableness, our perceptions of colors and tones must be shown to require an apprehension of a manifold by the imagination, unified in accordance with the representational conditions established by the forms of sensibility. In other words, a representation of a color or tone must contain a manifold of sensations that displays the spatiotemporal ordering characteristic of the form of an intuition. If that isn't so, colors and tones will have to be reckoned mere sensations, and our representations of them nothing but the specific qualities associated with mere sensations; there are no other options. But a mere sensation can provide only physiological gratification, and its specific qualities cannot be universally communicable.

This interpretation of Kant's aesthetic formalism affords a reply to Guyer. Drawing on his examples of Albers's *Homage to the Square,* and Dunham's remarks about the violence done to musical compositions by inattention to tone and orchestration, Guyer maintains that a diversity or confluence of colors or tones can occasion the free play, since it presents a manifold of sensations for the imagination to apprehend and unify. Guyer writes:

> Certain colors or tones, while nothing but sensations themselves, might be felt to belong together in just such a way as to satisfy the understanding's requirement of unity in the manifolds imagination presents to it; indeed, one might even suggest that the very fact that such features of objects are not pure *a priori* elements of their appearance . . . makes it all the more likely that they could serve for the felt synthesis without concepts which founds aesthetic response.[74]

From my perspective, Guyer's view makes at least two fundamental mistakes.

First, Guyer's flat assertion that colors and tones 'are nothing but sensations themselves' misses the point of Kant's investigation of the proper scope of his formalist strictures. In the third *Critique,* Kant does not reach a settled view whether colors and tones are 'nothing but sensations.'[75] That is the precisely question Kant raises in § 14 and ultimately admits he cannot answer with the requisite certainty in § 51. Kant is committed only to the conditional claim that *if* colors and tones can contribute to an object's beauty rather than mere agreeableness, *then* colors and tones cannot be mere sensations. Guyer purports to resolve a standing question that Kant himself never fully resolves. To that extent, his view distorts the inquiry of third *Critique.*

Second, Guyer's view suggests that a judgment of taste can be founded on the specific qualities of sensations alone. That cannot be Kant's view, since transcendental philosophy cannot rule out the variability hypothesis with the required *a priori* certainty and necessity. Thus, a judgment based merely on the specific qualities of a sensation cannot claim to be universally communicable. Now, Guyer will certainly protest that there is more to his view than this. In particular, Guyer acknowledges that our pleasure in the beautiful 'must be more than a merely physiological gratification in the sensory qualities of objects'; it must involve 'reflection upon a complex manifold of sensations.'[76] Crucially, for Guyer, the requirement that the manifold presented by the imagination for reflection be unified in some way does not imply that the features in terms of which it is unified 'may not themselves be such sensory qualities as color or tone.'[77]

Guyer thus claims that while a single sensation could never yield more than mere physiological gratification, a manifold or confluence of sensations can yield material suitable for reflection and thereby provide a basis for a pleasure that isn't just physiological gratification. Specifically, Guyer thinks that a manifold can be unified in the following sense: the various sensations present in the manifold are 'felt to belong together' by the subject who reflects upon the manifold and the variety of sensible features it presents. Likewise for Allison, who argues that any 'arrangement or ordering of sensible content' can provide the needed materials for aesthetic reflection.[78]

Guyer's (and Allison's) strategy of supplementing a single sensation with further sensations will not provide the needed basis for a judgment of beauty.[79] It is not at all clear how Guyer thinks that the harmonious feel of a confluence of sensations—the feeling that they belong together—will 'satisfy the understanding's requirement of unity in the manifolds imagination presents to it.'[80] Guyer never specifies what kind of unity the understanding requires from the imagination's apprehension of a manifold if it is to provide a basis for a judgment of beauty; indeed, his point is that Kant's aesthetic theory leaves this question entirely open. But not any old kind of unity will do; the understanding requires something quite specific of the imagination.[81] In contrast to Guyer, I have argued that Kant's aesthetic theory does provide an answer: the unity of the manifold required for a judgment of taste to be possible is the same kind of unity required for the application of a concept—any concept, undetermined which—to be possible. And that unity is spatiotemporality, the first *Critique's sine qua non* of cognition.

On Guyer's proposal, the required unity of a manifold of sensation is taken to be present if the sensations that the manifold comprises are pleasing when experienced in conjunction, when they feel like they belong together. But the fact that some sensations of green and some sensations of purple are pleasing when experienced together, or that the sensations of various pitches (say, those of a minor triad) are pleasing when experienced together, seems to have nothing to do with the understanding's requirements for the application of concepts in general. Unless, that is, having a representation of a color or tone itself requires the apprehension of a spatiotemporal form. But that is to give up on Guyer's assertion that colors and tones are nothing but sensations. I therefore do not see how Guyer's proposal for understanding the judgment of beauty can retain any intelligible connection to the conditions for the possibility of cognition that explain the judgment of beauty's universal communicability.[82] In short, Guyer's proposal cannot coherently characterize the judgment of beauty as making a legitimate normative demand, since it is based on nothing more than the pleasure one feels in the simultaneous and harmonious experience of the specific qualities of various sensations. Adding that there must be a manifold or diversity of such specific qualities, rather than merely one, will not help at all. Small wonder that Kant never countenances the option Guyer proposes.[83]

One might, however, object: although cognition in general requires that we can apprehend an object's spatiotemporal form, *empirical* cognition in particular requires that we can perceive an object as having qualitative features like color. This, in turn, requires that we can be sensibly affected by objects, that is, that we can receive sensations from objects, which give rise to representations of their sensible or qualitative features. It is therefore unclear why I privilege spatiotemporal form as the *only* necessary condition for cognition capable of grounding the kind of pleasure that licenses a judgment of taste—especially since Kant is concerned with empirical rather than *a priori* cognition in the third *Critique*.[84]

This objection assumes a mistaken version of the contrast between spatiotemporal form and qualitative features. More specifically, it mistakenly assumes that sensation alone can provide us with representations of certain qualitative features of objects, like color and tone. This is not to deny that we must receive sensations from objects in order to have representations of colors or tones. Nor is it to deny that we must receive sensations from objects and represent objects as having sensible or qualitative features in order to have empirical cognition. But it is to say that if judgments based on representations of these sensible qualities are to be universally communicable, then those representations (say, of redness) cannot be explained as merely receptive awareness of the specific qualities of sensations.

My view does not preclude all sensible features of objects from grounding a judgment of beauty. Rather, my point is that transcendental philosophy could never reach that result if it were to construe our perception of all sensible features as a receptive awareness of the specific qualities of sensations; it must construe our perception of at least some sensible features as manifesting an apprehension of spatiotemporal form. More generally, then, my view proposes a distinction between sensible features that require a spatiotemporal ordering of a manifold of sensations and sensible features that are merely our awareness of the specific qualities of sensations. The former can ground judgments of beauty; the latter cannot, since they are incommunicable. Such are the terms of Kant's inquiry—admittedly, one he ultimately finds inconclusive—into the aesthetic status of colors and tones.

Neither empirical cognition nor aesthetic experience would be possible if we were not sensibly affected by objects. For if we weren't, we would be unable to represent objects as having any particular spatiotemporal forms, even though sensation cannot afford us a representation of spatiotemporality per se.[85] But this requirement for empirical cognition and aesthetic experience cannot be the condition for the possibility of cognition that underlies the judgment of beauty: it renders a coherent account of the distinction between the beautiful and the agreeable impossible. This is so for two reasons. First, the specific qualities of our sensations are not universally communicable, so there wouldn't be any distinction between the beautiful and the agreeable; there would only be the agreeable. Taking our sensible affection by objects to be the relevant necessary condition for cognition throttles the very idea of the *beautiful* as Kant understands it. Second, if, *arguendo*, the specific qualities of sensations were universally communicable, this proposal would establish way too much: it would lack the resources to distinguish between the uptake of different sense modalities as Kant's distinction between the beautiful and the agreeable manifestly does distinguish.

Guyer's view lacks the resources to so distinguish. Guyer claims that I may feel an array of colors or tones to belong together, and that colors and tones are just sensations. Notably, Guyer *only* mentions colors and tones here. But if colors and tones are just sensations—as are tastes and smells—this selection is arbitrary. Think, for instance, of the pleasure of eating a Caprese salad: the tastes of tomatoes, mozzarella, and fresh basil leaves belong together. Finding different tastes (and smells) that belong together, that harmonize with one another, is the basis of good cooking. If nothing more than a confluence of sensations could occasion the free play, judgments of beauty could equally be made about tastes and smells. Guyer surely needs to provide further constraints on the features in terms of which a manifold of sensations can be unified in a judgment of beauty. The feeling that various sensations belong together, or go well together, or harmonize with one another, applies equally well to the uptake of all the sensory modalities. Indeed, Guyer's view allows any confluence of sensations, or any array of sensible features of objects, to be a potential basis for a judgment of beauty; Kant's conception of beauty does not. Guyer's view thus affords no basis for an answer to the traditional aesthetic question that can discriminate between different sorts of sensible properties—an answer that isn't vacuous because all-inclusive. It is no surprise, then, that Guyer complains Kant has *no* answer to this question at all.

Any interpretation of Kant's distinction between the beautiful and the agreeable that rejects restrictive formalism requires a distinction between representations of sensible features that are just specific qualities of sensations, and representations that involve something more than just sensation, namely, the form of an intuition. Otherwise, it could neither provide any basis for a nontrivial answer to the traditional aesthetic question nor capture the sensitivity to differences between sense modalities that Kant's distinction exhibits. These considerations decisively rule out that our sensible affection by objects is the necessary condition for cognition that underlies the judgment of beauty.

This general point can also be approached from the perspective of Kant's conception of aesthetic reflection. On Guyer's view, one can experience pleasure in the beautiful when reflecting on a manifold or diversity of sensations—say, an array of colors or tones—even though one cannot find an individual color or tone beautiful. This view fails to appreciate how Kant's notion of intuitive form is central to his account of reflection.

The pleasurable experience of beauty is grounded in reflection on the form rather than the matter of representations.[86] In a judgment of beauty, '[the] pleasure is connected with the mere apprehension of the form of an object of intuition,' an apprehension that requires the reflecting power of judgment to compare those apprehended forms 'to its faculty for relating intuitions to concepts.'[87] In a judgment of beauty, the imagination ('as the faculty of *a priori* intuitions') and the understanding ('as the faculty of concepts') are 'brought into accord through a given representation and without an aim' [*durch eine gegebene Vorstellung unabsichtlich in Einstimmung versetzt*], thereby arousing a feeling of pleasure.[88] Consequently, that object is called beautiful 'the form of which (not the material aspect of its representation, as sensation) in mere reflection on it . . . is judged as the ground of a pleasure in the representation,' and 'the faculty for judging by means of such a pleasure (consequently also with universal validity) is called taste.'[89] Most importantly, in a judgment of beauty, 'the ground of the pleasure is placed merely in the form of the object for reflection in general, hence not in any sensation of the object.'[90]

Kant emphasizes that we reflect on form, not matter. He speaks ubiquitously of a 'pleasure in mere reflection on the form of an object,'[91] a 'susceptibility to a pleasure from reflection on the form of things,'[92] and so forth. Strictly speaking, these passages are misleading. Since we reflect on representations, not objects, the material for reflection is the form of a representation. More precisely, it is the form of an intuition. We do not reflect, in Kant's sense, upon any old manifold of sensations; we reflect on a spatio-temporally organized manifold. Guyer's account therefore fails to square with Kant's description of the pleasure that grounds a judgment of beauty. That pleasure is one we take in reflecting (disinterestedly, and without any determinate cognitive aim) on the perceptual form of our intuitions. The problem, of course, is that Kant does not know precisely what that form comprises.

So it is not enough to point out that some combination or confluence of sensible features may be felt as pleasurable. That is surely plausible from a psychological or phenomenological point of view. But to be useful for the purposes of transcendental philosophy, psychological or phenomenological claims must be constrained by an analysis of the logical or epistemological conditions on judgments.[93] From Kant's perspective, there is only one way to show that a universally communicable pleasure grounds a judgment of beauty: show that, in a judgment of beauty, we reflect on a representation that involves not just (subjective) sensation, or even a manifold of sensations, but a manifold with the spatiotemporal form of an (objective) intuition. That is the question on which the aesthetic status of colors and tones, and thus the scope of Kant's aesthetic formalism, ultimately turns. Of course, there remains a question as to why, on Kant's view, cognition requires that I must be able to take pleasure in any of my intuitive representations, but I cannot hope to resolve that issue here.[94]

A proper interpretation of Kant's aesthetic formalism must show how it is anchored in some of the most fundamental tenets of his epistemology and metaphysics. Only then will it explain why he grapples with restrictive formalism, and the question of colors and tones, precisely as he does. Starting from the conception of intuitive form he had established in the 'Transcendental Aesthetic,' Kant initially concludes that shape and (temporal) 'play' are the only features that contribute to the beauty of objects. If he is to add colors or tones to this list, as a plausible aesthetic theory would require, he must show that our perceptions of colors and tones involve the imagination's apprehension of a manifold of sensation in accordance with the representational norms of spatiotemporality. And that is to show that our perceptions of these sensible features of objects are more than 'mere sensations'—precisely as Kant formulates the question in § 14. Restrictive formalism therefore stands or falls with the first *Critique*'s subjectivist and eliminativist view of colors and tones. Alas, Kant ultimately felt compelled to declare both questions—for they are at bottom the same—intractable by the lights of his philosophical system. This admission may well point to a fundamental indeterminacy in Kant's conception of an intuition, but that would be a topic to explore on another occasion.[95]

Section 6: Moral: The Centrality of Transcendental Idealism

In the end, Kant concedes that the scope of his formalist strictures is indeterminate. To be sure, Kant routinely speaks as though he has shown that restrictive formalism is correct, and there is no doubt that he takes it very seriously. Indeed, he takes it so seriously precisely because it is so deeply rooted in fundamental aspects of his epistemology and metaphysics. But for all the sophisticated philosophical argument that Kant brings to bear on this question, he is forced to admit that he cannot advance beyond our ordinary twofold conception of taste. With respect to judgments about colors or tones, Kant's theoretical distinction between the beautiful and the agreeable is neither more clearly demarcated, nor more solidly grounded, nor more entitled to claim certainty than common sense's ordinary twofold conception of taste. Substantive aesthetic theories aspire to provide convincing (or at least plausible) strictures about the kinds of properties of things that can contribute to their beauty. Formalism—of one variety or another—is Kant's attempt to provide these strictures. By his own admission, however, the scope of formalism's claims is indeterminate.

One might urge that Kant is too hasty to declare the question intractable; perhaps his formalist strictures are merely inchoate, not genuinely and insurmountably indeterminate. But it isn't even clear why this resolution should be welcomed as an improvement. Recall that Kant attempts to articulate the twofold conception of taste within the terms of his general and systematic philosophical theory. This articulation is shaped by the theoretical pressures of transcendental idealism: the doctrine of synthesis; the role of space and time as forms of sensibility and representational constraints on the synthesis of apprehension; and a subjectivist, eliminativist, ontology of sensible, or secondary, qualities. These aspects of transcendental idealism generate at least a prima facie commitment to restrictive formalism. To Kant's credit, he notices that this view yields implausible aesthetic strictures, and he searches, inevitably in vain, for a way to accommodate ordinary thought and speech's more plausible view within the terms of his philosophical theory. Along the way, these theoretical pressures force Kant into convoluted and abstruse inquiries, which end up rather far afield from the heart of the concerns that mark the human being's interest in matters of taste—even, in § 14, into an obviously empirical inquiry that is neither relevant to our aesthetic judgments nor an appropriate basis on which to rest the results of transcendental philosophy. Even if this line of inquiry were somehow brought to fruition, it would still be far from clear that it should be used to fund a philosophical conception of taste.

In this respect, Guyer makes a very sensible philosophical point: the doctrines of the first *Critique* are an intrusion into Kant's conception of taste, which should not be made to turn on the epistemological and metaphysical claims of transcendental idealism. It is not, however, open to Kant to have that attitude. We should not forget that transcendental idealism is at the very heart of Kant's thinking, and that transcendental idealism is a doctrine about space and time. We may hope, in a Strawsonian mood, that a plausible Kantianism can be constructed without any commitment to transcendental idealism; the search for one may indeed yield interesting philosophical claims. But we will not have a plausible reading of the historical Kant's substantive aesthetic doctrines without countenancing a central role for transcendental idealism's claims about space and time, even if they wreak no small amount of havoc with his conception of taste. Guyer is not unreasonable in hoping for a reconstruction of the core of Kant's theory that does not make essential use of those claims. But I doubt that any such detailed reconstruction is forthcoming—at least not one that makes sense of why Kant held the specific positions that he did, and struggled with them as he did—no matter how much his aesthetic theory suffers as a result. Such is the price of comprehensive philosophical system building.

Chapter 3

Sensations and Interests

In Chapter 2, I provided an account of the relation between Kant's criterion of *formality* for the judgment of taste and the criterion of *communicability*. That account has left the relation between formality and Kant's further criterion of *disinterestedness* unexplained. Moreover, the relation between these criteria is not clear from the text of the third *Critique*. In particular, it is not obvious whether these are independent criteria or whether they both result from a more fundamental and unitary conception of aesthetic experience. For a thinker as systematic as Kant, one would expect the latter to be the case. Indeed, both criteria appear to result from Kant's denial that the judgment of taste can be based on sensation, for Kant argues that a pleasure based on sensation—a pleasure in the agreeable—automatically counts as interested. In this chapter, I explain this puzzling claim, and explain how the linkage between sensations and interests reveals the basis for Kant's inference from the disinterestedness of the judgment of taste to its formality.

My explanation requires a distinction between two conceptions of interest—the *desire conception* and the *existence conception*, as I shall call them—which Kant runs together in the 'First Moment.' I explain this distinction in Section 1, building on a pair of helpful yet relatively unsubstantiated observations from Allison: first, Kant is wrong to suppose that one can remain truly indifferent to the existence of the object of her pleasurable contemplation; second, Kant does not, in any event, require a claim this implausibly strong.[1] In Section 2, I look in more detail at the existence conception and its relation to Kant's general claims about sensations. In Section 3, I argue that the existence conception erects a decisive yet unnecessary obstacle to Kant's search for a way to characterize colors and tones as elements of beauty rather than agreeableness. In Section 4, I provide a brief synthesis of the central interpretive difficulties canvassed in this and the preceding chapter. In Section 5, I conclude the discussion of these two chapters with some reflections on the philosophical interest of Kant's distinction between the beautiful and the agreeable, and his investigation of how this distinction ought to be applied to colors and tones.

Section 1: Two Conceptions of Interest

Certainly, some of Kant's examples of the agreeable are obvious cases of interested pleasures, on a natural and unforced conception of interest. Take, for instance, the taste of the palate. Enticed by a plate of food, I acquire an appetite that seeks active gratification—I grow hungry—and for that I must obtain a plate of the food and eat it. Merely contemplating the food will not afford me the pleasures I seek; in fact, too much mere contemplation of it will produce the very opposite of pleasure.

In this example, my pleasure in the food is interested because it is the satisfaction or gratification of a sensuous desire.[2] The satisfaction or gratification of a sensuous desire, appetite, urge, prompting, whim, and so forth—the lot of which Kant generally calls *inclinations* [*Neigungen*]—is a pleasure of the body that arises from its causal affection by objects. To obtain such a pleasure, I must acquire the object of my desire, so that I can actively use it, or do something *to* it, and thereby wring from it the pleasures it can afford me. In pursuing the gratification of an inclination or desire, there is something I want *from* the object of my desire.[3]

Although Kant's various characterizations of the interested pleasures of the agreeable are by no means univocal—or even consistent—there is a clear basis for the above characterization in his general conception of a desire. As we know from Kant's characterization of the pure judgment of taste, not all pleasures presuppose a desire or exercise of the will; if they did, all pleasures would be interested. Thus, pleasure and desire must in general be distinct: a pleasure is a state that tends to maintain itself; a desire is a state that attempts to produce or maintain something else, namely, its object. Desires are directed toward objects rather than self-perpetuation and thus involve an act of will; when we desire something, we want something from it that can be obtained or maintained only by our acting upon it in some overt way. A pleasure may be the result of satisfying a desire, however, a pleasure needn't require any such overt action upon an object.

A pleasure can, for instance, be a merely contemplative state. I may be content to linger over an object in contemplation without doing anything to it, without seeking to acquire it or employ it in some overt way to satisfy some end of mine. In the latter case, the pleasure will be disinterested; in the former, it will be interested. Interested pleasures require that I overtly use some object toward the satisfaction of some determinate aim or desire of mine, and where that aim or desire is the gratification of a bodily appetite, the resulting pleasure will be an interested pleasure in the agreeable.[4]

In the case of literal appetites like the desire for a food one finds delicious, this characterization of the agreeable seems uncontentious enough: the pleasure is interested insofar as I seek to acquire and use an object toward the gratification of a bodily appetite. Kant, however, often describes the pleasure taken in an object's color, or the pleasure taken in the tone of an instrument, as a pleasure in the agreeable, and hence as an interested pleasure.[5] The delight I take in an object's color need not—in fact, usually does not—have any connection to the satisfaction of an appetite or a desire. I may be perfectly content to admire an object's beautiful color disinterestedly—to leave it alone and passively allow it to serve me, as the object of my purely contemplative pleasure. If I admire the beautiful color of the autumn leaves, there is nothing I need to do to the leaves, nothing I want from them for the purpose of gratifying any appetite. It isn't even clear what I could want from them, or do to them, in any sense analogous to the case of a literal appetite for food. I may simply linger in contemplative delight over the sight of a beautiful color or array of colors. Given the above characterization of an interest as tied to the gratification of appetites or desires, such a pleasure is surely disinterested.

Granted, sometimes the pleasure afforded by color can be loosely connected to an appetite or desire. Consider, for instance, the use of color in the plating and presentation of food. As the old saying goes, 'we eat first with our eyes.' The visual presentation of a meal can contribute substantially to the pleasure one takes in the meal, and the use of color is (of course just one) aspect of that presentation. This is not a straightforwardly disinterested pleasure; rather, it is a pleasure that stimulates an appetite or further heightens a pre-existing appetite. One does not want just to contemplate the visual appearance of the well-plated and colorful food; one acquires a heightened desire or appetite that can only be gratified by eating.

This example, however, is not representative of our aesthetic experience of colors in general. Rather, it highlights the difference between the pleasure we generally take in colors and the appetitive pleasures that form the paradigmatic cases of the agreeable. By and large, the pleasure we find in the colors of things is contemplative, disconnected from the gratification of any bodily appetite or sensuous desire. Similarly for the case of tones: music provides an eminently contemplative pleasure, which has no basis in the gratification of any appetite or desire.

Thus, Kant's connection between the pleasures of the agreeable and the faculty of desire, introduced in the 'First Moment,'[6] becomes strained when one reaches the Second and Third Moments,[7] where he offers colors and tones as examples of the agreeable. But there are further aspects of Kant's characterization of the interested pleasures of the agreeable, on which it may be correct to count the pleasures taken in colors and tones as interested.

Kant often maintains that the pleasures of the agreeable involve an interest in the real existence of an object.[8] This conception of interest is distinct from the one we have seen so far, even though Kant generally introduces the two conceptions simultaneously and without distinction. Up to a point, it is easy enough to see a close relation between the desire and the existence conceptions of interest: the desire conception entails a limited version of the existence conception, since the existence of an object is necessary for the gratification of a desire or appetite. Thus, to the extent I have a desire, which can only be gratified by overtly acting upon some object, I thereby have an interest in that's object's existence. I simply can't act upon something that isn't there: if I desire some food of a particular kind, no mere representation of it will suffice; the satisfaction of my desire and the consequent pleasure I derive therefrom requires the real existence of some food of that kind. But it does not follow from the fact that I am interested in the existence of an object in this limited sense, that the object figures in the gratification of any particular desire of mine. These two conceptions of interest are therefore separable.

In one sense, I have an interest in the existence of any object in which I take pleasure or delight, even if that pleasure is purely contemplative, and so disinterested on the desire conception. Without additional constraints on the notion of an interest that it employs, an existence conception becomes all-encompassing. At a minimum, if an object affords me a contemplative pleasure, I have an interest in its existence, and its continued existence, in the following sense: I have an interest in its availability, and its continued availability, as an object of my contemplation. If I find a painting beautiful, it is not all the same to me whether it should suddenly vanish, so it is not all the same to me whether it is in fact a real painting, as opposed to an illusion or a fleeting trick of light.

As Kant describes pleasure, moreover, it is a state of mind that seeks or tends toward its own perpetuation. But we should not let such quasi-teleological descriptions of pleasure mislead us into forgetting that it is *we* who seek to extend our pleasures once they are underway. A pleasurable state is not a frictionless wheel which, once set into motion, keeps going of its own accord, until some external source of friction interferes with it. Rather, a pleasure is a state that we continually seek to renew, by continued or renewed engagement with—sometimes mere contemplation of—the object that affords us this pleasure. We naturally linger in contemplation over beautiful things, precisely because this contemplation affords us pleasure,[9] and we cannot linger very effectively over something that isn't, or is no longer, there.

Kant's rhetoric about the disinterested pleasure that grounds a judgment of taste invites conflation of the two senses of interest as well as a certain line of response to this objection to Kant's quasi-teleological description of pleasure. In describing the disinterested character of the judgment of taste, Kant writes:

> [I]f the question is whether something is beautiful, one does not want to know whether there is anything that is or that could be at stake, for us or for someone else, in the existence of the thing [*ob uns oder irgend jemand an der Existenz der Sache irgend etwas gelegen sei, oder auch nur gelegen sein könne*], but rather how we judge it in mere contemplation. . . . One only wants to know whether the mere representation of the object is accompanied with satisfaction in me, however indifferent [*gleichgültig*] I might be with regard to the existence of the object of this representation.[10]

The force of these remarks depends on how one takes Kant's rhetoric of judging 'mere representations' and being either 'indifferent to' or having something 'at stake' in the real existence of the objects of these representations.

There are two ways to take this rhetoric. The first involves having something at stake in the existence of the object in a strong and particular sense that aligns with the desire conception of interest. In this sense, I have something at stake in the existence of the object insofar as I have a desire or aim—beyond mere contemplation—in which that object, or a relevantly similar object, crucially figures. In other words, there is something I want from the object, which will satisfy whatever particular interest, desire, or perhaps literal appetite I have. This plainly requires the real existence of the object.

In the second and weaker sense, I might be said to have an interest, or to have something at stake, in the existence of the object to the extent that my contemplation of the object affords me pleasure. Hence, I am not indifferent to the object's continued availability as an object of contemplation. This is sufficient to show that I am not completely indifferent to the real existence of the object, even though there is nothing beyond mere contemplation—no desire or appetite—that requires me to act upon the object. This weaker sense just is a version of an unconstrained or independent existence conception, and its results are all-encompassing.

If one takes Kant's rhetoric about 'mere representations' and 'indifference to existence' at face value, one might object as follows: insofar as the pleasure I take in an object is merely contemplative, I require only the representation of the object for my contemplation. Whether it is a representation of something that really exists or is a figment of my imagination is irrelevant. And whether the object continues to exist is equally irrelevant. All that matters is whether my initial response to my representation is purely contemplative. If it is, I can remain indifferent to the real existence of the object.[11]

This objection makes two mistakes: first, it requires the implausible assumption that, as a general matter, purely imaginary representations are capable of affording us the same pleasures as representations caused by real objects; second, it overlooks the fact that pleasures, including contemplative ones, are sustained by us through continued or renewed engagement with the objects that afford us these pleasures. This would be a natural result of being misled by the quasi-teleological descriptions of a pleasure as having an 'inner causality' or a 'causality in itself' by means of which it simply perpetuates itself.[12]

First, from the perspective of the pleasures they can afford me, it is in general false that I am, or should be, indifferent between representations of the imagination and genuine perceptions of real things. Actually viewing Raphael's *Stanza della Segnatura*, for example, affords a pleasure (for the many of us who find it beautiful) that far outstrips whatever pleasure can be afforded by a figment of the imagination or some purely imaginary representation that 'looks like' Raphael's *Stanza della Segnatura*. Putting aside any further issues that may arise about continued existence, and confining ourselves to questions about one's initial response to some mental state, it is still true that genuine perceptions of real objects are, on the whole, more forceful—hence more pleasurable, when they are perceptions of beautiful things—than purely imaginary representations. So, too, of music: there is, in general, more pleasure to be had from genuinely hearing an actual sonic realization of a beautiful composition than from 'hearing it,' so to speak, with the mind's ear.

Granted, there are some people whose mind's eyes and ears are vivid and forceful enough to serve as sources of contemplative pleasures on par with real things that provide us with genuine perceptions. These lucky people might have sufficient reason to be indifferent to the real existence of such objects, and might be equally content to contemplate what they find in their own mind's eyes and ears. But to assume that we all have reason to be genuinely indifferent in this matter is to assume that we all have mind's eyes and ears that conjure up representations capable of affording us pleasures equal to those afforded by Raphael's actual paintings or actual sonic realizations of Villa-Lobos's string quartets. This is hopelessly glib; we are simply not, in general, anywhere near that lucky. What's more, it is to assume that we are not, in general, capable of telling whether we are actually looking at a painting or merely imagining one, or actually hearing a string quartet as opposed to listening to our own mind's ears. This is not the place to mount a serious attack on a view of perception that has these results; in cases like these, however, its overstatements are sufficiently plain. None of this is to deny that purely imaginary 'representations' can serve as sources of contemplative pleasures. My point, rather, is that it is confused and severely overstated to maintain that, in general, we are or should be 'indifferent' to the real existence of the objects of our contemplative pleasures. We would not, by and large, have those same pleasures without them. 'Mere representations' are not adequate as a wholesale substitute.

Second, more than just my initial response to a representation is at stake in aesthetic experience. I don't simply notice something that affords me pleasure and then remain in that state unproblematically, at least until something more pressing intrudes and forces me to reorient my attention accordingly. On the contrary, I must *renew* my pleasurable state, by renewed or continued engagement with the object that affords me this pleasure.[13] Kant's quasi-teleological descriptions of pleasure as a state that tends toward its own self-perpetuation can be misleading in this regard, and make the most sense when read to say that a pleasure is a state that provides me with a prima facie (motivating) reason to seek its perpetuation.[14] Here the difference between genuine perception of real objects and merely having representations becomes salient, as does the difference between real objects and such things as mirages and tricks of light. Neither 'mere representations' nor mirages have the same constancy—the same staying power—as real objects. To the extent that I find something beautiful and prefer to linger over it, I will prefer a real object to a mirage or a 'mere representation,' since these things have habits of suddenly fading or disappearing. I have an interest in the object's real and continued existence, in the thin sense of an interest in its continued availability as an object of contemplation and hence as a source of pleasure. An object, or even a mirage or trick of light, may afford me a pleasurable representation for contemplation, but if it does not stick around for my continued engagement with it, my representation will not have the same staying power to sustain my pleasurable state. Cut off from its source, my pleasurable state will dry up sooner than it otherwise would.

Some might object that I do not take seriously enough the distinction between representations produced by voluntary exercises of the imagination and genuine hallucinations.[15] While voluntary exercises of the imagination may not have the same force or liveliness as genuine perceptions, full-blown hallucinations do; that is what makes them indistinguishable from genuine perceptions. Thus, we may prefer real Raphael paintings and actual sonic realizations of Villa-Lobos's string quartets to voluntary exercises of the imagination, and therefore we may properly have an interest in the real existence of such things. We can, however, remain 'indifferent' between their real existence and full-blown hallucinations of them.

Even granting the truth of this view of perception for the sake of argument, this line of objection is insufficient to establish that we are or should be indifferent between genuine perceptions and hallucinations of beautiful things. There are two reasons why this is so. First, hallucinations—like mirages and tricks of light—do not have the same constancy or staying power as real objects. Here, too, my pleasurable state, if grounded in a hallucination, will dry up sooner than one grounded in the existence of a real object. Second, a pleasure grounded in a hallucination cannot be universally communicable; it is intrinsically private rather than publicly available, just as the hallucination itself is. A pleasure that is intrinsically incommunicable cannot be the basis of a judgment of taste; at best, it can be the basis for a mistaken belief that I have in fact made a judgment of taste. Hallucinations—however forceful, lively, or pleasurable they may be, or indeed, for however long they manage to last—can never ground a judgment of taste. Since a judgment of taste is both universally communicable and disinterested, the proper conception of disinterestedness cannot tolerate, much less encourage, the claim that I have no interest in the real existence of the objects of my pleasurable contemplations.

Thus, there are at least two reasons why even a purely contemplative pleasure entails an interest in the real existence of an object: it entails an interest in its availability (and continued availability) as an object of contemplation and hence as a source of pleasure—even though the object has no role in the gratification of any desire or appetite. The possibility of drawing a coherent distinction here is sufficient to show that the desire and existence conceptions of interest are distinct. More specifically, it is possible to have the existence conception without the desire conception, even though the desire conception entails a restricted version of the existence conception.

One might object that the thin, weaker form of an existence conception—on which my interest is merely in the availability of an object for my contemplation—is so thin that it's uninteresting. In one sense I think that's true. But that does not show that this conception cannot be prized apart from the desire conception. More importantly, the thinness of this conception of interest should not be taken to provide an objection to anything I have said. On the contrary, it shows that the legitimate force of the existence conception depends on the stronger and more limited desire conception. To be sure, given the desire conception, a restricted version of the interest conception follows. But the interest conception should not be framed in such a way that it can be prized apart, or applied independently, of the desire conception. That will introduce needless confusion that Kant's, or any, aesthetic theory is better off without. Happily, this separation can be achieved.

On my view, then, all that Kant should say about the disinterestedness of a judgment of taste is that I do not need to act upon the object of my judgment so as to gratify some desire or appetite. Beyond the object's continued availability for my pleasurable contemplation, there is nothing I want or desire from it. Before I am entitled to this conclusion, however, I must clear another textual hurdle. Kant clearly intends the existence conception to be limited to the agreeable, for the abstruse reason that the interested nature of a pleasure in the agreeable arises from its grounding in sensation. So we must see how, if at all, Kant can limit the scope of the existence conception by tying it to his notion of mere sensory gratification, and thereby avoid the all-encompassing result that an unconstrained existence conception would otherwise entail. Without presupposing some version of a desire conception—either in its standard form as I have already presented it, or in an alternative, strained form that we shall see shortly—I do not see that he can. This will be the topic of Section 2.

Section 2: Existence, Interest, and Sensation

The desire conception of interest is by no means new to Kant; it is Kant's reformulation of a standing theme of philosophical aesthetics in the seventeenth and eighteenth centuries. It was, in one particular form or another, common philosophical currency at least since Hutcheson argued that properly aesthetic pleasures are independent of any use we might make of an object, or any personal advantage we might derive from it. The desire conception naturally and intelligibly locates Kant within the broader dialectic of philosophical aesthetics that began with Shaftsbury and Hutcheson, and continued through Kant into the nineteenth century—philosophical theories of taste framed by the idea that genuine pleasures of taste need to be sharply distinguished from pleasures tied to the satisfaction of personal interests or desires.[16]

The existence conception, however, is a Kantian novelty, and some further explanation of its appearance in Kant's aesthetic theory is certainly needed. It will not suffice to note that an interest in the existence of an object is required or entailed by the desire conception, as I explained in Section 1. For there, the desire conception does the real explanatory work: my interest in the real existence of an object is a trivial consequence of the fact that the object itself is required if I am to use it to satisfy some inclination of mine. This point hardly warrants emphatic insistence on 'indifference to existence,' which Kant's repeated formulations of the existence conception betray; if this were all he had in mind, the point would perhaps be worth mentioning once, along the way. Kant must have had some further, perhaps (to his mind) more fundamental reason for radically reformulating the notion of aesthetic disinterestedness.

In its general form, Kant's reasoning to the existence conception can be captured by the following inference:

1. The pleasures of the agreeable are forms of gratification, that is, purely sensory pleasures.
2. Sensations are indicators of the real existence of objects.
3. The pleasures of the agreeable are forms of gratification, and hence interest, in the real existence of objects.[17]

The premises should be uncontroversial as a matter of Kant-interpretation. As we saw in Chapter 1, judgments of the agreeable are expressions of the bodily, sensuous, animalistic side of our nature. The pleasures in the agreeable are nonreflective pleasures, in which one is awash in the pleasant feel of a sensation. These pleasures, as we further saw in Chapter 2, are based solely on our susceptibility to causal affection and determination by outside forces, and it should not be controversial to say that this susceptibility is a matter of receiving sensations from the impingement of objects on our sense organs. A sensation, Kant tells us, is 'the effect of an object on the capacity for representation, insofar as we are affected by it.'[18] And if sensations are the effects that objects have on us, then having a sensation is a matter of standing in a causal relation to an object. The presence of sensation therefore indicates the real existence of some material object by which one is causally affected.[19] When the effect of some material object on our sense organs is pleasurable, Kant describes the pleasure as the object's agreeableness to our senses. If my pleasure is a form of gratification in the thing's effects on my body, then failing its real or material existence, there wouldn't be any such source of sensations to provide me with this pleasure. Thus, sensations require the real or material existence of objects.

The characterization of the agreeable as a form of sensory pleasure, along with the characterization of sensation as that which corresponds to the real existence or actuality of material objects, jointly entail a characterization of the agreeable as a form of gratification, and therefore interest, in something's existence. But this does not yet restrict the applicability of an existence conception to purely sensory pleasures, for it provides no response to the objections posed in Section 1 concerning the all-encompassing scope of an existence conception that is not subject to additional constraints. The linkage between sensations and existence requires further articulation if it is to restrict the scope of an existence conception of interest.[20]

By elaborating on the relation between existence and sensation—as opposed to the formal aspects of our intuitive representations—the Kantian taste theorist has a line of reply, albeit an unsatisfactory one. The reply distinguishes matter and form, and thereby distinguishes sensory pleasures, that is, forms of gratification, from pleasures taken in the purely formal features of our representations. These purely formal features are spatial and temporal features, which are due to the pure forms of intuition rather than the matter of an intuition, that is, sensation. We don't sense space and time directly; space and time do not themselves impinge on our senses. Rather, the spatial and temporal features of our representations are due to the activity of the imagination in synthesizing representations in accordance with the conditions on representations established by the forms of sensibility. In this way, spatiality and temporality are not indicators of the real existence of material objects.[21] And so, even on the existence conception—once it is tied explicitly to the presence of sensations—a pleasure taken in purely spatial and/or temporal features will not count as an interested pleasure.

This reply cannot fully vindicate the existence conception. Take again the view of color present in the 'Transcendental Aesthetic' and some (though not all) sections of the third *Critique*, on which the representation of a color is described as a mere sensation rather than a 'formal determination of the unity of a manifold of [sensations].'[22] On the existence conception, my liking for a particular shade of green, as a form of sensory gratification, counts as an interested pleasure. In contrast, my liking for a particular kind of triangle counts as disinterested. This is wrong: a liking for equilateral triangles is neither more nor less interested than a liking for a particular shade of green. The linkage between interest and sensation creates the strain: the sheer fact that my representation of green is a mere sensation (on this conception of color, anyway) has nothing intelligible to do with whether or not I have an interest—in any natural and nonmetaphorical sense—in which this or any other green object figures. Certainly it is no less forced to speak of an 'appetite for hunter green' than it is to speak of an 'appetite for equilateral triangularity.'

Any distinction here would require that we take the gratification of an appetite to be present simply because I am enjoying the pleasant feel of a sensation, say, of hunter green. This does seem to be Kant's view:

> Now that my judgment about an object by which I declare it agreeable expresses an interest in it is already clear from the fact that through sensation it excites a desire for objects of the same sort, hence the satisfaction presupposes not the mere judgment about it but the relation of its existence to my state insofar as it is affected by such an object. Hence one says of the agreeable not merely that it **pleases** [*gefallen*] but that it **gratifies** [*vergnügen*]. It is not mere approval that I give it, rather inclination is thereby aroused.[23]

This view puts too much strain on the ideas of arousing and satisfying a desire or appetite. Again, the linkage to sensation creates the strain: the fact that a liking for hunter green or for minor thirds is (on this view) a sensory pleasure, does not make it at all appropriate to speak of an 'appetite for hunter green' or an 'appetite for minor thirds'; no inclination is either gratified or aroused. But without this general claim about the linkage between sensation and desire or appetite, it is not possible to limit the scope of interested pleasures—on the existence conception, that is—to sensory pleasures only, or indeed, to any subset of aesthetic pleasures. Without this linkage, the existence conception remains all-encompassing. Here, the existence conception still depends on a version of a desire conception to block its otherwise overreaching generality, but the particular version of the desire conception presupposed here—as the cases of colors and tones make patent—appeals to a contrived and unnatural conception of when a desire, appetite, or inclination can appropriately be said to be either gratified or aroused.

Even if we grant that a pleasure based on sensation automatically entails the presence of an interest, it still wouldn't be at all clear why that kind of interest would render such pleasures incommunicable. The presence of an interest, as construed by the existence conception, provides no reason to think that pleasures in the agreeable thereby fall within the to-each-his-own conception of taste. The sheer fact that my pleasure requires the existence of a material object provides no reason to think that the pleasure is therefore not available to all on the same terms, and no reason to think that a difference in taste would thereby amount to a mere disparity, rather than a genuine disagreement. An inference to the incommunicability of the pleasures of the agreeable can proceed from the characterization of these pleasures as purely sensory, by means of the variability hypothesis explored in Chapter 2. But that leaves the notions of interest and incommunicability without any direct relation to one another. For on this strategy, it is the characterization of the pleasure as *sensory* that provides the needed premise for an inference to its incommunicability. Its further characterization as interested, in the sense of the existence conception, accomplishes nothing; it becomes a mere by-product with no independent explanatory value. As we'll see more clearly in Section 3, the existence conception does provide the needed linkage between disinterestedness and formality, but in doing so, it leaves us with no reason to think that there is any direct and intelligible linkage between the notions of interest and incommunicability, which Kant clearly intends them to have. Without equivocating on the notion of an interest, Kant cannot construct the systematic theoretical relations between the disinterestedness, universal communicability, and the formality of the judgment of taste that he intends.

Unlike the existence conception, the desire conception has no difficulty recognizing a pleasure taken in an object's color (or in a tone) as disinterested. Since it takes the notion of an appetite in a more literal and plausible sense, it can recognize that the pleasure one takes in the color of an oak tree's leaves in autumn neither gratifies nor arouses any alleged 'appetite for scarlet,' simply by dint of construing a representation of scarlet as a mere sensation. Because the leaves figure in no desire, appetite, or noncontemplative aim of mine, the desire conception—for reasons we saw in Section 1—can straightforwardly count this pleasure as disinterested.

Furthermore, the connection between appetitive desire and the incommunicability associated with the to-each-his-own conception of taste is natural and uncontrived. When it comes to the pleasures that this conception of interest will associate with the agreeable—the taste and smell of an enticing food being the paradigmatic examples—it is already part of our ordinary conception of taste that such pleasures are purely personal, and that nobody else's normative claims are entitled to speak for our own bodily appetites. When it comes to bodily appetites and desires, taken in the literal sense, we are dealing with personal likes and dislikes; on virtually nobody's view are they subject to universal normative demands. Simply by dint of the bodily, appetitive nature of the pleasures countenanced by the desire conception of interest, the pleasures it associates with the agreeable are linked right from the start with a nonnormative or to-each-his-own conception of taste. In contrast, the existence conception provides no reason to think that the notion of an interest with which it operates has any direct and unforced connection to incommunicability. Not only does the desire conception intelligibly locate one of the starting points of Kant's philosophical aesthetics within a broader historical dialectic, it also preserves a clearer and more natural connection to the starting point of Kant's aesthetic theory, as I explained it in Chapter 1—his conception of what our ordinary views about taste come to.[24]

So far, then, I see no good reason for an aesthetic theory to insist on the existence conception. To be sure, a pleasure that is tied to the gratification of a desire does entail an interest in the existence of what one desires. But here the interest in an object's existence is both parasitic on, and constrained by, the more fundamental desire. The pleasure I take in an object should count as interested in a way that precludes its universal communicability, only when I need the object to exist so that I can use it to satisfy some bodily, sensuous, noncontemplative desire or appetite of mine. Cut off from this constraint, an independent existence conception becomes either all-encompassing or hopelessly contrived.

Last but not least, taking an interest to be automatically generated by the presence of sensations still leaves colors and tones cut off from a Kantian conception of beauty. The desire conception does not have this result, yet it does preserve the core conception of the agreeable as purely personal, bodily pleasures, and leaves all the paradigmatic examples of such pleasures squarely within its purview. In the next section, I further substantiate my claim that Kant's aesthetic theory would be better off sticking with the desire conception and dropping the existence conception altogether. I argue that even on the revised conception of colors and tones that Kant grapples with in the third *Critique*, the existence conception still leaves him unable to countenance colors and tones within the scope of the beautiful. We have encountered here one of the principal stumbling blocks to Kant's ultimately failed attempt to provide a satisfactory reconciliation of his developed aesthetic theory with the ordinary, pretheoretical conception of taste from which it begins. Precisely in this stumbling block, however, we also encounter the theoretical linkage between the judgment of taste's features of disinterestedness and formality, strictly construed.

Section 3: Colors and Tones: One Last Difficulty

As I argued in Chapter 2, Kant devotes considerable attention to the question whether our representations of colors and tones are mere sensations or rather 'formal determinations,' which require an activity of synthesis to unify a manifold of sensations into an intuition with spatiotemporal form. If the latter option is correct, Kant argues in § 14, judgments about colors and tones could be construed as judgments of the beautiful, because they would be made on the basis of form, rather than mere sensation. And, as we've seen, a judgment made on the basis of (perceptual) form both avoids the difficulties that render sensations incommunicable and retains its connection to the conditions for the possibility of cognition, which, according to Kant, are required for there to be norms that govern such judgments.

But if an aesthetic judgment must be disinterested in order to be communicable, or normative, then judgments made about colors and tones cannot be communicable—not if the existence conception provides the relevant standard of interest, anyway. The reason for this is quite simple. Even on the revised view of colors and tones that Kant struggles with in the third *Critique*, the representations of colors and tones are not, and obviously cannot be, instances of *pure* perceptual form. In contrast to spatiality and temporality, they are not aspects of our representations that are due solely to the pure forms of sensibility, such that they do not count as indicators of something's real, or material, existence. On the contrary, they necessarily involve an exercise of receptivity whereby we receive sensations. They may no longer be construed as *mere* sensations, but they remain, nonetheless, indicators of something's real existence.

On this revised view, representations of colors and tones are empirical intuitions, complexes of sensation and pure intuition. But the pleasures they afford—even though these pleasures are now said to be based on the intuition's perceptual form—still count as interested on the existence conception: concerning these representations, it is not possible to abstract away from all matter of the empirical intuition and merely judge its form. Though these representations are now said to have a form, one cannot abstract away from all matter of sensation and be left with anything that could reasonably be called a representation of a color or tone.[25] A pleasure taken in a color or tone will always be based, at least in part, on sensation. It will therefore always count as interested on the existence conception, whichever view of our representations of colors and tones—mere sensations or empirical intuitions—one ultimately adopts.[26]

The intrusion of the existence conception into Kant's aesthetic theory provides the primary motivation for his initial, albeit hesitant, classification of colors and tones within the agreeable. After all, on the desire conception, this classification is obviously implausible. If, however, one thinks of sensations as indicators of an object's existence, and takes this to provide the relevant standard of interestedness, one will count a pleasure taken in a color or tone—on either construal of our representations of them—as interested. No matter which construal Kant were ultimately to settle on, the existence conception would always block these pleasures from being properly described as disinterested; it would, therefore, always block the corresponding judgments from counting as judgments of the beautiful.

But the existence conception, along with the underlying view of sensation to which it is tied, does explain the systematic link between the disinterestedness and the formality of the judgment of taste. More specifically, the existence conception explains how Kant concludes that only a judgment based on formal features, in the strict sense, could have the disinterestedness required of the pure judgment of taste. The inference is actually quite simple. Any pleasure based on sensation will count as interested on the existence conception. So a disinterested aesthetic pleasure can only be based on *pure* perceptual form, since that is the only remaining aspect of our (intuitive) representations that does not correspond to anything's real existence. A pleasure based solely on sensation—for instance, the taste of one's favorite food—will obviously count as interested in this sense. But so will a pleasure taken in a color or tone, since one cannot abstract away from all sensation and be left judging anything that could rightfully be called a representation of a color or tone. Only purely spatial or temporal features can escape the existence conception's sweeping proclamation of interestedness. That, I believe, motivates Kant's initial, highly restrictive, presentation of his formalism, on which a disinterested aesthetic judgment must be based on spatiotemporal form in the strictest sense. Although Kant tries to find a way to reintroduce the notion of form into our representations of colors and tones, this strategy will never suffice, so long as the existence conception remains. The desire conception, however, removes this otherwise insurmountable obstacle. I conclude, then, that the existence conception of interest provides the theoretical linkage between the disinterestedness and the formality (in the strict sense) of the pure judgment of taste. So much the worse for this systematic connection, based as it is on a hopeless construal of interest.

Section 4: Synthesis of the Difficulties

In this chapter, I have argued that Kant's aesthetic theory is better off without the existence conception, even though Kant needs it to forge a direct connection between the disinterestedness and the formality of the judgment of taste. Kant's readers thus face the following general interpretive difficulty: his characterization of the judgment of taste involves the quasi-sensory, or as-if subjective, features of being grounded on pleasure and being nonconceptual; and the quasi-cognitive, or as-if objective, features of formality, disinterestedness, and universal communicability.[27] I have been concerned to explicate the relations between the quasi-cognitive features of the judgment of taste, and I conclude that intelligible connections between these three quasi-cognitive features cannot be systematically explicated without equivocating between the two separable notions of an interest. To see why this is so, let's recall the two main lines of argument I have offered concerning Kant's reasoning to his restrictive notion of formality. While I endorse neither one philosophically, I do believe they make sense of the trajectory of much of Kant's argumentation in the third *Critique.*

First, transcendental philosophy is unable to assert that the variability hypothesis is false. For all that transcendental philosophy can know or establish—since the variability hypothesis and its denial are empirical rather than transcendental claims—material objects cause qualitatively different sensations in different people, thereby undermining any basis for the communicability of the pleasures that attend to those sensations. The pleasures anyone derives therefrom are pleasures he just *happens* to have, rather than pleasures it is in any (normative) sense *necessary* to have. The universal communicability of a pleasure requires that it be equally available, on the same terms, to all. It must be rooted in a fundamental capacity or set of capacities that transcendental philosophy can ascribe to us all as a matter of necessity.

The representation of spatiotemporality by the pure forms of intuition fills this role. This representational capacity is not merely sensory, and not a contingent feature of the human brain, but rather a characterization of what our cognitive faculties must be like if cognition is to be possible. In light of the nonconceptual status of the judgment of taste, the forms of intuition are the only possible candidate for this role in Kant's epistemological scheme. Thus, Kant can argue from the 'privacy' of sensation and the universal communicability of a judgment of taste to the grounding of that judgment in a pleasure taken in the formal features of our intuitive representations. In essence, it is argument by elimination, by means of which an inference from universal communicability to formality becomes possible.

Second, Kant appears to believe that only pleasures taken in formal features can be disinterested. This inference requires the existence conception. Since sensations are construed as indicators of real existence—and this is taken to establish the presence of an interest—only a pleasure taken not in sensations, but rather in something that is not an indicator of anything's real existence, could count as disinterested. Argument by elimination again reveals the pure forms of intuition as the only possible candidates. Although this forges a connection between disinterestedness and formality, it provides no reason at all to think that there is any direct and natural connection between interest and incommunicability. This result can be avoided as a matter of course on the desire conception, but on that conception, the claim that only a judgment based on purely spatiotemporal features could count as disinterested once again becomes mysterious.

In sum: we can choose the desire conception or the existence conception. If we choose the desire conception, we can plausibly argue that interested pleasures fail to be universally communicable. But the claim that only purely spatiotemporal features can ground a disinterested pleasure then appears false, and is certainly unexplained. To generate this formalist claim, on the desire conception, we have to appeal to an independent set of requirements on communicability, and to the variability hypothesis, to show that sensory pleasures fail to satisfy those requirements. That would leave pure perceptual or intuitive form as the only remaining candidate, generating an inference from communicability to formality. In other words, on the desire conception, disinterestedness and formality are independent.

If we choose the existence conception, we can indeed argue—within the context of transcendental idealism's characterization of our representations—that only formal features satisfy the requirements of disinterestedness. But we will have no grounds for a direct inference from the interestedness of many judgments, on this conception, to their incommunicability. No matter what, some inference will remain unexplained, unless we equivocate on what I have argued are two separable conceptions of interest. We have run up against the limits of the philosophical systematicity that Kant's aesthetic theory can achieve.

Kant's own predilections aside, I do not believe this should be cause for much anxiety. Kant should simply drop the existence conception in favor of the desire conception. It isn't clear to me that anything of value will be lost. On my reading, disinterestedness properly registers the fact that the aesthetic pleasure that grounds a pure judgment of taste is a contemplative

delight—a delight taken in the perceptual form of an object in a nontechnical, nontheoretical sense, without implying any restriction to purely spatiotemporal features. This further, unfortunate restriction is generated by
the role of spatiotemporality in providing a necessary condition for the possibility of cognition. This should not be surprising, since the most fundamental aspect of Kant's formalism is not an idiosyncratic and problematic
conception of 'interest,' but the connection he seeks to forge between the
formality of the pure judgment of taste and his analysis of the conditions
for the possibility of cognition.

Even if we were to adopt the existence conception, the connection forged
between disinterestedness and formality would still require the view that
the representations of spatiality and temporality—since they are due not to
sensation but to the *a priori* forms of intuition—are not indicators of anything's real or material existence. Otherwise put, on either the desire or the
existence conception, transcendental idealism, not disinterestedness, is the
driving force behind Kant's aesthetic formalism. On an existence conception, one can directly connect the notions of disinterestedness and formality, provided that one is already willing to accept transcendental idealism's
conception of an *a priori* form of intuition. But a transcendental idealist
doesn't even need the notion of disinterestedness to be an aesthetic formalist. The existence conception merely adds the claim that *only* a pleasure
based on purely spatiotemporal features could be disinterested, and that
result, on any natural and uncontrived notion of interest, seems false
anyhow.[28]

That much is well confirmed by the cases of colors and tones. What's
more, the existence conception would immediately render Kant's investigation of the epistemological and aesthetic status of colors and tones irrelevant. On the desire conception, which naturally construes the pleasures
taken in colors and tones as disinterested, this investigation—inconclusive
and problematic as it is—at least has an intelligible point. Given the disinterestedness of these pleasures, they are natural candidates for inclusion
within a conception of beauty. But given the further restriction of beauty to
formal spatiotemporal features, Kant must show that our representations of
colors and tones have these formal elements, or else they cannot ground a
judgment of taste.

Ultimately, the problem is not simply that the aesthetic resources available in the third *Critique* are too thin to fund a more robust conception of
aesthetic form on independent grounds, although I think that is true. An
attempt to augment these resources—so as to construct a more tolerant
notion of aesthetic form, as Guyer and Allison suggest we ought—must

remain within the parameters set by transcendental idealism, if the claim that the judgment of taste manifests a necessary condition for the possibility of cognition is to made out in a distinctively Kantian way. That is why Kant's investigation proceeds as it does, by searching for grounds on which to apply the notion of intuitive or spatiotemporal form to our representations of colors and tones. Anything but this strategy, whatever its difficulties as a piece of substantive aesthetic theory, would be tantamount to an attempt to prize apart the aesthetic theory from transcendental idealism's characterization of our representations. Small wonder, then, that Kant's investigation proceeds as it does. But this investigation would immediately lose all point and prospect on a conception of interest that blocked the pleasures taken in colors and tones from ever counting as disinterested in the first place.

In this and the preceding chapter, I have offered an interpretation of Kantian aesthetic formalism that takes seriously its grounding in transcendental idealism. Unlike Guyer, I do not believe that Kant's identification of aesthetic and perceptual or intuitive form—its problematic results for his aesthetic theory notwithstanding—is either gratuitous or avoidable. If any prominent aspect of Kant's aesthetic theory is gratuitous and avoidable, it is the existence conception of interest. In light of the largely negative philosophical results of this interpretation, however, one might reasonably ask whether it has any positive philosophical interest, especially for contemporary inquiries. I conclude this aspect of my interpretation by sketching a modest proposal that speaks to this concern.

Section 5: The Significance of the Beautiful and the Agreeable

The aesthetic questions about colors and tones that Kant raises in the third *Critique* are part of his broader epistemological investigation of our representations of these sensible qualities, namely, whether such qualities are simply presented to us, or given through sheer receptivity. This question, in turn, can be viewed as part of a more general interpretive question about the extent of Kant's sympathies toward empiricism. Consider what Kant calls an empiricism of taste, the view that 'taste always judges in accordance with empirical determining grounds, and thus in accordance with those that are given only *a posteriori* by means of the senses.'[29] This amounts to a wholesale classification of aesthetic pleasures as pleasures in the agreeable. The distinction between the agreeable and the beautiful marks a distinction between pleasures that are, and pleasures that are not, straightforwardly made available by that which is simply presented to us, or given to us through sheer receptivity.

Kant is gesturing here toward more than just the thought that an 'empiricism of taste' would involve a denial of any *a priori* determining ground for judgments of taste, such that they would one and all be determined by that which is 'given only *a posteriori* by means of the senses' [*nur a posteriori durch Sinne gegeben werden*]. I think the word 'given' [*gegeben*] *is* as philosophically loaded as it will sound to contemporary ears.[30] An empiricism of taste is grounded in an empiricist conception of sense experience and, in particular, of our representations of sensible qualities. I submit the following: Kant construes the paradigmatic cases of the agreeable—tastes and smells—as qualities that are simply presented to us through sheer receptivity. In the problematic cases of the agreeable—colors and tones—Kant undertakes to oppose the remnants of a broadly empiricist view. For a variety of reasons, he suspects that the empiricist view is wrong in these cases; he searches for a reconstrual of our representations of these qualities on which they could count as beautiful, which is to say, a construal on which they are not simply presented to us through sheer receptivity, but are rather constructed in accordance with the cognitive norms that the *a priori* forms of intuition provide for the imagination's synthesis of the manifold. To say that a representation has an intuitive form, for Kant, is precisely *not* to say that it is simply presented to us through the senses.

Consider, for instance, Locke's view of our ideas of sensible qualities:

> First, our *Senses*, conversant about particular sensible objects, do *convey into the Mind*, several distinct *Perceptions* of things, according to those various ways, wherein those Objects do affect them: And thus we come by those *Ideas*, we have of *Yellow, White, Heat, Cold, Soft, Hard, Bitter, Sweet*, and all those which we call sensible qualities, which when I say the senses convey into the mind, I mean, they from external Objects convey into the mind what produces there those *Perceptions*. This great Source, of most of the *Ideas* we have, depending wholly upon our Senses, and derived from them to the Understanding, I call *SENSATION*.[31]

There are three points to note here. First, Locke conceives of sensation as sufficient for delivering to us ideas of sensible qualities ('depending *wholly* upon our Senses'); no further operations of the intellect are required for us to have an idea of yellow or white, or bitter or sweet. For Locke, our ideas of these qualities are 'simple ideas,' which require nothing beyond sensation. They are given to us as is in experience. Second, Locke conceives of sensation as a causal relation between an object and a perceiver: objects 'affect' our sense organs and thereby 'convey' into the mind various ideas of objects and qualities. Simple ideas, therefore, are the mental states that are caused in us when objects impinge on our senses. Third, Locke marks no distinction between colors and tastes. Both concerning their status as secondary qualities, and concerning their status as simple ideas, which sensation alone can provide, Locke sees no relevant difference between the sensible properties associated with different sense modalities. What holds for a taste or a smell holds for a color or a tone. It is worth asking after Kant's reasons for becoming suspicious of the empiricist assimilation of our representations of these various sensible qualities. It is here that the most instructive lessons are to be learned.

We can begin by noting that Kant had long been suspicious of this assimilation on what we might call cognitive grounds, as evidenced by his various attempts to work out a distinction between 'objective' and 'subjective' sensation in the *Metaphysics* lectures. As we saw in Chapter 2, Kant consistently holds that some sense modalities, in particular, smell and taste, are at the very least far less 'objective,' that is, 'related to cognition,' than the modalities of hearing and especially sight. This same attitude toward the noncognitive status of the sense of taste appears elsewhere, including Kant's examples of taste (the sweet taste of sugar, the repugnant taste of wormwood) in his discussion of judgments of experience and of perception in § 19 of the *Prolegomena*. Kant admits that these are examples of judgments of perception that *cannot* become judgments of experience. 'Everyone acknowledges,' he says, that tastes are 'merely subjective,' that they 'refer merely to feeling,' and that 'they express only a relation of two sensations to the same subject, namely myself.'[32] In contrast—notwithstanding his view in the 'Transcendental Aesthetic'—Kant often recognizes judgments about color as judgments of perception that *can* become judgments of experience, that is, that can subsequently be related to objects. They do not merely express the relation of sensations to a subject; they articulate objective, judgeable content.[33]

From one perspective, this distinction between different sensible qualities may appear gratuitous. Why couldn't a judgment about sweetness admit of the same cognitive value, the same objectivity, as a judgment about redness? Put the other way around, if tastes cannot be thought of as objective or as 'related to cognition,' what allows colors to be? From an empiricist standpoint such as Locke's, the distinction can look unmotivated, even question begging. To be sure, there is more that could be said, against a flat-footed empiricist, about the differences in cognitive status between colors and tones on the one hand, and smells and tastes on the other. But I suspect that considering the difference in their *aesthetic* status threw into sharper relief for Kant some salient differences between them, sharply calling into question the empiricist assimilation of the whole lot of sensible qualities under a single general model. And whether it did or not, for the historical Kant, there are good reasons for thinking that it should have.

The desire conception makes patent a substantial difference between qualities like taste and qualities like color or tone. If the pleasurable character of a mere sensation gives rise to a desire or appetite, or is the gratification of a desire or appetite, as in the taste of the palate, then it should make perfect sense—if colors are examples of the agreeable—to speak of an 'appetite for hunter green.' But this so-called appetite is not like an appetite for chocolate or lamb or beer; it is like an 'appetite for equilateral triangularity,' which is to say, it is no appetite at all. The kind of pleasure we take in colors or tones is not the same kind of pleasure we take in literal tastes; they are not pleasures of mere sensation. For if they were, we could speak freely and comfortably of our desires or appetites for hunter green and minor thirds. The inappropriateness of speaking of desires, appetites, or inclinations in the case of colors or tones suggests that the kind of representations we have here must be different because the kind of pleasures we have here are different: they are contemplative rather than appetitive pleasures, forms of delight that are not the gratification of sensuous desires. In lingering over the beautiful coloration of an oak in autumn, I am not acting on the basis of any appetite or inclination that has been caused to arise in me by sensations I have received from some object. That description is contrived, and leaves out something essential, namely the pleasure or delight I take in my disinterested contemplation of the perceptual form (speaking in a nontechnical sense) of my representation of a beautiful color.

The pleasures of the agreeable involve the gratification of desires, appetites, or inclinations that are aroused by the sensations an object causes us to have. These are heteronomous, animalistic pleasures; the capacity to take pleasure in the agreeable does not presuppose any cognitive capacities that we do not share with other animals: 'Agreeableness is also valid for nonrational animals.'[34] Our susceptibility to the agreeable presupposes only sensation and appetitive pleasure; given Kant's general characterizations of the agreeable, it cannot presuppose any uniquely human cognitive faculties. What this means, on my view, is that our susceptibility to the agreeable cannot presuppose the capacity to have an intuition. Mere receptivity, the passive capacity to be causally affected by objects, such as other animals have, is not sufficient to endow us with intuitions.

For Kant, our susceptibility to the contemplative pleasures of the beautiful presupposes uniquely human cognitive capacities, whereas our susceptibility to the pleasures of the agreeable does not.[35] When we take pleasure in the agreeable—for instance, in tastes or smells—we deploy only capacities we share with other animals, for they are susceptible to these pleasures just as we are. And that is because such qualities are available unproblematically—presented or given, so to speak—in mere sensation. The aesthetic status of tastes and smells causes no problem for an empiricist view of sensible qualities, but the aesthetic status of colors and tones does. It calls into question rather sharply the assimilation of these various sensible qualities under a single univocal model.[36]

In Chapter 2, I argued that for Kant, what is crucial to the possibility of universally communicable judgments is the presence of a rule-governed activity of the imagination. In the case of the beautiful, the rule governedness of the imagination's activity consists in its conformity to the 'universal laws of sensibility,' which derive from the *a priori* forms of sensibility.[37] The investigation here casts further light on the significance of this aspect of Kant's account. To say that a representation is the product of a rule-governed activity of the imagination is to say that this representation is not straightforwardly available in our mere sensory uptake. Whether a representation is available in our mere sensory uptake is, on my reading, the most fundamental basis of Kant's distinction between the beautiful and the agreeable. That is why his investigation of colors and tones takes the overall shape of an inquiry into whether our representations of these qualities are part of objective intuitions. Only then will they require the operation of the distinctively human forms of sensibility.

The investigation of Chapters 2 and 3 reveals some important general morals about interpreting Kant, and about contemporary inquiries in epistemology and perception. There has been much debate in recent years about the question whether Kant believed, in the fashion of a Lockean empiricist, that our awareness of any sensible qualities is or can be given through the senses, and hence whether our perceptual states do or could contain any so-called nonconceptual content. Following the standard language of the debate, I will call a reading of Kant that denies the existence of such forms of awareness a 'conceptualist' reading, and the alternative a 'nonconceptualist' reading.[38] Much of the debate has focused on the significance of Kant's notion of an intuition, and in particular, whether this kind of representation, or this aspect of our representations, is evidence of such nonconceptual content. I have no wish to enter into this debate in any detailed way here, but I will say that, construing the issue in this way, I find the conceptualist reading to be correct. But there is also something that this debate, on both sides, seems to me to be overlooking: the significance of Kant's category of the agreeable, and his struggle over the question of the aesthetic status of colors and tones.

Although Kantian intuitions are not evidence of unconceptualized (or even less, unconceptualizable) elements of perception, the sensible qualities in which we find the pleasures of the agreeable, which lack intuitive form, *are* independent of discursive mental activity. Nonconceptualist readings are correct that some of the mind's awareness of sensible qualities is achieved independently of any discursive activity. They are wrong, however, to identify these states with Kantian intuitions. In that regard, the conceptualist readings are correct. But they ought not be overstated. Denying that *any* of our representations of sensible qualities can be independent of discursive mental activity will leave them unable to explain how there could be the category of the agreeable at all. In particular, if the sensible qualities that afford these pleasures require some kind of discursive mental activity, the conceptualist will be unable to explain why the pleasures we take in them are not, and cannot be, subject to norms as well. To the extent conceptualists have focused on the notion of an intuition, however, they should not have much philosophical difficulty taking this point.[39]

So much for the significance of Kant's general distinction between the beautiful and the agreeable. His more pointed investigation of colors and tones also offers, to my mind, two general lessons. First, those interested in contemporary versions of the question about our representations of sensible qualities that arises from Locke's theory of perception should not be overhasty in assimilating all such qualities to a single general model. One of the epistemological morals of Kant's aesthetics is precisely that the empiricist assimilation of all sensible qualities, as we saw it in Locke, is suspect and ultimately problematic. And that point should be taken whether one's own model is empiricist or not. What works for some sensible qualities may well not work for others, and Kant does well to resist the craving for generality in philosophical explanation that plagues the Lockean view.[40]

Finally, there is a moral about the relevance of aesthetics to these general issues in epistemology and perception. I have argued throughout that the epistemological and metaphysical strictures of transcendental idealism do much damage to the particular results of Kant's substantive aesthetic theory. Turning the point on its head, there is a valuable contribution in the other direction, that of aesthetics to epistemology. I've claimed that Kant's investigation of the aesthetic status of colors and tones brings into sharpest relief the need to separate the account of these representations from an account of our representations of other sensible qualities, like tastes and smells. It is a familiar Kantian theme that a characterization of our representations takes as a starting point the kinds of claims, usually discursive but more generally normative claims, in which those representations figure. Extending this line of thought to our aesthetic claims provides us with good reasons for suspecting, within the context of a broadly Kantian view, that our representations of colors and tones couldn't correctly be described as qualities that are made available through sheer receptivity: this leaves no explanation of how such claims could ever be governed by genuine norms. Our account of these representations must intelligibly connect them to whatever we take the ultimate source of such norms to be.[41]

For Kant, such norms are to be found in the activity of the imagination in the synthesis of representations. The specific set of norms that, for Kant, govern aesthetic judgment—norms articulated in the doctrine of formalism, shaped as it is by transcendental idealism—turn out to be too constricted to provide a satisfactory aesthetics. But we needn't accept transcendental idealism to take the general point. To the extent that philosophers are still engaged in the project of providing a nonnaturalistic account of our capacity to represent and make judgments about sensible qualities like color, Kant's investigation in the third *Critique* reaffirms the relevance of our aesthetic claims to this ongoing philosophical project. His sometimes unfortunate or damaging demands for philosophical system aside, we would do well to recover Kant's sense of the intrinsic interconnectedness of philosophical questions, especially given the extent to which philosophical aesthetics seems to have fallen out of fashion as of late.

Chapter 4

Some Varieties of Normativity

In Chapter 1, I claimed that disagreement in matters of taste is a stubborn and widespread fact of human life, one all the more striking against the backdrop of the agreement we enjoy in our everyday linguistic and cognitive affairs. Despite this disagreement, we persist in making normative demands in some matters of taste, those in which, as Kant puts it, we judge something to be beautiful rather than agreeable. If my claim that we do not achieve widespread agreement or consensus in matters of taste is correct, and Kant's claim that judgments of beauty make legitimate normative demands is correct, it follows that an explanation of how these normative demands are possible cannot require or presuppose that there is any significant degree of agreement or consensus in our judgments of beauty.

The normative demand made by a judgment of beauty is the claim that the pleasure one takes in beholding some particular object exemplifies a standard of correctness for anyone's response to that same object. If I take it that I am correct in finding an object beautiful, then I take it that everyone else ought to find it beautiful too. I take those who respond differently than I do to the object to be wrong, or not to be responding as they ought to respond. Given this construal of the normative demands of taste, it follows that an explanation of how I am entitled to take my aesthetic response to an object to be the correct response to that object cannot require, as a precondition, that my response conform to or exemplify any reasonably widespread or shared response among those who judge that same object. The possibility—that is, legitimacy—of the normative demands made by judgments of beauty cannot require that there be any general agreement among human beings concerning which things are correctly taken to be beautiful. Any account that makes general agreement or consensus into a precondition of taste's normative demands must be mistaken.

Indeed, one should accept this point even if one believes that there is general agreement concerning which things are beautiful: general agreement is not a precondition for the exercise of taste. My entitlement to take my aesthetic response to an object to be appropriate does not depend on whether or not people in general, or even anyone at all, responds to that object as I do. More generally, we could all take ourselves to be responding appropriately to an object, even if everybody responded to it differently, and no two people ever found the same things, or more or less the same things, beautiful. Of course, a denial that there is much consensus in matters of taste needn't go to such extremes, and I don't put this forward as a description of the facts. My point is simply that one can allow disagreement between people to be as ubiquitous and pervasive as one likes; this will never show that the exercise of taste is impossible—that normative demands or genuine claims of taste are not in principle legitimate.

If one accepts these reflections, one has good reason to believe that an explanation of how we can consider an aesthetic response to an object to be correct or incorrect cannot be modeled very closely on an explanation of how standards of correctness or incorrectness are possible in either the linguistic or cognitive domains. A recent and prominent interpretive approach to Wittgenstein's later philosophy, exemplified by Stanley Cavell, Cora Diamond, Edward Minar, and Barry Stroud, to name a few of the best of such commentators, has undertaken to show that the general notion of 'following a rule' only makes sense if one takes an extensive backdrop of human agreement—Wittgenstein's elusive notion of 'agreement in judgments' [*Übereinstimmung in den Urteilen*]—to be in place.[1] More specifically, this interpretive approach maintains that without general patterns of agreement among human beings in the performance of an activity—the existence of what Wittgenstein calls a 'practice' or a 'custom'—be it the use of a natural language or the formation and application of empirical concepts, there wouldn't be any such thing as 'following a rule'; there wouldn't be any such thing as a standard of correct or incorrect performance for the activity. Stroud concisely sums up the central thought here, as it applies to the use of language:

> In the case of speaking and understanding a language, there must at the very least be some regularity, some general pattern of activity, for one's performance to conform to. Otherwise there would be no such thing as correctness or incorrectness, no following a rule or failing to follow it.[2]

In contrast, I have claimed that the possibility of normative standards for taste in no way depends on the presence of any regularity or general agreement in the results of its exercise among human beings at large. Thus, there appears to be a substantive disanalogy between the kind of normativity found in matters of taste and that found in the linguistic and cognitive domains.

This disanalogy is particularly pressing for Hannah Ginsborg's interpretation of Kant's epistemology and its application to his aesthetic theory. Ginsborg provides a powerful account of the possibility of empirical concepts in terms of what she calls a 'primitive recognition of normativity.'[3] Ginsborg's account is especially notable for its sensitivity to some of the central philosophical lessons of this interpretive approach to Wittgenstein and its ability to make sense of the commitments of Kant's theory of perceptual synthesis in light of them. Ginsborg, however, subsequently constructs an explanation of how judgments of beauty are possible within the terms set forth by her model of a primitive recognition, as it functions in the case of perceptual synthesis, along with an account of the possibility of norms for a natural language, which she uses to elucidate it. In this way, Ginsborg's explanation of how the judgment of beauty is possible threatens to run afoul of precisely the disanalogy I have just sketched.

In the present chapter, I argue that a consequence of applying Ginsborg's model of a primitive recognition to the judgment of beauty is that some general regularity or agreement or consensus in the results of the exercise of our capacity for taste must be taken as a precondition of the normative demands made therein.[4] I do not claim that Ginsborg actually believes this to be a precondition of taste, but rather that she is faced with a choice: she must either accept the charge that she has (perhaps unwittingly) committed herself to this mistaken conception of the conditions for the possibility of taste, or she must acknowledge that there are at least two different conceptions of normativity, and two different conceptions of a primitive recognition, that her general model needs—but fails—to distinguish. Otherwise put, I defend the following conditional claim: if Ginsborg wants to construct a general model that explains the possibility of normativity both in matters of taste and in the linguistic and cognitive domains, as I believe she does, then she is committed to this mistaken conception of the preconditions for normativity in matters of taste.

Here is the plan, in the small, for the present chapter. In Section 1, I present an overview of Ginsborg's model of a primitive recognition and its intended application in the linguistic, cognitive, and aesthetic domains. The philosophical issues involved are rather complex, and for the sake of providing a surveyable sketch of the overall problem with which I am here concerned, I will slough over some of the finer and more intricate features of the model until Section 4. In Section 2, I argue that Ginsborg's criticism of Guyer's 'ideal prediction' interpretation of the judgment of beauty obscures the role of agreement in her account of normativity in matters of taste, although there is no real conceptual tension between her model and this criticism. In Section 3, I try to get clearer about the kind of agreement that the model of a primitive recognition requires, and explore some aspects of the contrast between a primitive recognition and what Ginsborg calls a recognition of normativity in a 'derivative' sense. In Section 4, I examine some of the more intricate details of Ginsborg's model as it applies in the cognitive realm and explore a deep tension between two aspects of her view. I present reasons to choose one of these aspects over the other in Sections 4–5. In Section 6, I return to the application of the model of a primitive recognition to judgments of taste.

Section 1: Overview of the Problem

A cornerstone of Ginsborg's view is the distinction between *rule-governed* and *rule-guided* activities.[5] For Ginsborg, it is crucial that perceptual synthesis be understood as governed but not guided by empirical concepts. She illustrates her distinction with the example of norms for speaking a natural language. The question is how we can discover the rules that determine whether or not a given linguistic usage is correct. Ginsborg quite reasonably says that the methods we employ all involve some appeal to the actual linguistic behavior of the native speakers of that language; the actual linguistic practices of native speakers in general are normative—are the source of rules or standards—for speakers of that language in general. There is, as she puts it, 'a general reciprocity according to which each of us can in principle serve as an authority for the others.'[6]

Put differently, the rules that determine how to speak a natural language correctly are not available prior to or independently of there being an actual practice of speaking that language. This point holds both at the individual and at the collective level. A natural language does not arise out of the conscious application of rules; no such rules even exist before there is the practice of speaking that language. The rules can only be derived after the fact, from reflecting on and codifying the way the practice is actually carried out: the practice itself is the ultimate source of its rules. While the practice of speaking a natural language is not (for native speakers) explicitly guided by antecedently available rules, it is nonetheless governed by rules that can be formulated by codifying the actual practices of native speakers. Hence, there are still standards of correctness for linguistic usage—standards set by the way the practice is actually performed, in general, by native speakers of the language. As Ginsborg puts it, 'the rules governing how English *ought* to be spoken can be discovered only through reflection on how English *is* spoken.'[7] Ginsborg sometimes frames the point at the individual level. At that level of description, the crucial point is that in acquiring the ability to use a language, a native speaker does not first learn general rules and subsequently learn how to apply them. Native speakers are not, in that sense, guided by rules in their use of the language. But their speech is still rule governed: they catch on to the way the language is spoken by the other native speakers, and to what the other native speakers consider to be correct speech, 'through a natural and unstudied process in which the imitation of others plays a central role.'[8] In time, their own linguistic behavior will by and large exemplify or conform to those standards.

This is a rich and plausible explanation of how the activity of speaking a natural language can be simultaneously understood as both natural and normative. For present purposes, I want to focus attention on the crucial role that a presupposition of a general agreement plays in the argument. This presupposition is packed into Ginsborg's use of the phrase 'in general': the way in which native English speakers *in general* speak sets the standards of correctness for use of the English language. Ginsborg relies on the fact that there is such a thing as the way native English speakers *in general* speak. Of course, differences and disagreements do emerge, people sometimes make mistakes, and so forth. The actual linguistic behavior of any given native English speaker is by no means an infallible guide to the rules of English.[9] But mistakes and disagreements over what would be the correct, or best, or most appropriate, usage exist against the backdrop of an extensive general consensus. Indeed, in the absence of such general agreement or regularity in the way native speakers speak, there *wouldn't be* anything recognizable as a natural language at all. The presupposition that native speakers enjoy a general agreement about how to speak their language correctly is incontrovertible, as is the claim that the native speakers themselves are the ultimate source of the rules for speaking the language correctly.

But Ginsborg's main interest is not in the norms for a natural language; ultimately, she wants to explain how the activity of the imagination in perceptual synthesis can be taken to conform to normative standards. If perceptual synthesis is conceived in terms of the rule-guided model, one would need to grasp empirical concepts before perceptual synthesis could ever take place. To make a long story short, there couldn't be any such thing as an empirical concept, for there could be no way to learn or acquire a concept through perceptual experience. This problem can be avoided if we think of perceptual synthesis as governed by empirical concepts but not as guided by them. As in the case of the rules for correct linguistic usage, empirical concepts could then be understood as discursive rules—what Kant calls 'reflected representations'[10]—that are formed by reflecting on the way in which perceptual synthesis actually or naturally occurs for people in general. Empirical concepts could then be understood as such 'reflected representations' of the perceptual uptake of the world on the part of human minds in general. Ginsborg explains:

> We can think of [the synthesis of imagination], in the way we think of a natural language, as subject to rules which are not imposed externally but rather determined by the very activity they govern. What our imagination in fact does in the perception of a given object may be regarded as setting the standard for what our imagination ought to do in the perception of that object and others of its kind.[11]

The standards for how one's imagination *ought* to perceive an object, according to Ginsborg, ultimately derive from how human imaginations, in general, actually perceive it. In that sense, the norms for perceptual synthesis should be understood on the model of the norms for a natural language—just as Ginsborg's use of the first-person plural phrase '*our* imagination' suggests.

A consistent general model, one which applies equally to natural language and to perceptual synthesis, is possible only if perceptual synthesis exhibits general patterns of agreement, just as natural-linguistic usage does. There must be some such thing as the way that human beings in general perceive the world, some such thing as the typical or characteristic human perceptual uptake of the stuff that surrounds us on a daily basis; our perceptual uptake or sorting of that stuff must proceed in a more or less uniform way. We must agree, in the main, about which of the concepts we could form on the basis of this perceptual uptake or sorting are the most natural, most useful for human practical and theoretical purposes, make the most sense, and have the most intelligible routes of application; we must in general agree about which occasions are the appropriate or correct occasions for applying the concepts we form on this basis. As in the case of linguistic usage, no single person's way of sorting out and characterizing the objects of her perceptual experience, and no single person's stock of empirical concepts formed on its basis, will ever be decisive or infallible. There will always be local misunderstandings, disagreements, and disputes. But for Ginsborg's modeling of norms for perceptual synthesis on norms for a natural language to be correct, or even intelligible, it has to be the case that disagreement and error here emerge against the backdrop of a widespread and extensive agreement—at least if we limit ourselves to fairly ordinary, routine cases. For without a broad and general background of agreement, there wouldn't be the 'general reciprocity' that allows each of us to serve as an authority for the others.

If I am right, Ginsborg's analogy between natural languages and perceptual synthesis presupposes that there *is* broad, general agreement in our ways of synthesizing, or our cognitive dispositions, which are the basis for the explicit concepts we go on to form and use to make matter-of-fact claims. This presupposition seems to me unproblematic. We do, by and large, find that agreement about matter-of-fact questions is easy to achieve in simple and ordinary cases, though of course there is often substantial dispute about a variety of difficult and less mundane matters of fact. As Ginsborg recognizes, what falls under the rubric of perceptual synthesis is a host of empirical, natural, psychological processes (that can and must, according to Ginsborg, also be regarded in normative terms), that yield the same results for (more or less) all of us because they take the same subjective course in (more or less) all of us. And they take the same subjective course in (more or less) all of us because we are (more or less) all the same kind of creature, and share an extensive background of natural reactions to, and needs and interests in, the world we all inhabit and perceive. The concepts we go on to form are ways of codifying those natural reactions; expressing our own needs and cognitive interests; and giving determinate shape to our thought, inquiry, and communication. Without some broad and general background of agreement, as Wittgenstein is keen to remind us, we wouldn't have what we call inquiry, judgment, and communication at all; whatever it is that we would have in the absence of general agreement would be something else, something that lacked the de facto regularity of these practices as we know them.[12]

So far so good, for Ginsborg's model. I have tried to sketch in broad strokes the general features of a primitive recognition of normativity, which Ginsborg takes to apply equally to linguistic usage and perceptual synthesis. In this primitive recognition, an activity itself is taken to exemplify its own rules or standards of correctness; there are no determinate, *antecedent* standards for how the activity ought to be performed.[13] I have tried to show how the presupposition of general agreement functions in cases where this model of a primitive recognition makes sense. In the case of linguistic usage, there needs to be such a thing as how, *in general*, native speakers of a language speak, for that is what provides the standards for how one ought to speak the language. In the case of perceptual synthesis, there needs to be such a thing as (roughly speaking) how, *in general,* people sort the things presented to them in experience. If controversy in these matters were the norm, and general agreement were not a real feature of these activities, Ginsborg's model of a rule-governed activity, or of a primitive recognition, could not get the explanatory foothold it succeeds in getting. If native speakers of English did not in general agree about how to speak English, someone's brute insistence on taking her own usage to exemplify the standard for how it ought to be would be a sham; there *wouldn't be* any such standard. If this predicament were representative of human noise-emitting behavior generally, then this behavior would be just that: noise-emitting behavior, without the regularity, constancy, and general agreement that is characteristic of anything we could ever recognize as a language. An individual's own usage would not, in such circumstances, exemplify a norm; it would merely be a personal inclination, perhaps even a personal idiosyncrasy. Similarly, if this were the general predicament in perceptual synthesis—if, for instance, few people could ever reach agreement about which things were windows and which things were shoes, or more generally, about which things were appropriately taken to be the same as other things—someone's brute insistence on taking her own way of perceiving, or sorting, or conceptualizing an object to exemplify the standard for how it ought to be perceived, or sorted, or conceptualized would not amount to the kind of normativity we understand our cognitive activities to be governed by. Once again, the missing element is the regularity, or constancy, or agreement that is characteristic of our cognitive activities. Indeed, apart from this element, our notion of a cognitive norm in general, or of a concept in particular, would have no intelligible point at all. The proper scope and force of these thoughts will, I hope, become clearer in Section 5.

I want to note two things I am *not* saying. First, I am not saying that nobody ever disagrees about correct linguistic usage—about what is or is not either a correct or a (more) appropriate way of perceiving an object or applying a particular concept. Disagreements arise, on particular occasions, for particular reasons. The crucial point is that they could not be ubiquitous, or we wouldn't have the linguistic and cognitive practices we do have. In Section 3, I will get clearer about what kinds of disagreements do not threaten the legitimacy of Ginsborg's primitive recognition model and its presupposition of general agreement. Second, I am not attempting to provide or suggest a reduction of normativity to regularity or agreement, or claiming that Ginsborg has any such intention.[14] I am merely claiming that, in the case of the activities that Ginsborg seeks to describe through the model of a primitive recognition, the operative idea of normativity would have no real sense or force in the absence of general regularities or patterns of agreement on the part of the human beings who engage in those activities. The presence of a broad and general agreement is *part of* our conception of linguistic and cognitive norms.

We now reach the question whether Ginsborg's general model—a model of normative standards for an activity that are derived from reflection on how, in general, human beings conduct themselves in the performance of that activity—can be applied to matters of taste. If I am right that the applicability of this model within the linguistic and cognitive realms requires the fact of general human agreement, then I must, at the very least, be skeptical of its applicability to judgments of taste. There are two reasons for this skepticism. First, I have denied that we are entitled to presume much agreement in matters of taste. Second, I have claimed that agreement—whether we partake of much of it or not—is not an essential part of or precondition for taste. This marks a deep difference between taste on the one hand and the linguistic and cognitive realms on the other; it is the disanalogy with which I began.

As I've argued, and will continue to argue in more detail in Sections 3–5, the presence of general agreement is essential to an explanation of the possibility of normative standards in the linguistic and cognitive realms. If there were no such thing as the way English speakers in general speak, there would be no such thing as English at all. If there were no such thing as how human beings in general were inclined to think of, or classify, the objects of the sensible world presented to them in perception, there would be no such thing as concepts—or even cognitive norms in general—as we know them. But the same thing cannot be said of taste. If there were no widespread agreement in human aesthetic response, if there were no general agreement about which things are beautiful, or in what way they are beautiful, there would still be such a thing as taste: the presence of such agreement is not a precondition of taste. In both the linguistic and cognitive cases, it would be a sham to take oneself to be exemplifying a norm—to take one's own linguistic usage or synthesis to be as it ought to be—if there weren't general human agreement in these practices. But taste is very different. If we all took our aesthetic responses to an object to be as they ought to be, even though there were scant agreement among those responses, that would be no sham. Indeed, that's not far from the way matters of taste often look. To that extent, taste does not fit the model of normativity that can be derived from Ginsborg's other two cases, in which the fact of agreement is essential to making any sense of the practices as rule governed. In matters of taste, human agreement is neither a clear fact of the matter nor an essential part of the notion of taste, in the way it is an essential part of the notions of linguistic and cognitive norms—including the very notion of a concept. Thus, there are prima facie reasons for doubting Ginsborg's entitlement to subsume taste under the same general model as linguistic and cognitive activities.

Section 2: Agreement and Predictions

Ginsborg's criticisms of Guyer's interpretation of the judgment of taste obscure the role that agreement in matters of taste potentially plays in her own interpretation. In particular, Ginsborg objects to Guyer's interpretation of the judgment of taste as being or containing a prediction about the agreement of others with my judgment. For Guyer, of course, a judgment of taste is not a straightforward empirical prediction but rather an 'ideal' prediction, or a prediction about an 'ideal observer,' who has achieved both 'ideal circumstances of response' and 'ideal knowledge of one's own response.'[15] Guyer does not claim that in a judgment of taste, I predict that others *will* agree with my judgment—as though I expect agreement in matters of taste to be the norm. Rather, Guyer claims that in a judgment of taste, I predict that others *would* agree with my judgment, if only they would cultivate the right stance toward the object we are both judging (so as to be susceptible to the pleasure it affords), and if only they would command a clear view of the basis of their own response to the object (so as to discern whether or not that pleasure licenses a pure judgment of taste). Naturally, people often fail in one or both of these respects, but if they were to succeed, then we would all, or nearly all, agree about what is beautiful. As Guyer puts it, 'the judgment that a particular object x is beautiful amounts to the claim that everyone who perceives x should . . . take pleasure in it, or that under ideal conditions . . . everyone who perceives x will take pleasure in it.'[16] On textual as well as philosophical grounds, Ginsborg has sharply criticized Guyer's interpretation of the judgment of taste as making a predictive rather than a purely normative claim.

Ginsborg and Guyer are equally eager to cite the following passage from § 22 in support of their respective interpretations of the judgment of taste: concerning the judgment of taste, Kant writes, 'er sagt nicht, daß jedermann mit unserem Urteil übereinstimmen **werde**, sondern damit zusammenstimmen **solle**.'[17] Guyer cites this passage as evidence that the judgment of taste makes an ideal rather than empirical prediction; that is how he

understands the sense of the verb *sollen* in this context, and, more specifically, the contrast between *sollen* and *werden*. Ginsborg, however, takes passages such as this one to show that the judgment of taste contains only
a normative demand, with no prediction whatsoever, empirical or ideal.
Ginsborg's response to Guyer, in denying that a judgment of taste contains
any prediction that others will agree with my judgment, tends to obscure
the role that her own view potentially requires for a presupposition of
human agreement in matters of taste.[18]

Ginsborg denies that the judgment of taste makes any sort of prediction
about the responses of others; she emphatically claims that it makes only a
normative demand on how those responses ought to be. This may give the
impression—perhaps even to Ginsborg herself—that she can remain neutral concerning the question whether there is general agreement in matters
of taste. If the judgment of taste only says that others *ought* to agree, and not
that they *will* (or *would*) agree, the latter question may seem neither here
nor there for an analysis of the judgment of taste or for an explanation of
the possibility of its normative claims. What matters is whether a normative
demand is present, not whether we have any reasonable expectation that
the demand will be met.

That appearance is misleading. Ginsborg's claim against Guyer, strictly
speaking, is that no prediction about agreement, whether empirical or
ideal, is *part of the content* of a judgment of taste; the content of a judgment
of taste is simply a normative demand. And that is how I think the quote
from § 22 above should be taken, namely, as a specification of the content
of a judgment of taste. Textually speaking, Ginsborg's objection seems to
me decisive, when understood in the strict sense just specified. Philosophically, too, Ginsborg's point is well taken. It is just not plausible to think that
when I claim that some object is beautiful, I am predicting that others will
agree with my judgment. That is simply not what I am claiming. And with
all that experience has taught me about the prospects for finding or achieving widespread consensus in taste, that is the last thing I would ever take
myself to be entitled to claim when pronouncing upon the beauty of an
object, even in the attenuated sense of Guyer's ideal prediction.

Ginsborg's critique of Guyer decisively shows that Guyer's account mislo-
cates the issue of human (dis)agreement in matters of taste. A specification
of the content of a judgment of taste is the wrong place in one's account for
this issue to arise, and it leads to a distorted account, in Guyer's case, of
what a judgment of taste actually claims. For Ginsborg, as for Kant, the issue
of agreement needn't be settled in order to specify the content of a judgment of taste. But that is not to say it needn't be settled at all, if one seeks to

provide a philosophical explanation of how judgments of taste are possible. Hence this issue arises, in Ginsborg's account, not in her specification of what a judgment of taste claims, but rather in the general model of normativity she deploys to explain how such judgments are possible.

To see this more clearly, it will help to compare the content of a judgment of taste with the content of a claim, for example, that some object is a toothbrush. Here the issue can be construed either in terms of the correct use of a word or in terms of one's 'perceptual synthesis' with respect to some object. I can be described as using the word 'toothbrush,' and hence claiming to use it correctly; or I can be described as perceiving some object *as* a toothbrush, and hence claiming to perceive it correctly; or I can be described as applying the concept *toothbrush*, and hence claiming to apply this concept correctly. Any one of these descriptions will suffice for the present point.[19] On any construal, the content of my claim that some object is a toothbrush implies a normative claim: I take myself to have done something correctly, and thus I take it that others ought to do it the same way. As Ginsborg puts the point, 'the application of a concept to an object carries with it a normative implication, namely that there is a certain way in which the object ought to be perceived.'[20] In this way, my claim that something is a toothbrush is like a claim that something is beautiful, with the following qualification: the former involves a claim that I have lived up to some determinate, specifiable normative standard, whereas the latter does not.

The content of my claim that something is a toothbrush contains no prediction that others will agree with me. Nor does it contain a prediction that others would agree with me, if only, say, they would view the object under ideal perceptual conditions. Like the content of a judgment of taste, the content of this claim makes no prediction about the responses or judgments of others. When I say or claim that something is a toothbrush, I am not asserting that others will apply the word or the concept *toothbrush* as I have, or that they will perceive the object *as* a toothbrush, as I have. Even though my claim says nothing about the linguistic or cognitive practices of others, and so makes no prediction about them, it does not follow that I can take my claim that something is a toothbrush to be correct in the absence of a general agreement, or consensus, or regularity in the practices of others, for then there wouldn't be a standard of correctness or incorrectness for me to conform or fail to conform to. There would be no rule for me to follow or fail to follow, and hence there would not be the normativity that characterizes the notion of a rule, a normativity that attends either to the use of a term in a language or to the application of a concept to an object in perception. Putting the point in linguistic terms, Stroud writes:

There must be a general practice or custom in effect for there to be such a thing as a correct or incorrect move, or a rule that is followed or broken. Such consensus could also therefore be called a 'pre-condition of the language-game'. But this consensus or uniformity of practice in the employment of our words is typically not asserted when we say things in the language. I say or imply nothing about my or anyone else's linguistic community when I say that it is raining, or when I say that 68 plus 57 equals 125.[21]

Stroud's point is clear: although saying something in a language (typically) does not assert the presence of any consensus among speakers of that language, the presence of some general patterns of agreement or consensus is nevertheless a precondition for there to be correct or incorrect uses of that language. The question of agreement or consensus in linguistic practices does not arise at the level of the content of particular assertions made within the language. Similarly, the question of agreement or consensus in matters of taste does not arise at the level of the content of particular claims that an object is beautiful. Rather, it arises, as in Ginsborg's model of a primitive recognition (which, recall, takes as its starting point the norms for a natural language), at the level of the preconditions for there be normativity in the first place. It does not follow from Ginsborg's denial that the content of a judgment of taste involves any prediction about the agreement of others, that her explanation of the possibility of correctness or incorrectness of response in matters of taste can remain neutral about whether there is such agreement. Indeed, to the extent that her model of a primitive recognition is meant to apply to judgments of taste along with conceptual and linguistic practices, it cannot remain neutral on this point.

I will be refining and defending this claim over the course of the next four sections. Two issues in particular call for immediate attention. First, we need to be clearer about what kind of agreement is required for the possibility of norms in the linguistic and cognitive cases, and what kinds of disagreements pose no threat at all to the possibility of them, or to the possibility of legitimately taking oneself to conform to them. This will allow us to understand more clearly what Ginsborg means by a 'primitive' recognition of normativity, and how it differs from what she calls a 'derivative' recognition. Second, one might object that my grouping of cognitive norms with linguistic norms itself stands in need of further defense. Perhaps that is already unfaithful to Ginsborg's intentions, and perhaps she has resources for objecting to my representation of her position so far. I will treat the first of these issues in Section 3.

Section 3: Primitive and Derivative Recognitions
of Normativity

An important clarification is needed. One might mistakenly think that I
have proposed, either on my own behalf or on Ginsborg's, a principle to
the effect that: (1) It can be correct or incorrect to count some object x as
an F only if there is general consensus or agreement about whether x is correctly counted as an F. For the time being, I will formulate the point generally, so that 'counting some x as an F' (for instance, counting something as
a toothbrush) can be construed as the use of a linguistic predicate or as the
application of a concept. The principle is thus to be taken as applicable
both to linguistic and to cognitive norms. I claimed in Section 1 that it
would be a sham to take oneself to be performing an activity correctly when
there isn't any standard for how that activity is to be performed correctly;
Stroud, too, makes the same point. If that is right, it follows that: (2) One
can appropriately take oneself to count some object x as an F correctly or
incorrectly, only if there is general agreement about whether x is correctly
counted as an F. That is one way to interpret the thought that it can be correct or incorrect to count or call something a toothbrush only if there is a
general practice that establishes what is correctly counted as or called a
toothbrush. It is easy to see that these principles are implausibly strong: in
too many cases, they will preclude the possibility of genuine disagreement.

   To be sure, disagreements about whether something is a toothbrush are
quite rare, but more plausible examples are not far to seek. Suppose a fos-
silized skeleton of a hitherto unseen type is discovered, and paleontologists
descend upon the site to examine it. They find they cannot reach a consensus about how to classify this newly discovered animal: some believe it is
correctly thought to be a new variety of dinosaur; others believe it to be a
new variety of prehistoric bird; others think that neither classification is
appropriate or warranted.[22] The correct application of at least the concepts
or terms 'dinosaur' and 'bird' has come into dispute, and no consensus can
be reached about which, if either, is correct or appropriate to apply in the
present case. If we accepted (1), we would describe this as a case in which
there isn't any standard of correctness for the application of these concepts
or terms to this particular object. It doesn't follow from this that there are
no standards of correctness for their application to any object, but none
would be fixed for this particular case. If that were true, then none of the
paleontologists could appropriately take his own classification of the skeleton to be correct. And so none could take any competing classifications to
be incorrect. The paleontologists could not understand themselves to be

engaged in a genuine disagreement. Any plausible interpretation of the thought that agreement or consensus is required for there to be a standard of correctness or incorrectness—for 'following a rule'—clearly must avoid this consequence.

This example helps us to articulate more precisely what kind and extent of agreement is required for there to be standards of correct or incorrect applications of concepts or terms. The paleontologists do not agree on the application of 'bird' and 'dinosaur' to some particular object, but that provides no reason to think that they do not routinely agree about how to apply these concepts or terms in a vast array of cases. We should distinguish two kinds of agreement in the application of concepts or linguistic predicates, which I will call the strict and the loose senses of agreement. In the strict sense, there is agreement among members of a community regarding the application of some concept or term 'F' only when there is a general consensus that 'F' is correctly applied to some particular x that is now the object of judgment or investigation. In the loose sense, this particular agreement is not required. There is agreement in the loose sense provided that there is a general consensus regarding the correct application of 'F' to an array of cases (either routine, paradigmatic cases, or more difficult ones that have already arisen and been settled), even though some particular object now under investigation presents a difficult case, concerning which agreement cannot be reached. Only the loose sense of agreement is required for there to be a standard of correctness for the use of an empirical concept or its linguistic surrogate, and so for individuals using them to take themselves to be conforming to a normative standard.

We can, then, make coherent sense of the paleontologists as engaging in a genuine disagreement, legitimately taking their competing classifications to be subject to normative standards, and thus legitimately taking their classifications to be correct or incorrect. Given their mastery of concepts like 'dinosaur' and 'bird,' they can each take themselves to be applying (or withholding) those concepts as they ought to in this particular case. Each is entitled to take there to be a standard for the correct use of these concepts, given the grasp of these concepts that has already been achieved. Their disagreement concerns how that standard is to be met or adhered to in this particular case. Sometimes, discerning what a normative standard requires is a difficult and sophisticated cognitive task, in which we are apt to disagree. But that does not imply that no such standard exists.

Some kinds of disagreement—even if there is little prospect of resolution anytime soon—therefore do not call into question the applicability of normative standards. Otherwise put, a general lesson to be taken from this example is that the sense in which normative standards require agreement should not be taken to be completely thoroughgoing or unrelenting. Sometimes, there will be disagreement about the application of a concept in some specific case, where the question posed to those inquiring is *how* our shared understanding of the relevant concepts, and our agreement about how they are to be applied in an array of other cases, is to be brought to bear in this particular case. Disagreements, like that among the paleontologists, exist against the backdrop of much general consensus concerning how the disputed concepts are correctly understood and applied in a wide range of cases; that is why the paleontologists can take there to be a standard for the application currently at hand. Their task, an admittedly difficult one, is to discern what that standard requires.

There are further senses in which the paleontologists' disagreement exists against the backdrop of a more general consensus. For example, while they may be unable to agree whether this skeleton ought to be thought of as a bird, or as a dinosaur, or perhaps as something else altogether, there are presumably a whole host of concepts on whose application in the present case they will agree: 'fossil,' 'skeleton,' 'bone,' 'prehistoric animal,' 'vertebrate,' to name but a few rather basic ones. Their specific disagreement about whether it is a bird or a dinosaur will turn on a number of questions involving the application of these and other concepts: the investigators will examine the size, shape, and density of the bones; the animal's dentition and cranial capacity; and so forth. This is just to reiterate a familiar point about the intrinsic interconnectedness of concepts: determining whether or not something is to be counted as an F requires one to ascertain whether or not it is a G, or an H, and so forth. Recognition of the applicability of one concept provides grounds for applying or withholding other concepts. In determining whether this animal is to be regarded as a bird, or as a dinosaur, or as something else entirely, the paleontologists will draw on their mastery of many other concepts, concepts whose applicability will help to determine what they should conclude concerning their specific disagreement about the classification of this animal. This, too, is part and parcel of the claim that the paleontologists can each take themselves to be classifying the animal correctly, or as they ought to. They can appeal to the applicability of a host of other concepts, on which the applicability of concepts like 'dinosaur' and 'bird' depends, to defend their claims to have applied these particular concepts correctly in the case at hand. Of course, some disagreements may emerge among them at this level, too, but I do not think it is problematic to suppose that there is also much they will agree on: that the skeleton has bicuspid dentition, or a cranial capacity of such-and-such volume, and so forth. The point here is of a piece with the point made in the previous paragraph: it is not always easy to discern *how* a standard for the application of a term or concept is to be brought to bear in a particular case, but in difficult cases we can still take it that our (linguistic or conceptual) practices *do*, in general, set such standards—even if we find that there is little agreement, for the time being, concerning precisely what it requires in the present case.

I readily admit that these remarks are somewhat sketchy. But the specific details of how paleontologists do their work are not important here. The important point is to understand what general features of a kind of rather common disagreement about the application of a concept or linguistic term allow us to take ourselves to be using a concept or term correctly, even in the absence of any general agreement about its correct use in a particular case. My claim is twofold: first, that such disagreements exist within the context of a more general pattern of agreement about the correct use of both the specific concepts or terms currently under dispute and of many other concepts or terms as well; second, that these patterns of general agreement are what allow us to take there to be a standard for the current case. The problem, once again, is that the standard is—as standards sometimes are—difficult to grasp clearly and apply in a challenging case.

I do not want to overstate this point. In particular, I do not want to suggest that our agreed-upon uses of words or concepts determinately or absolutely fixes their correct application *for every possible case*. My point is a more modest one, namely, that our agreed-upon uses of words or concepts—the meanings with which they have been invested by our usage so far—are sufficient to show that their application in difficult, unprecedented cases is *not arbitrary*. In that sense, the meanings of 'bird' and 'dinosaur,' along with the meanings of many related concepts or terms, establish standards for how they are to be projected into difficult or unprecedented cases. Not any old projection we may try to make will be intelligible to us as a use of *those* concepts. That is not to say that such projections are always obvious or easy to make, or that we will sometimes fail to agree, pending serious and competent investigation, about which ones we ought to make. It is, however, to say that there are standards governing those projections, standards that are ultimately derived—sometimes in very subtle or insightful or intellectually sophisticated ways—from the general patterns of agreement that our practices exhibit. It is, moreover, to say that in such cases the parties to a disagreement can still intelligibly take themselves to be governed by normative standards.[23]

I think most of us would agree that the paleontologists are engaged in a genuine disagreement, in which their proposed projections of various concepts are governed by normative standards, and we would agree that the paleontologists should be seen as entitled to take themselves to be governed by normative standards, even if some of the paleontologists turn out, upon further investigation, to be wrong in the specific claims they have made. I take this to show that principle (1) is false. Hence the reasoning to (2), even if valid, is not sound, and so we needn't accept any principle like (2). Thus, the example of the paleontologists does not defeat the claim that general agreement in a practice or activity is required for the possibility of a primitive recognition. Indeed, the paleontologists' disagreement concerns what Ginsborg calls a recognition of normativity in a 'derivative' sense. The same goes for principles like (1) and (2): they do not capture the sense of agreement required by the model of a primitive recognition. Neither I nor Ginsborg needs to accept them.

When the paleontologists take their classifications of the animal to be correct, or as they ought to be, they make what Ginsborg calls a 'derivative' recognition of normativity. This follows from the fact that they are taking some particular use of language or application of a concept to be correct. Ginsborg denies that taking any *particular* use of an empirical concept or a linguistic predicate to be correct qualifies as a primitive recognition of the normativity of this piece of behavior.[24] In this derivative sense, 'judging that something is as it ought to be requires the antecedent assumption that there is some determinate way it ought to be.'[25] That will be true of any particular act of empirical cognition or any particular utterance: the meanings of the concepts or terms to be applied will set a determinate standard for how they ought to be applied.[26] That is the basis of the paleontologists' claim to be applying these concepts as they ought to. In the primitive sense, however, recognizing an activity to be subject to normative standards involves no such antecedent assumption that the activity conforms to some determinate way it ought to be. We take it to conform to a standard simply 'as a trivial consequence of its exemplifying the standard.'[27] This is the kind of judgment we make when we say that the practice of speaking English, as a whole, is 'as it ought to be.' The point of this claim is not to say that most people speak English correctly rather than incorrectly, but rather to point out that the activity of speaking English, as a whole, sets the standard for its own correct performance.[28]

Central to Ginsborg's argument is her claim that the possibility of a derivative recognition of normativity presupposes the possibility of a primitive recognition. In the case of linguistic usage, she claims that 'the possibility of taking a given use of English to be as it ought to be in the derivative sense presupposes that we can take the linguistic practice as a whole to be as it ought to be in the primitive sense.'[29] In Section 1, we saw how a primitive recognition in the case of a natural language relies upon the assumption of general agreement among native speakers of the language: there must be such a thing as how English is—'as a whole' or 'in general'—spoken. Since the activity of speaking English sets the standard for its own correct performance in any particular case, if there is no uniform way in which the activity in general is performed, then there simply isn't any standard for its correct performance in any particular case, and hence nothing for one to take one's performance to conform to. There must be a general practice of speaking English, which I am entitled to take as setting determinate standards for its own correct performance, and against which I can judge the correctness of any particular use anyone makes of it. In this way, the possibility of a primitive recognition is more fundamental than and required for the possibility of a derivative recognition.

To capture Ginsborg's idea of a primitive recognition, we need principles, unlike (1) and (2) above, that apply to linguistic or cognitive activities in a *completely general* way, not to some particular case. I propose to distill the core of this idea into the following generalized versions of the previous principles: (1´) There can be linguistic or cognitive norms *at all* only if there are general patterns of agreement, or consensus, or uniformity that obtain among people in the performance of linguistic or cognitive tasks. Note that, in the linguistic case, this is just a restatement of Ginsborg's claim that a natural language exemplifies normative standards, or sets the standards for its own correct performance, with this claim's presupposition of agreement made explicit. Hence: (2´) One can appropriately take there to be linguistic or cognitive norms *at all* only if there are general patterns of agreement, or consensus, or uniformity that obtain among people in the performance of linguistic or cognitive tasks. This is easy to see in the linguistic case: if everyone spoke differently, there would be no such thing as a natural language, and therefore no such thing as norms that govern how it would be correct or incorrect to speak.

I take these principles to be faithful to Ginsborg's description of the possibility of normative standards for a natural language and the role of a primitive recognition as it applies in that case. I take it that she would accept (1´) and (2´) for linguistic norms, but a more difficult question is whether she would accept them for cognitive norms as well, that is, norms for empirical cognition or perceptual synthesis. It is not obvious whether Ginsborg thinks that norms for such activities require the same intersubjective agreement as norms for the use of a natural language. And one might, for independent reasons, take it to be less obvious that these principles correctly apply to cognitive norms. I explore these questions in Sections 4–5.

Section 4: The Tension in Ginsborg's View

According to Ginsborg, an individual's 'imaginative activity . . . with respect to the objects that are given to [her]' is taken to be normative, or as it ought to be.[30] Alternatively, Ginsborg sometimes describes this imaginative activity (i.e., ways of performing perceptual synthesis) as 'associative' or 'sorting' behavior, which is in turn to be understood as the actualization of underlying associative or sorting dispositions.[31] What has normative significance, then, is how an individual sorts the objects presented in sense experience, so as to take them to be instances of various general kinds of things. Our dispositions to perform this imaginative or synthesizing activity, that is, to sort as we do, underlie our capacity to make matter-of-fact claims, as they are the basis for the formation of empirical concepts, with which I can explicitly judge that an object is, say, a pencil, or a window, or a shoe. Now, any particular act of synthesis is taken to be normative in the derivative rather than primitive sense, for in any particular act of synthesis, as Ginsborg says, 'I regard my imaginative activity as governed by a determinate concept.'[32] Hence, I judge my imaginative activity to conform to some specific, determinate rule. It is my imaginative, or synthesizing, activity as a whole—or the sorting dispositions that underlie it—that I take to be exemplary of rules in the primitive sense, just as it is the practice of speaking English, as a whole, that I take to be exemplary of the rules for its correct performance. Moreover, it must be legitimate for me to take my imaginative activity (or sorting dispositions), as a whole, to be as it ought to be, in the primitive sense; otherwise, I could not take any particular feature of my imaginative activity (or any particular actualization of my underlying sorting dispositions) to be as it ought to be, in the derivative sense. The legitimacy of a primitive recognition of this sort is thus a condition for the possibility of empirical concepts.[33] Ginsborg writes:

> It is only because I am entitled to take my imagination in general to be exemplary of rules that I can take some specific feature of its workings . . . not merely as characteristic of how my imagination actually *does* perform under a given set of circumstances, but also as exhibiting a rule determining how it *ought* to perform, and hence as yielding an empirical concept.[34]

If this primitive recognition were not legitimate, I could only regard my imagination as a purely psychological faculty—as opposed to a genuinely cognitive faculty that exemplifies, and hence is governed by, normative standards.[35] Crucially, the standards for what the imagination *ought* to do are set by what the imagination *in fact does*.[36] That is the core of the analogy between norms for perceptual synthesis and norms for a natural language.

There does, however, appear to be a difference between norms for a natural language and norms for synthesis on Ginsborg's account, a difference which can be seen in the passage quoted above. The apparent difference is this: in the case of linguistic norms, Ginsborg's account makes reference to standards exemplified by a *community* of language users, say, the native speakers of English; in the case of synthesis, however, her account here makes reference to *my* imaginative activity or *my* dispositions to sort as I do—although she is not consistent in her formulations.[37] Perhaps this shows that Ginsborg takes linguistic and cognitive norms to differ in following way. In the linguistic case, the possibility of taking one's own usage to be as it ought to be requires the presence of normative standards that are, de facto, intersubjectively shared: there must be a way that native English speakers, in general, actually speak English. Put differently, the linguistic case requires intersubjective agreement as a precondition of normativity. But on this suggestion, the cognitive case does not. I can take my own imaginative activity to be as it ought to be regardless of whether others synthesize or sort as I do. De facto intersubjective agreement is not required. All that is required is that my imaginative, or synthesizing, or sorting behavior does not change wildly from moment to moment; there must be some general regularity or constancy in my behavior over time, so that, as it were, my present self largely agrees with my past selves. Of course, I can come to make local adjustments over time, realizing that I was wrong in the past in some particular case. I just cannot behave randomly or willfully; my behavior must manifest some regularity or constancy if I can intelligibly be taken to be behaving as I think I ought to. One could call that a requirement of intersubjectivity, I suppose, in a very thin and attenuated sense. It does not, however, require my behavior or underlying dispositions to be the same as those of others. It does not require agreement among people in the same sense as the argument about linguistic practices does. If this is how we are to think of the possibility of cognitive norms on Ginsborg's account, then (1´) and (2´) must be restricted to linguistic norms. But if Ginsborg has one general and univocal model of a primitive recognition, then the ideas captured by (1´) and (2´) should apply equally to linguistic and cognitive norms.

In other words, if Ginsborg thinks that cognitive norms require only the thin sense of intersubjective agreement, her conception of cognitive norms is substantively different than her conception of linguistic norms; her model of a primitive recognition is therefore not the same in the two cases. This conception of cognitive norms would allow her to align her model of synthesis more closely with what I take to be an appropriate view of taste, on which agreement is not understood to be a precondition of taste, but it would do so at the price of disengaging her model of synthesis from the analogy to linguistic practice from which she begins. Either way—unless Ginsborg is willing to take agreement to be a precondition of taste—the notion of a primitive recognition cannot be univocal throughout its various applications in her argument.

The question, then, is whether Ginsborg's model of norms for synthesis or sorting behavior is to be construed on the same terms as her model of norms for speaking a natural language. We've seen that there are at least prima facie reasons to doubt that it is. One might try explicate the difference in the following way. I owe the proposal to Ginsborg herself, but it is to be taken as a proposal only, and not as a definitive statement of her settled view. It is nevertheless worth exploring on its own merits, and I shall try to explain why I think it fails.[38]

One might try to maintain that an individual could take her sorting behavior to exemplify normative standards even in the absence of any general agreement or regularity in the behavior of human beings. We might, in other words, all sort differently, yet it would still be the case that each of us would be entitled to claim that her own way of sorting, in general, exemplifies the standard for how it ought to be done. All that the lack of general agreement would show is that we would never be able to arrive at concepts with determinate, settled meanings, not that one couldn't take her sortings to have normative significance for everybody. Our disagreements would, to be sure, remain irresolvable, but that would not show that one couldn't take her own sortings to have normative significance for everyone else. This proposal does, indeed, appear to square well with Ginsborg's claim that the legitimacy of a primitive recognition of the normativity of synthesis in general is a condition for the possibility of forming particular empirical concepts.

At first blush, this proposal also seems to square well with certain aspects of Ginsborg's account of sorting dispositions and behavior. Ginsborg says that what 'makes' an individual's sortings or associations rule governed is 'the fact that we *take* them to have normative significance.'[39] The word 'makes' suggests that, according to Ginsborg, the fact that a person takes her associative or sorting dispositions to have normative significance is sufficient to establish that they do: nothing else is needed for one's associative or sorting dispositions to *be* rule governed than the fact that she *takes* them to be rule governed. That seems to be the point of the passage that follows as well: 'The rule-governedness of my associations is thus a function of my taking them to be rule-governed, which is in turn a function of my taking my natural dispositions as exemplifying a universally valid norm.'[40] If this is all that is required, one could appropriately take her own associative or sorting behavior to be as it ought to be, even in the absence of any robustly intersubjective agreement in our dispositions; that agreement is only required for us to arrive at shared concepts with determinate contents or meanings, not for the possibility of normativity per se. Even though there would be no particular standard to which one could take her dispositions or behavior to conform, one could still appropriately take her behavior to be as it ought to be, in the primitive or indeterminate sense. If the current proposal could be sustained, Ginsborg could reject the cognitive aspects of (1´) and (2´) and restrict these principles to linguistic norms. That would allow her to have a conception of a primitive recognition that does not require any general patterns of agreement. But it would be a different conception of a primitive recognition than she deploys in describing and accounting for natural-linguistic norms.

Ginsborg's suggestion—that *taking* one's performance of an activity to be rule governed thereby *makes* one's performance rule governed—immediately calls to mind Wittgenstein's reminder that '"obeying a rule" is a practice. And to *think* one is obeying a rule is not to obey a rule. Hence it is not possible to obey a rule "privately": otherwise thinking one was obeying a rule would be the same thing as obeying it.'[41] The simple point of this passage is that in the absence of a 'practice'—some de facto standard for the correct performance of an activity—there wouldn't be anything that counted as following a rule or failing to follow it; there wouldn't be anything that counted as performing the activity either correctly or incorrectly. In the absence of an actual standard for correct performance, anything could be taken to accord with a rule, that is, to be a correct or appropriate way to perform the activity.[42] The idea of conforming to rules, or being rule governed, would be empty, for anything that one took to conform to a rule would have the same claim to do so as anything else. There would be no distinction between actually conforming to a rule and merely thinking that one has done so. Note that nothing in this line of reasoning requires a judgment that something conforms to any particular, determinate standard; it requires only that there must be some standard(s) in place, if the notion of following a rule, or taking oneself to be following a rule, is not to be empty. This line of reasoning should not, in other words, be taken as restricted to derivative judgments of normativity.

In the context of the current proposal, one might suspect that Ginsborg's position allows anything—anybody's way of synthesizing or sorting—to be taken as being as it ought to be, or as appropriate, and hence as exemplifying an intersubjective standard for how the imaginative activity of others ought to be. I could legitimately take any way of synthesizing or sorting objects, to which I just happen to be disposed, to exemplify a standard for how everyone ought to synthesize or sort. That would indeed make the claim to rule governedness empty: it would fail to distinguish between *any* two ways of sorting.

Supplementing a disposition with an inherent or perhaps innate sense of its appropriateness will not help. So it will not help simply to say, for instance, that children have not only an awareness of their own mental or psychological propensities but also a 'primitive appreciation' of their appropriateness.[43] To the extent that what an individual is disposed to do comes naturally, as a matter of course, without her entertaining, much less having to think through alternatives, what she finds herself disposed to do *will* thereby feel appropriate. What comes naturally, what simply strikes her as so, is something she will thereby feel to be appropriate, simply by virtue of its naturalness, its seeming obviousness, or its coming as a matter of course. This alone will not distinguish between any two instances of taking something she finds herself disposed to do to be rule governed; further constraints on the idea of what one is naturally disposed to do are sorely needed. Thus, if we are allowing, as per the proposal, that the dispositions of each individual vary ubiquitously from those of others, this 'primitive appreciation' will be of no help. Nor could Ginsborg explain any such sense of the appropriateness of one's synthesizing or sorting as an appreciation of its being objectively correct, and, for that reason, exemplary of a rule that everyone ought to follow. For on her view, the capacity to take one's mental activities to be intersubjectively valid is prior to, and more fundamental than, the capacity to take them to represent the way things objectively are. Indeed, on her view, it is the former that makes the latter possible.[44]

The possibility of a primitive recognition requires that I can take my behavior as a whole, or my underlying dispositions as a whole, to exemplify cognitive norms without actually judging that I am in conformity or agreement with others; this may seem to imply that I am entitled to take my behavior as a whole, or my underlying dispositions as a whole, to exemplify cognitive norms independently of whether or not they *actually* agree with or conform to those of others. Thus, the very idea of a primitive recognition may seem to imply that agreement in the robust intersubjective sense is not required for claims of normativity with respect to my sorting behavior as a whole, or my underlying dispositions as a whole. And that is precisely what the proposal under scrutiny also suggests: agreement in the thin intersubjective sense is all the agreement needed for there to be legitimate claims that my behavior or dispositions exemplify cognitive norms that are applicable to everyone.[45]

But the fact that I do not explicitly judge my imaginative activity or sorting to conform to a shared standard does not imply that there needn't be any shared standards for my performance of those activities to have normative significance for others. In particular, it doesn't follow that I am entitled to take *anything* my imagination is disposed to do—however regularly or consistently it does it—to exemplify a normative standard that applies in the robust intersubjective sense. As in the case of a natural language, there wouldn't be any standards at all if everybody sorted, and were disposed to sort, in a completely different manner. That is the sense in which taking oneself to conform to—in the trivial sense of exemplifying—a normative standard would be a sham: one could equally well take any behavior or set of underlying dispositions to be normative, as long as one were stuck with it over time. Any such taking would be equally legitimate, no matter how idiosyncratic—or even incomprehensible to everyone else—one's cognitive behavior or dispositions happened to be. But not any old bundle of idiosyncrasies or cognitive lunacy sets a standard that is valid for all, and we should not think ourselves entitled to take any old bundle of idiosyncrasies or cognitive lunacy to set a standard that is valid for all.

Thus, some genuine constraints on the legitimacy of taking one's behavior or dispositions to be normative, or alternatively, some constraints on the claim that one has a 'primitive appreciation' of their appropriateness, are clearly needed if the claim of rule governedness is not to be applicable willy-nilly and so ultimately empty. The need for these constraints is precisely what principle (2′) encapsulates, and why I have claimed that we should accept it. The sheer fact that my own behavior or underlying dispositions are more or less constant over time does not provide a sufficient constraint, since it will allow me to take anything that I habitually do to be rule governed. It is indeed hard to see how the notion of a rule, in the sense of a cognitive norm, will have any point at all if I can legitimately take any manner of persistent behavior that I please to exemplify one.

Ginsborg has resources to provide the needed constraints, resources which are very telling in the present context. Following the previous line of objection, one might accuse Ginsborg of allowing any arbitrary or idiosyncratic tendency to be taken as exemplifying a normative rule for human mental activity, which would make the very idea of rule governedness empty. But Ginsborg denies that her position has this consequence by explicitly connecting her account of sorting behavior to Kant's analysis of taste. She takes her lead from Kant's claim that the judgment of taste is disinterested, which means, among other things, that the pleasure I take in an object does not depend on any 'private conditions,' conditions which are idiosyncratic to me and thus set me apart from other human beings.[46] Ginsborg's account of sorting dispositions—or as she also calls them, 'natural dispositions'—is meant to embody an analogous thought. Our natural dispositions to sort this way or that do not depend on private, idiosyncratic features of our individual mental lives. Rather, they are expressions, one might say, of human nature—of natural, shared human propensities to be responsive to the world in one way rather than another. Ginsborg suggests:

> As long as my mental activity is not influenced by any factors which set me apart from other human beings, Kant appears to suggest, then I can legitimately take it as representing a standard which all human beings, myself included, ought to meet. And if that is so, then to the extent that my dispositions to associate representations are independent of my desires and other contingent features of my psychology, I can take them as exemplifying normative rules that apply to all human beings.[47]

Here the possibility of taking one's dispositions to exemplify normative standards is made to depend on the fact of agreement or commonality among human beings: our stock of empirical concepts, according to Ginsborg, is built up from dispositions that are 'shared' and 'natural,' rather than from dispositions that are merely peculiar features of our own personal psychological constitutions.[48]

Ginsborg's 'suggestion,' as I will call this line of argument, is in genuine tension with the proposal under scrutiny. If I can take my associative or sorting dispositions to exemplify norms only to the extent that they are 'independent of my desires and other contingent features of my psychology,' and are thus 'shared' and 'natural,' it follows that I can take my associative or sorting dispositions to exemplify norms only to the extent that they reflect general human agreement. Ginsborg's suggestion therefore precludes the possibility that there is widespread disagreement among us, or that we are all substantially different, with respect to those dispositions that can be taken to exemplify norms. Hence, her account of natural dispositions can constrain the applicability of any putative 'primitive appreciation' of the appropriateness of one's behavior, or of any taking of it to be normative, but only by making essential use of the notion of cognitive dispositions that are generally shared by human beings at large: the behavior that flows from our cognitive dispositions is natural, persistent, habitual, and strikes us as appropriate because *that* is simply how human beings respond cognitively to the world presented in sense experience. Where that is the case, there will be a standard—set by general patterns of intersubjective agreement—that can underwrite a claim that one's behavior or dispositions exemplifies a standard for all to follow. The notion of being rule governed will no longer be empty or applicable at will.

Whereas Ginsborg's proposal characterizes our cognitive dispositions as potentially varying ubiquitously from one person to the next, her suggestion characterizes our cognitive dispositions as 'shared' and 'natural,' as if they are expressions of a common human nature. It is therefore difficult, if not impossible, to ascribe a settled view to her. But clearly we cannot accept both of these claims, for they are plainly incompatible. And if an individual's dispositions can be taken to exemplify normative standards only insofar as they are shared, natural dispositions, it couldn't be the case that we were all be entitled to take our dispositions to exemplify normative standards if our dispositions were vastly disparate. Indeed, if we all had different dispositions, we *wouldn't* be entitled to take our dispositions to exemplify normative standards at all—not even with the proviso that we wouldn't arrive at determinate, shared empirical concepts. Ginsborg's reliance on shared, natural dispositions is required for more than just the possibility of determinate concepts; it is required for the possibility of cognitive norms *tout court.*[49] Or so I will argue more explicitly in Section 5.

Ginsborg's suggestion construes sorting dispositions, along with the empirical concepts we arrive at by reflecting on and codifying these dispositions, on the same model as she uses to describe natural language. That is to say, in taking our way of performing an activity to exemplify normative standards in the primitive sense—in either the linguistic or cognitive case— we rely on the fact of general human agreement in the performance of these activities. The judgment of normativity is still primitive in that an individual does not explicitly judge any particular piece of behavior to conform to any determinate or antecedent standard or rule. Yet in both cases, there *is* some actual standard: there is a way that these practices are, as a matter of fact, carried out. My claim, to be clear, is that this is a *requirement* in both the linguistic and cognitive cases. Furthermore, Ginsborg's conception of shared, natural dispositions not only connects it back to her model of norms for a natural language, where the presupposition of general agreement was both explicit and uncontroversial, but also directly indicates a connection to Kant's conception of taste, as she wants to understand it. This suggests that Ginsborg intends to produce a univocal model for all three cases. If so, the fact of agreement or consensus will have to play a crucial role throughout.

If, however, we accept Ginsborg's initial proposal for understanding cognitive norms, we will be at a loss to find univocal conceptions of normativity and of a primitive recognition consistently deployed throughout her argument. The difference, as we've seen, can be put in terms of whether agreement is a precondition for the possibility of cognitive norms, as it surely is for linguistic norms. Alternatively, it can be put in terms of the sense in which agreement is thought to be intersubjective in each case. On the initial proposal, one's cognitive activity could be taken to be exemplary of norms in the absence of its agreement with the cognitive activity of others: all that is required is for the behavior, or the underlying dispositions actualized in that behavior, to remain more or less stable, or invariant, from moment to moment. On this thin, and indeed somewhat metaphorical, sense of 'intersubjective,' the required agreement is only an agreement between (so to speak) my present self with my various past selves—which is compatible with all of my various 'selves' being wholly unlike those of anybody else. But that is not the conception of intersubjective agreement at work in the model of natural-linguistic norms, which makes essential use of the way in which a community of native speakers actually speaks.

There are two points to be taken from the discussion in this section. First, Ginsborg's two proposals for understanding cognitive norms are incompatible, and so we must choose one or the other. Second, Ginsborg's suggestion is the one to choose, both because it preserves the univocality of her model of a primitive recognition, as it applies to both linguistic and cognitive norms, and because it is correct. The fact that there *is* general agreement in our cognitive activities and dispositions is essential to the possibility of our legitimately taking them to exemplify universally valid normative standards. Of course, as in the example of the paleontologists, we may find disagreements in particular cases that don't promise to be resolved any time soon; no requirement or precondition of agreement can be completely thoroughgoing or unrelenting. I take that point to apply as well at the level of a primitive recognition. Furthermore, one may sometimes incorrectly take her cognitive activity to exemplify normative standards—perhaps because she hasn't noticed that she's subject to some psychological idiosyncrasy or desire, or that she's a lunatic—without that threatening our *general* entitlement to take our mental activities to exemplify cognitive norms that are valid for all. But none of this shows that general agreement, in the robust intersubjective sense, is not a requirement or precondition for cognitive norms.

So far, then, we have seen that *for us*—just as Ginsborg's suggestion indicates—the fact of general agreement is an essential part of our entitlement to take ourselves, in general, to exemplify linguistic or cognitive norms. Against this backdrop of agreement, we can make sense of particular errors, unfounded claims of normativity, or cases of individuals inventing rules for themselves that nobody else's cognitive activities are (or ever will be) governed by. But here we are still imagining *ourselves*, and we are not beings of whom it is true that our cognitive dispositions vary ubiquitously from person to person. For such beings, there would be no analogue of Ginsborg's shared, natural dispositions; there would be only what she calls 'contingent features of [one's] psychological makeup.' In the next section, I explore the question of what role this conception of normativity would have in the lives of beings whose cognitive dispositions *did* vary ubiquitously from one individual to the next. It will emerge that this very conception of normativity—cognitive norms valid for everyone, not just the various selves, as it were, of a single creature—has no serious function within their lives and activities. I take this to show, in turn, that the fact of agreement in the robust intersubjective sense is *part of* the conception of a universally valid cognitive norm that *we* take ourselves to exemplify and to be subject to.[50]

Section 5: Thought Experiment: The Idiosyncratic Sorters

Recall the two main features of Ginsborg's original proposal. First, everybody sorts differently, so that we never arrive at determinate concepts by means of which we can settle our disagreements. Second, everybody still takes, and is entitled to take, her own sorting dispositions to exemplify normative standards. The claim I will defend in this section is the following: if the sorting dispositions of beings did not exhibit a general uniformity or agreement—if they varied from individual to individual as ubiquitously as the proposal allows—then such beings would have no serious use for a conception of genuinely intersubjective or universally valid cognitive norms. This conception is one that finds its home within the lives of beings—human beings—who are largely alike, who are attuned to one another in terms of their cognitive responsiveness to the world, who therefore do, to a very significant extent (though obviously not entirely) have the same cognitive dispositions. In short, *we* all share a vast array of natural reactions to the world we experience, and it is within *this* context that the idea of those reactions being normative for one another has a place. We cannot straightforwardly project our conception of cognitive norms into the lives of beings who differ from us in this radical way.

To help show this, I will attempt to describe some essential features of what we might call the 'characteristic surroundings' of our conception of genuinely intersubjective or universally valid cognitive norms, and show that these characteristic surroundings are, in important ways, missing in the lives of the beings we are trying to imagine.[51] For ease of reference, I call them the Idiosyncratic Sorters, for among them each is disposed to sort in her own way, different from that of anyone else. If the Idiosyncratic Sorters have anything recognizable as a conception of universally valid cognitive norms at all, which is doubtful, it won't be *our* conception of them.

First, *our* conception of normativity finds its place within the lives of beings who are correctable or teachable. It isn't clear how the Idiosyncratic Sorters will be able to teach or instruct one another in anything at all, given that their natural reactions to the world of sense experience vary to such extremes. Consider one example of a natural reaction on which our ability to instruct one another, or even to communicate at all, routinely depends: the gesture of pointing to something for the purposes of ostensive training or explanation. We all naturally react to the gesture of pointing with the hand by looking in the direction of the line from wrist to finger-tip.[52] This gesture serves as a way of indicating where one person would like another to direct his attention, or to look. There are, of course, other ways we accomplish this than by pointing with a finger. For instance, we all naturally react, just as well, to the gesture of motioning with the head—a nod—by looking in the direction that the head is moving *toward*. Reacting to a gesture as pointing one way rather than another is itself an example of a natural reaction or a disposition to sort some item of sense experience. Since, by hypothesis, the Idiosyncratic Sorters are all disposed to respond differently to what is presented to them in sense experience, it follows that they will all react to, or take, a pointing of the finger or a nod of the head as a gesture in a different direction. A teacher attempting to point to a multiplication table on the blackboard will routinely find that every student looks in a different direction. One looks in the direction of the line from wrist to finger-tip, and so looks at the blackboard; another looks in the direction of the line from finger-tip to wrist, and so stares out the window; two others look in directions perpendicular to the finger, always, and so look at the floor and ceiling respectively, no matter where the teacher points. Unless, that is, she is pointing either to the floor or the ceiling, in which case they both seren-dipitously look at the blackboard.

If we take seriously the thought that the natural dispositions of the Idio-syncratic Sorters differ drastically from Sorter to Sorter, then we will find that we do not quite understand how it is that these beings manage to teach, instruct, and correct one another. Indeed, it is hard to imagine how they arrive at any shared language, or how they communicate with and under-stand one another at all. It is more than just the possibility of determinate empirical concepts that is threatened: it is the possibility of communication and understanding *tout court*. One might respond that we don't know enough about the Idiosyncratic Sorters to come to any firm conclusion about how they communicate. The example is left somewhat indeterminate, and there is much that we do not know about them. But it is true that unless they manage to find some set of reactions that they can rely upon them-selves to share with one another generally, they will not find any reliable way to instruct and correct one another. Even the simplest attempts at ostensive training or explanation will be plunged into confusion and chaos. We don't even really understand what these beings would be doing, or hoping to accomplish, at their schools (assuming they have any) in the first place.

The first point, then, is that we are attempting to project our conception of normativity into a scenario that lacks the ordinary context of scenes of instruction, training, and correction within which that conception, for us, is naturally situated. These are social and intersubjective scenes, which the Idiosyncratic Sorters lack. Their attempts to teach or instruct or correct one another seem to be severely stymied. Correlatively, their attempts to learn from one another seem equally threatened. A child who is naturally dis-posed to sort things one way will not find that other people are in general a consistent source of approval or disapproval of her sortings; nor will the disapprovals she will inevitably encounter be of a consistent kind or con-tent. There will not be the regularity or uniformity in the instruction she receives from others that *we* routinely enjoy, and that allows us to learn from each other, particularly as children. She would, of course, be naturally dis-posed to sort things one way rather than another, but she would not find that her behavior elicits consistent general patterns of agreement, rejec-tion, encouragement, correction, and so forth from others. Checking her own behavior against that of others would not have the effect it does with us, for whether she is told that she is correct or not will depend on whether she asks Mommy, Daddy, or Teacher. For *us*, an essential part of our concep-tion of being correct is that whether one is correct or not is independent of whom one happens to ask, a conception which makes the sense that it does for us because, by and large, it doesn't so depend—not at any rate, for the simple kinds of questions about their sorting behavior that can arise for children. What I put on the table for everybody to eat the chicken soup with is not something I ever took to depend on whether Mommy or Bubby had asked me to put spoons on the table, and whether I could tell solids from liquids from gases correctly never depended on whether I asked Daddy or Science Teacher about my homework. The constancy or regularity of the instruction, approval, and correction that we receive as children from parents, teachers, and other elders is essential to our formation of some conception of what it is correct to do. Young Idiosyncratic Sorters only find out how Mommy wants them to act, or Daddy, or whoever happens to be Teacher this semester. It is extremely difficult to see what role for a stable conception of 'what it is correct to do' could emerge, for a Young Idiosyncratic Sorter, from amid the general disorder of everyone's reactions.

As Cora Diamond has persuasively argued, *our* conception of a rule or a norm applies 'anonymously.'[53] Correctness and incorrectness are not tied to this-or-that particular person. The existence of a rule or norm that governs what it is correct to do has consequences, the same consequences, for anyone. This conception of an intersubjective norm is crucially tied to two aspects of our life-with-norms: first, that after instruction or training, we engage in cognitive practices that are typically characterized by the relative absence of discordant results in their performance. Sorting medium-sized dry goods—taking some such good to be a certain kind of thing, or taking it to be the same kind of thing as another—can, to a great extent, be separated in our lives from who did the sorting. Second, and because of this, we can and do rely on the results of each other's sortings in an anonymous way. We ask questions like 'How many chairs are in the kitchen?' or 'Are there spoons on the table yet?' and, in general, we rely equally well on the answers we receive no matter whether Mommy, or Bubby, or Grandpa, or someone else answers the question. Because we can rely on the results of these simple sorting tasks in an anonymous way, we don't usually ask questions like 'Did Bubby take anything on the table to be a spoon when she looked?' or 'How many things in the vicinity of the table did Sister count as chairs?' But those seem like the only kinds of questions that will be helpful, or even make sense, for the Sorters to ask. *Our* kinds of questions don't appear to have any real application for them.

To see what our conception of a genuinely intersubjective cognitive norm comes to, we need to attend to the features of our life-with-norms, to look and see what it is like to follow a rule, to teach others how to follow it, to correct others when they are wrong, to invent new rules or creative projections of old rules into unprecedented applications, to rely on the uptake of others, and to suffer the consequences of being someone on whose uptake others find they cannot rely. *That* is what the conception of a norm looks like in *our* lives; that shows its grammar. Our conception of a norm is intricately woven into a pattern of life: in which we take the results of an inquiry, especially a simple sorting task, not to depend on who performs it; in which we find regular patterns of encouragement and correction from our elders; in which we find that we can—luckily, because we must—routinely rely on each other's uptake of the world; in which we find that there are procedures of instruction and training that are generally reliable in helping others to perform tasks as we perform them, indeed, as we are relying on others to perform them. These aspects of our life are *part of* our conception of norms; they are the 'characteristic surroundings' within which that conception has the place, and makes the sense, that it does. These surroundings are not, at least not in any obvious way, in place within the lives of the Idiosyncratic Sorters. If they have some conception of their mental activity being subject to 'norms' at all, whatever it might be, it isn't ours. It isn't clear that we would even be able to recognize it.

If we attend to the functioning of our idea of intersubjective norms within our lives, even in such a cursory way as this, we find that conception to be situated within the context of a shared way of life with characteristic patterns of reaction, training, reliance, and agreement. What I have tried to show with this cursory sketch is that our conception of norms or rules that govern our sortings, or eventually our use of full-blown discursive concepts, is inextricably tied to shared, social, and robustly intersubjective proceedings in which we can, and usually do, just blindly take for granted that others are the same as we are, that they share our natural reactions and dispositions in a way that allows us to reason and communicate together, to instruct and correct each other, and to rely on each other in the business of everyday life. These proceedings, which the Idiosyncratic Sorters lack, are essential to the very idea of an intersubjective norm with which we operate. Our participation in a shared life of following and teaching rules—with all the constancy and regularity, all the unspoken and unhesitating reliance on one another, and all the consequences of failure, that this shared life brings with it—is what gives our conception of intersubjective norms the sense and the point that it has. The way in which others respond to our behavior, undertake to correct it or encourage its further development, and rely upon it to be or develop a certain way, on pain of sometimes severe consequences, forms the essential background within which we come to think of our own mental activity as subject to norms that are equally applicable to anyone and everyone.

Beings whose lives lacked these characteristic features wouldn't have the conception of a universally valid cognitive norm that we have. Whatever conception of a cognitive norm they might have simply wouldn't be ours; its function and its grammar would be different. The proposal we have been investigating—in which the cognitive dispositions of beings lack the general uniformity, regularity, or agreement of our own, but in which those beings still take their mental activity to exemplify intersubjective norms applicable to all—is an attempt to take *our* conception of norms and project it into the lives of beings whose lives lack the context in which our conception functions. In this way, the attempt to imagine beings who do not share an extensive array of natural reactions and dispositions yet still operate with *our* conception of an intersubjective cognitive norm runs aground. It does not make the sense it might, on the surface, seem to make.

Here is how *not* to understand what I have claimed in this section. I have offered the *hypothesis* that if certain facts about us were different than they are, we would have a different conception of cognitive norms.[54] For instance, we wouldn't have the appropriate causal histories required to form this conception on the basis of our experience. If I were offering such an hypothesis, one would indeed have to wonder how, on the basis of what we know about the Sorters, I could establish that. Rather, the point I have tried to make is about the grammar of our conception of cognitive norms: that it has *this* place in our lives. That there isn't *this* place in the lives of the Sorters is something we can know from the terms of the proposal. So I am not denying that the Sorters could entertain, perhaps as a logical possibility, the idea of a cognitive norm that is valid for everyone; I am denying that 'making a claim of normativity,' in the lives of the Sorters, is the same thing as making a claim of normativity in *our* lives. Whatever we imagine them doing with such 'claims' is not what we do with them. Indeed, we simply don't know what such beings would be doing with them, to the extent that we can understand them to be 'making claims of normativity that are valid for any and all of them' in the first place. We have not, on the basis of the terms set forth by the proposal, managed to form a clear conception of what we are trying to imagine here.

It will not help, then, to protest that the Sorters could form a conception of cognitive norms like ours. Forming a conception—perhaps entertaining something as a logical possibility—is one thing. But adopting it as one's own, as one that has a serious application within one's life and practices, is quite another.[55] For us, the conception of a cognitive norm that is universally valid certainly does have a serious application. That is because we are, one might say, 'normative beings,' beings capable of being instructed, corrected, and relied upon to perform various cognitive tasks without arriving at ubiquitously discordant results.[56] Our practices of training, explanation, correction, and relying on one another's uptake of the world are all part and parcel of the life of a 'normative being.' Indeed, it matters tremendously to our lives and our daily activities that we can rely on the others to be like ourselves, to have, by and large, the same responsiveness to the world of experience. We wouldn't lead the kinds of lives that we do, with the practices and activities that we have, if we found that we could not. But the Sorters, apparently, are managing to get by without doing so. They may have formed a conception of cognitive norms like ours, but it is not something around which their lives and activities depend as ours do, or around which they are structured as ours are. For them, this conception may be a speculative philosophical curiosity or tool: perhaps their philosophers 'invent fictitious natural history,' as some of ours do, for the purpose of coming to better understand their own practices by a kind of reverse projection;[57] it may appear to them as hopelessly and uselessly utopian theorizing appears to us; it might be a joke, or a way of parodying creatures like us, whose lives and activities are so frail that they depend upon our sharing the same general forms of responsiveness and uptake. We don't, again, know what they are doing with this conception, but it is, at the very least, exceedingly hard to envision any way in which it has a serious application for them, around which their ordinary lives and activities are structured.

To the extent that we try to describe the lives and practices of the Idiosyncratic Sorters as having a place for universally valid normative claims to be woven into, we must describe them as participating in a form of life which, by hypothesis, they do not have; we have projected more of ourselves and our life-with-normativity into their lives and practices than the terms of the proposal actually allow. In that sense, the attempt to describe the envisioned scenario—or, *a fortiori*, to pose within it a question of whether such beings would be 'justified' in claiming to exemplify universally valid cognitive norms—comes to nothing. That seems to me a good reason to abandon the proposal under scrutiny and opt instead for something like Ginsborg's suggestion, but without limiting the role of agreement to the formation of explicit empirical concepts. Indeed, our claims of normativity, not just our empirical concepts, are inextricably tied to the fact of our agreement in basic cognitive dispositions and responsiveness—our *Übereinstimmung in den Urteilen*. This agreement, or better yet, this attunement is part and parcel of the very practices that give our 'cognitive norms that are valid for anyone and everyone' the sense and the point that they have. Our conception of cognitive norms—like our conception of linguistic norms—cannot coherently be prized apart from it.

Section 6: The Disanalogy between Taste and Cognition

In Section 4, I extracted two lines of thought about cognitive norms from Ginsborg's writings and argued that they are incompatible. I have presented reasons to favor Ginsborg's 'suggestion,' rather than her 'proposal,' on which we could legitimately take our mental or imaginative activity to exemplify universally valid cognitive norms in the absence of any general or widespread patterns of agreement. Unless Ginsborg opts for her suggestion, she will not have a consistent general model of a primitive recognition that applies to both cognitive and linguistic norms. We come now to the application of this model to judgments of taste, and the same general predicament recurs. Either Ginsborg treats an analogous notion of agreement as a precondition for the normative claims of taste, or she has no consistent general model of a primitive recognition that applies to all three cases. I have suggested that Ginsborg does intend to offer such a model; this much was intimated by the way she attempts to simultaneously link her analysis both to linguistic norms and to a reading of the Kantian judgment of taste. The difference here, however, is that the conception of norms and of a primitive recognition that first emerges in Ginsborg's discussion of natural languages should not be applied to aesthetic norms, although, I have argued, it should be applied to cognitive norms.

First, recall the parallel between the analysis of 'natural dispositions' and the judgment of taste. One who makes a judgment of taste, according to Kant, 'cannot discover as grounds of the satisfaction any private conditions, pertaining to his subject alone.'[58] A pleasure that takes as its ground such a private condition—a 'mere sensation' for instance, or an idiosyncratic psychological trait to which the pleasures of involuntary memory, like the Taste of the Madeline, appeal—does not license a normative claim that others ought to share my pleasure.[59] This is analogous to a disposition to sort objects in some idiosyncratic way, perhaps because my dispositions are grounded in a psychological quirk or personal desire of mine. Dispositions that are thus tied to features of my own personal psychology do not, on Ginsborg's suggestion, license the claim that they exemplify universally valid normative rules or standards. Shared, natural dispositions, which are not tied to features of my own personal psychology, do license such claims, since they are expressions of the mental or psychological constitution that I share in common with human beings at large. Similarly, one who makes a judgment of taste must 'regard [the pleasure] as grounded in those [conditions] that he can also presuppose in everybody else.'[60] The pleasure that grounds a judgment of taste is based on conditions that are common to all, rather than conditions that are peculiar to some particular individual. In other words, the pleasures that we are entitled to take as normative are precisely those pleasures that are based on something common to human beings in general.[61]

In the case of sorting dispositions, the appeal to natural dispositions was needed to sustain a meaningful distinction between exemplifying a normative rule or standard and merely taking oneself to exemplify a normative rule or standard, a distinction which, I have argued, cannot be sustained in the absence of some actual rule or standard. That is not to say that one must explicitly judge oneself to conform to some particular rule or standard; the very possibility of a primitive recognition requires that this is not the case. Nor is it to say that to take one's mental activity or linguistic usage to exemplify a normative rule or standard is to make a prediction that others will (or would) produce the same mental activity or linguistic usage. As Ginsborg's critique of Guyer has shown, the content of a judgment of taste involves no such prediction. And as Stroud has shown, saying something in a language does not typically involve an assertion that there is agreement among the members of a linguistic community. But we saw in Section 2 that this is compatible with the claim that the presence of patterns of general agreement is still a precondition for normativity. I take Ginsborg to be committed to this conception of a precondition in the case of linguistic norms, and argued in Sections 4–5 that she should accept the line of thinking present in her work that leads to a construal of cognitive norms on the same model. So, if her conception of a primitive recognition is to remain consistent throughout the various cases to which she applies it—and indeed, if that model, as it is developed in the contexts of linguistic and cognitive norms, is to illuminate the judgment of taste—then the presence of general patterns of human agreement will have to be taken as a precondition for the normativity involved in judgments of taste. Hence the main thesis of this chapter: either Ginsborg is committed to the claim that agreement is a precondition of norms for taste, or there are two conceptions of normativity, and two conceptions of a primitive recognition, that need to be, but aren't, clearly distinguished in her argument. If we are to make sense of the judgment of taste in terms of the same model as these other activities, I do not see how an appeal to a similar conception of agreement can be avoided.

It is worth looking briefly at the application of the model of a primitive recognition to judgments of taste. Recall that in any particular act of empirical cognition, I do not take my imaginative activity to be exemplary of rules in the primitive sense, because I regard that activity as governed by some determinate empirical concept. Yet, the possibility of this derivative recognition presupposes the possibility of a primitive recognition: it is only because I am entitled to take my imaginative activity in general to be as it ought to be, in the primitive sense of exemplifying rules, that I can take any particular aspect of that activity to be rule governed in the derivative sense. This primitive recognition is thus a condition for the possibility of empirical cognition, but not something that I do in any actual instance of empirical cognition. It is, however, something that I do when I make a judgment of taste; there, I do take my imaginative activity to be exemplary of rules *simpliciter*. I do not take my imaginative activity to conform to any specific or determinate rule for how it ought to be. I do not take the activity of my imagination to be governed by any empirical concept of the object that has elicited that activity, and I do not perceive that object as having any particular or determinate property. Hence I do not take my imaginative activity and the object that elicits it to be mutually appropriate to one another in any specific or determinate way; rather, I take there to be 'an irreducible harmony or fit' between them that is completely general or indeterminate.[62] In a judgment of taste:

> I take the activity [of my imagination, which is elicited by some object] to be exemplary *simpliciter* of how the object ought to be perceived. I take it—as I am entitled to take my imaginative activity in general—to set a standard for how my or anyone else's imagination ought to function with respect to the object which elicits it . . . I take my imaginative activity in the perception of the object to be as it ought to be in the primitive sense, which means that I have no conception of *how* it ought to be except that afforded by the example of my activity itself: namely, the indeterminate conception that it ought to be *this way*.[63]

In a judgment of taste, my actual imaginative activity sets the standard for how that activity ought to be, either in myself or in others, without there being any determinate or antecedent conception of how it ought to be.

When I take my imaginative activity to be exemplary of rules in this primitive way, I take my imagination and understanding to stand in the relation characteristic of aesthetic judgment, which Kant calls the 'free play of the cognitive faculties.'[64] Crucially, Kant takes the free play to manifest a condition for the possibility of empirical cognition in general, and we can now see how, on Ginsborg's reading, that claim is to be understood. The possibility of a primitive recognition of the normativity of my imaginative activity in general is a condition for the possibility of empirical cognition, and most specifically, for Ginsborg, of empirical concepts. Accordingly, Ginsborg claims that there is a 'general principle of judgment' that applies both to cognitive and to aesthetic judgments, the principle that 'I am entitled to take my imaginative activity as exemplary of how it ought to be.'[65] This principle—that of our entitlement to a primitive recognition—is applied directly in judgments of taste, where the imagination and understanding are in free play. In empirical cognition, the role of the general principle of judgment is 'exhausted . . . in allowing us to think of our imaginative activity on any particular occasion as governed by determinate concepts.'[66] The application of determinate concepts 'prevents us from thinking of our imaginative activity on any *particular* occasion in the way we must think of it *in general* if those concepts are to be possible.'[67] But that is still to say that this principle governs the possibility of empirical cognition, by articulating a condition that is actually and directly satisfied in a judgment of taste.

Now, we have here a general model for explaining the possibility of both aesthetic and cognitive norms. The crucial aspect of this model is the idea of taking the activity of the imagination to be exemplary of norms. In Sections 4–5, I set forth reasons to think that the fact of general patterns of human agreement is essential to making sense of the possibility of this primitive recognition, reasons which are patent in the case of norms for a natural language. With respect to cognitive norms, my claim was that it is only in the context of general patterns of agreement in the synthesis or sorting of human beings at large—in other words, in their imaginative activity—that we can make sense of this primitive recognition; hence, this agreement is essential not only to the formation of determinate concepts with settled meanings, but also to the very idea of cognitive norms that govern the mental activities of anyone and everyone. If general patterns of agreement in our imaginative activity are essential to making sense of our entitlement to this primitive recognition, then it is unclear how they could fail to be part of the idea of a primitive recognition of the normativity of imaginative activity when that primitive recognition is *actually* made in the context of a judgment of taste.

However, it seems to me that this approach to explaining the possibility of norms for taste makes a critical error about the grammar of the concept *taste*. The presence of widespread or general patterns of agreement is not essential to or a part of the notion of taste, in the way it is essential to or a part of the notions of linguistic and cognitive norms. We could all—and legitimately so—take our aesthetic responses to be normative for others, even if everybody responded differently, and disagreement in matters of taste were ubiquitous. The question is not, ultimately, about how much agreement in matters of taste we actually do achieve. We aren't exactly Idiosyncratic Tasters, but neither is agreement in matters of taste anywhere near what it is in either linguistic or cognitive matters.[68] Whatever the case may be about how much agreement there is in matters of taste, the fundamental problem is that agreement is not part of the very conception of taste, in the normative sense, in the way it is part of or a precondition for our very conception of linguistic and cognitive norms. While the attempt to imagine beings like the Idiosyncratic Sorters, who make serious claims about their cognitive activity being normative for all, runs aground— because it projects into their lives a social context of agreement, instruction, and correction that, by hypothesis, they lack—an attempt to imagine Idiosyncratic Tasters would not similarly run aground. There is no difficulty in describing beings who exercise taste, even though they cannot ever agree about what is beautiful. They may still make serious claims to one another about the normativity or appropriateness of their own aesthetic responses.

My claim has been that our conception of linguistic and cognitive norms is tied to the idea of agreement in the robust intersubjective sense. These norms are part of and grow out of a shared life of training, instruction, correction, and general patterns of agreement. Without that social context, the idea of normative standards that are held to be valid for the linguistic or cognitive behavior of everyone would have no serious application and no real point. At the very least, such claims—for whatever reason one imagines them being made—wouldn't be the kinds of normative claims that *we* make; their grammar would be that of something very different. Linguistic and cognitive norms, for us, aren't just regularities in an individual's own behavior that she simply 'takes' to exemplify standards that are valid for everyone else; they are regularities in human behavior that we do largely share with one another. And it is the characteristic patterns of each other's agreement and encouragement; our efforts to instruct one another; our attempts to correct each other when there is a disagreement; and, most importantly, our mutual dependence on each other to share largely the same uptake of the world, which frame our conception of standards of correctness that apply to a person's linguistic or cognitive behavior, no matter who that person happens to be. Learning what it is to take, or to be entitled to take, one's natural behavior or dispositions to exemplify standards that are valid for all takes place within a social context of instruction, agreement, communication, and correction: to conceive of linguistic and cognitive norms as something that can be abstracted from the shared social context within which these norms have their distinctive function and point is to make them far too individualistic.[69]

Taste, however, *is* individualistic. Our conception of taste is not rooted in the same shared social context of instruction and correction. We are not, for instance, taught what is beautiful at school in the way we are taught how to conjugate a verb, or how to distinguish solids from liquids from gasses, or what the word 'spoon' means. We are not taught that such-and-such things are 'what we call beautiful,' as we are taught that *this* is what we call obeying the rule '+2,' or what we call a verb agreeing with its subject, or what we all count as a chair. In linguistic and cognitive matters, we are, from our earliest days, instructed in the ways of others: our teachers and parents and elders want us to speak, to sort, to add as they speak, and sort, and add. And it is true, of course, that we largely find it natural to do these things as they do them; our cognitive dispositions are attuned deeply enough for their instruction to routinely take root.[70] Not so in matters of taste. We are not only allowed but also encouraged to develop our own tastes, to find out what each one of us likes rather than to learn what others like, or what they think we 'ought' to like. Indeed, this is not an arbitrary feature of our lives; it is part of the very grammar of the concept *taste*. There is no such thing as taste submitting to authority; there cannot be instruction and correction in matters of taste in the same sense in which there is instruction and correction in linguistic and cognitive affairs. To like what one 'ought' to like is *not* to exercise taste. To follow others in what they like, or find beautiful, is not to cultivate one's taste but to suppress it. Taste, by its very nature, is robustly individualistic and autonomous. It is not and cannot be situated within the same social context of instruction and correction as linguistic and cognitive affairs.

Essential aspects of our life-with-linguistic-and-cognitive-norms are therefore lacking in our lives-with-taste.[71] It is not true that the conception of normativity that applies to matters of taste has as an essential part a shared social context of instruction that displays widespread, general patterns of agreement. It is not part of the very idea of taste that we enjoy widespread, general patterns of agreement, whereas it is part of the idea of a natural language, or the idea of a cognitive norm, that we do. As I've argued, in the lives of beings whose cognitive dispositions varied ubiquitously like the Idiosyncratic Sorters, the idea of robustly intersubjective normative standards would have no serious application at all. But in the lives of beings whose tastes varied ubiquitously, the normative claims of taste would. General agreement is part of the idea of linguistic and cognitive norms; it is not part of the idea of the claims of taste. Even if everybody's tastes were dramatically different, they could still exercise taste in the normative sense. But if everybody spoke differently, there wouldn't be any natural languages. If everybody sorted, or perceived, or synthesized differently, we wouldn't have our life of forming and applying rules, teaching them to one another, and relying on others to be the same as we are. It is this life-with-rules that not only allows us to form determinate concepts but also frames our very conception of a cognitive norm that applies equally well to anyone. Norms for taste, however, do not display these general features; principles along the lines of (1´) and (2´), which I have maintained should be accepted for both cognitive and linguistic norms, should not be taken to apply to norms for taste.

Two things must be noted in Ginsborg's defense. First, it is by no means obvious that she intends there to be principles along the lines of (1´) and (2´) for taste. Second, and more importantly, there is much that her primitive-recognition model succeeds in capturing about the overall logic of Kant's solution to the problem of taste, and so much to recommend it as a reading of Kant. It is beyond question that Kant wants to construe cognitive norms and the normative claims of taste within the terms of a single general model. That is fundamental to Kant's theory of taste, which seeks to explain the possibility of aesthetic norms by establishing that the judgment of taste satisfies a condition for the possibility of judgment in general.[72] But to the extent that aesthetic and cognitive norms are subsumed under one general model of norms, deriving from a general conception of the normativity of the imagination's activity, either cognitive and linguistic norms will need to be construed as individualistic in an inappropriate and distorted way, or the normative claims of taste will be made to require some general agreement as a precondition. Following through on Ginsborg's suggestion, with its linkage to Kant's analysis of taste, will lead to the second kind of distortion. Adopting her proposal for understanding cognitive norms will lead to the first. Acknowledging that there are essential differences between the conceptions of normativity involved in these cases, along the lines I have been exploring here, will undermine the applicability of a general and univocal model of a primitive recognition. Something, somewhere, will have to give.[73]

To my mind, then, the problem uncovered in this chapter is a problem for Kant's theory of taste, not for Ginsborg's interpretation. The overall logic of Kant's solution to the problem of taste cannot preserve an adequate sense of the difference between the kinds of normative claims made by taste and those made in the cognitive realm. A general conception of normativity through which cognitive and aesthetic norms are to be linked as Kant intends is indeed too general, and will inevitably lead to a distortion of at least one of them. I have been concerned throughout this book to trace to their roots the distortions in Kant's conception of taste. As we've seen, the idea of the activity of the imagination as the ultimate source of both cognitive and aesthetic norms is central to Kant's approach, providing both the lynchpin of the claim that the judgment of taste manifests a necessary condition for the possibility of cognition as well as the basis for Kant's theoretical articulation of the twofold conception of taste, that is, his distinction between the beautiful and the agreeable. The connection Kant forges here is too tight, the conceptions of normativity and imaginative activity are ultimately too thin and general, to capture anything distinctive about the claims of taste and their place within our lives.

I'll say in closing—and programmatically, to be sure—that reflection on the significance of taste might fruitfully begin by appreciating the capacity of aesthetic disagreement to expose the fragility and the limits of our mutual attunement, on which our capacities to reason and communicate together, to make ourselves intelligible and known to one another, ultimately and ubiquitously depend. Indeed, we might ask whether 'I don't understand you'—that is, I don't understand *how* you could fail to have a certain experience of an object; *how* you could miss what I see, or claim to see what I apparently miss—isn't what we really (mean to) say in the face of aesthetic disagreement. At the very least, 'you are *wrong*' is not a claim we can take at face value in this context.

'You are wrong' is of course what we ordinarily say when disagreement arises in our cognitive and linguistic practices; within those practices, our shared natural reactions prove too deeply attuned, our methods of training, instructing, correcting, and convincing each other prove too reliable, for us to ever notice the attunement on which they rest. In philosophy, as in ordinary life, we routinely see right through it. One way to get it back into view is to 'invent fictitious natural history.'[74] Another way, perhaps, is to reflect on the ways in which our mutual attunement, our shared natural responsiveness to the world—so blindly taken for granted in our linguistic and cognitive affairs—so often goes missing in matters of taste, and what the procedures of aesthetic discourse and criticism can hope to do in response. Whether such procedures can assemble, for the epistemologist, more than just this very general reminder about the basis of our cognitive norms, is a question about which I remain open minded.[75]

Notes

1. The Twofold Conception of Taste

[1] For a different view of the structure of the concept *taste*, see Schaper, 'The Pleasures of Taste,' in Schaper, ed., *Pleasure, Preference and Value*, especially pp. 39–40. Schaper argues that its apparent twofold structure is nothing more than a 'non-fortuitous ambiguity,' and that our failure to achieve a sharp enough separation has led to 'oversimplifications to the point of caricature' throughout the history of aesthetics. On my view, Kant's aesthetic theory offers caricatures all its own—his descriptions of judgments about colors and tones—which result from his attempts to frame a fully general and completely sharp distinction on theoretical grounds.

[2] See Cavell, 'Aesthetic Problems of Modern Philosophy.' Especially relevant is the section titled 'Aesthetic Judgment and a Philosophical Claim,' pp. 86–96.

[3] See Guyer, *Kant and the Claims of Taste*, pp. 118–30. Guyer notes the connection between this aspect of his interpretation and Cavell's discussion at p. 120 n. 57.

[4] §§ 1–5 ('First Moment') and §§ 6–10 ('Second Moment') of *Critique of the Power of Judgment*.

[5] I use the phrases 'judgment of beauty,' 'judgment of taste,' and 'pure judgment of taste' interchangeably throughout. Generally, they translate Kant's standard term (*reine*) *Geschmacksurteil*, although Kant occasionally uses phrases like *das ästhetische Urteil über das Schöne*. It is generally agreed that there is no substantive distinction here.

[6] Strictly speaking, I base my judgment on my felt pleasure along with my best (yet eminently fallible) assessment of the motivational sources of my pleasure. But the issues raised by the latter requirement are not relevant to the present discussion.

[7] My own view is that Kant's all-or-nothing model of aesthetic normativity is ill-conceived. Even putting aside obvious cultural variations that might call this model into question, normative demands come in varying degrees of generality; not all normative demands are genuinely *universal*. There is a type of aesthetic criticism that could be summed up by saying '*You of all people . . . .*' We expect people who have certain forms of mastery—or certain interests—to be susceptible to beauties that we don't expect others to be susceptible to, or at least to have a heightened susceptibility to them. Think for instance of jazz improvisations where at least some of the beauty is only accessible to listeners who can hear the *interaction* between the musicians. An excellent example is the album *Undercurrent* by Bill Evans and Jim Hall. While there is a beauty in the music that I, for one,

would think everyone ought to be susceptible to, there are certain aspects of the music that aren't equally accessible to all. Especially interesting in this context is Evans's use of silence as a structural element in improvisation, which he uses to urge Hall on to fuller elaborations of his own melodic line. The responsiveness to this beauty that one could reasonably demand of a listener depends on the extent to which the listener is capable of hearing the interaction between Evans and Hall. I'm not sure that this dimension of aesthetic responsiveness and criticism fits neatly into the overall architecture of Kant's theory, but I suspect it finds its most natural (or least contrived) place within the category of so-called dependent beauty, which I discuss briefly in Section 4.

8 *Critique of the Power of Judgment*, § 7, 5: 212.

9 Ibid.

10 The notion of 'rational opposition' is admittedly not fully clear. It is, in effect, a placeholder for whatever sense in which judgments of beauty can claim intersubjective validity—and therefore be correct or incorrect—without being either true or false. Since judgments of beauty, like judgments of the agreeable, also lack truth values, characterizing judgments of the agreeable as not *logically* opposed to one another would fail to distinguish them from judgments of beauty.

11 Note that, in the third *Critique*, Kant's conception of judgment must be substantially broader than in earlier works, especially the 'Transcendental Analytic' of the first *Critique*. There Kant construes a judgment as a *claim* in the dual sense of (1) 'objective validity,' a claim about the way things are, and (2) 'intersubjective validity,' a claim to the agreement of others. While neither judgments of beauty nor judgments of the agreeable make claims about the way things are, judgments of beauty do make claims to the agreement of others. For Kant, that is the more fundamental characterization of judgment. Judgments of the agreeable, however, make no claims at all; they are expressive uses of language. Even given Kant's broader conception of judgment in the third *Critique*, it is unclear why—by his own lights—they are properly called 'judgments' at all.

12 *Critique of the Power of Judgment*, § 7, 5: 212–13.

13 See Guyer, *Kant and the Claims of Taste*, pp. 123–5, for helpful discussion of the difficulties in rendering the subtle differences in sense between these German verbs.

14 Cavell, 'Aesthetic Problems of Modern Philosophy,' p. 89, n. 8.

15 A point of substantial scholarly dispute lurks here—namely, whether Kant intends to distinguish aesthetic *response* from aesthetic *judgment* proper. For references to the leading literature in the contemporary debate, and a programmatic sketch of my own view, see note 61 in Chapter 4.

16 Cavell, 'Aesthetic Problems of Modern Philosophy,' p. 91.

17 Guyer, *Kant and the Claims of Taste*, p. 119.

18 *Critique of the Power of Judgment*, § 7, 5: 212.

19 Ibid., § 8, 5: 214.

20 Guyer, *Kant and the Claims of Taste*, p. 121.

21 Ibid.

22 For documentation, see the Yiddish Radio Project, www.yiddishradioproject.org.

23 Hannah Ginsborg forcefully pressed this line of objection. Chapters 2 and 3 should make clear why I think it ultimately fails.

24 Compare the example of the pianist who plays Beethoven as if it were Chopin in Cavell, 'Aesthetic Problems of Modern Philosophy,' pp. 91–2.

25 *Critique of the Power of Judgment*, § 7, 5: 212.

26 Ibid., § 14, 5: 224.

27 Kant pervasively confuses different senses of the word 'tone.' One sense aligns with *pitch*; in that sense, tone is properly distinguished from mere noise by a regularity or constancy of vibration that makes the sound identifiable as an instance of a general type, like a C#. But Kant often uses 'tone' in the sense of *timbre* or *tone color* [*Klangfarbe*], which, as distinct from pitch, is the character or quality of a sound that distinguishes one instrument from another. A full account of Kant's views on music would have to sort out the constant equivocations in the text, but that would not repay the effort in the present context. For disambiguation of the various senses of 'tone,' see the entries 'Acoustics,' 'Pitch,' 'Timbre,' 'Tone,' and 'Tone Color' in Randal, ed., *The New Harvard Dictionary of Music*.

28 *Critique of the Power of Judgment*, § 14, 5: 224.

29 *Critique of Pure Reason*, B44.

30 Ibid., A29/B44–5.

31 *Critique of the Power of Judgment*, § 14, 5: 224.

32 Ibid., § 39, 5: 291.

33 Ibid., § 14, 5: 224.

34 A Humean might object: we can control the way our senses are causally affected by objects, in the sense that we can cultivate our capacities for sensory discrimination. That is the heart of Hume's description of the difference between the good and the bad critic. See Hume, 'Of the Standard of Taste.' Perhaps we could then articulate a normative dimension of the taste of the senses in terms of a requirement that people ought to cultivate these capacities, and become capable of finer discrimination between (sometimes subtle) differences in the sensory qualities of objects. But this line of argument is not available to Kant, since it requires the assumption that objects reliably produce qualitatively identical sensations in different subjects— namely, the contrary of what I call the *variability hypothesis*. See Chapter 2 for discussion.

35 *Critique of the Power of Judgment*, § 16, 5: 230.

36 Ibid., § 16, 5: 230. Surprisingly, Nietzsche misses the mark. In *Genealogy of Morals*, Essay 3, § 6, he remarks:

> If our aestheticians never weary of asserting in Kant's favor that, under the spell of beauty, one can *even* view undraped female statues 'without interest,' one may laugh a little at their expense: the experiences of *artists* on this ticklish point are more 'interesting,' and Pygmalion was in any event not necessarily an 'unaesthetic man.' Let us think the more highly of the innocence of our aestheticians which is reflected in such arguments; let us, for example, credit it to the honor of Kant that he should expatiate on the peculiar properties of the sense of touch with the naïveté of a country parson.

But Galatea (or more precisely, her ancestral statue) gave Pygmalion occasion to make a judgment of dependent beauty, and the requirement of 'disinterestedness' applies only to judgments of free beauty, that is, to pure judgments of taste. See generally the 'First Moment of the Judgment of Taste,' *Critique of the Power of Judgment*, §§ 1–5, 5: 203–11. I discuss the requirement of disinterestedness in more detail in Chapter 3.

[37] *Critique of the Power of Judgment*, § 51, 5: 324–5.

[38] A judgment of dependant beauty need not be disinterested, although it can be. See note 36 in this chapter.

[39] See McDowell, *Mind and World*, Lectures I–IV.

[40] See Strawson, *The Bounds of Sense*. Chapter 1 of Part 1 provides a helpful summary of Strawson's dissatisfactions with transcendental idealism, and expresses his central claim that 'The doctrines of transcendental idealism . . . are undoubtedly the chief obstacles to a sympathetic understanding of the *Critique*' (p. 22). I hope to defend the view that, whatever difficulties transcendental idealism may cause for Kant's aesthetic theory, a failure to take seriously its systematic role will erect a serious obstacle to understanding much of Kant's argument in the third *Critique*.

[41] Ginsborg defends this interpretation throughout her writings. Especially relevant, however, are 'Lawfulness without a Law,' and 'Thinking the Particular as Contained under the Universal.'

[42] I have in mind, of course, the kind of 'instruction' or 'training' [*Abrichtung*, in Wittgenstein's curiously harsh phrase] that is the focus of much of Wittgenstein's discussion in *Philosophical Investigations*. The relevant parameters of these ideas will become clearer in Chapter 4.

2. The Beautiful and the Agreeable

[1] See especially *Critique of the Power of Judgment*, § 7, 5: 212–13; § 14, 5: 223–6. For the sake of simplicity, this chapter will ignore complications attending to the distinction between free and dependent beauty.

[2] Ibid., § 14, 5: 224.

[3] For useful discussion, see Allison, *Kant's Theory of Taste*, Chapter 6, § III, especially p. 131. The 'limited way' refers to the apparent restriction of judgments of beauty to 'pure' or 'unmixed' colors and tones. For details, see note 85 in this chapter.

[4] *Critique of the Power of Judgment*, § 13, 5: 223.

[5] Ibid., § 14, 5: 224.

[6] Ibid., § 14, 5: 224.

[7] Ibid., § 14, 5: 225.

[8] See Guyer, *Kant and the Claims of Taste*, p. 205.

[9] Ibid.

[10] Ibid., p. 206.

[11] *Critique of the Power of Judgment*, § 14, 5: 224.

[12] For example, ibid., § 41, 5: 297.

[13] Ibid., § 16, 5: 229.

[14] *Critique of Pure Reason*, B44.

[15] Ibid., A29/B44–5.

[16] The terminology of 'perceptual form' is from Guyer, *Kant and the Claims of Taste*, Chapter 6.

[17] It is likely that colors should be thought of as properties, while tones should be thought of as entities or particulars, rather than as properties; hence the disjunctive formulation. This question will resurface later in the chapter.

[18] *Critique of Pure Reason*, A29/B44–5; *Critique of the Power of Judgment*, § 14, 5: 224; § 39, 5: 291–3.

[19] See notes 13–14 in this chapter.

[20] See Locke, *Essay Concerning Human Understanding*, Book II, Chapter viii, § 10.

[21] *Critique of the Power of Judgment*, § 39, 5: 291.

[22] I do not mean to imply that a contrast between necessary versus contingent features is either the ultimate point or the only content of a transcendental characterization of our cognitive faculties.

[23] *Critique of Pure Reason*, A28/B44–A30/B45.

[24] This reading is in sharp contrast to Guyer, *Kant and the Claims of Taste*, pp. 208–9. Guyer believes that Kant asserts the variability hypothesis as true, and uses this assertion as a ground for excluding qualities such as color and tone from the proper elements of beauty. Thus, Guyer charges that Kant allows his aesthetic theory to lapse into the realm of the 'merely empirical and psychological.' In contrast, my interpretation funds no such charge.

[25] One might object: having a representation of an object as being of some *particular* shape requires sensations just as a representation of an object as having, say, a color or a smell does. Thus, the problems raised here concerning secondary qualities would arise in the same way for primary qualities. I begin to address the intricate questions raised by this objection in Chapter 3.

[26] *Critique of Pure Reason*, B44. Only the B-Edition of the 'Transcendental Aesthetic' contains an explicit denial that sensations allow us any cognition of an object at all. Further references to the view of the 'Transcendental Aesthetic' in this section should be taken as concerned with the B-Edition unless otherwise indicated.

[27] See editorial note *d*, p. 155, of the Guyer-Wood translation of *Critique of Pure Reason*.

[28] *Critique of the Power of Judgment*, § 3, 5: 206 (my italics).

[29] Ibid.

[30] Ibid., § 39, 5: 290.

[31] Pluhar concurs. He notes the equivalence of the two terms in note 19, p. 157 of his translation, *Critique of Judgment*. I have opted for the more literal translation of *Sinnenempfindung* as 'sensory sensation,' even though Pluhar's 'sensation proper' avoids some of the awkwardness of the literal translation.

[32] I follow the dating of Ameriks and Naragon in their translation of Kant's *Lectures on Metaphysics*, which contains all of the lectures cited in this chapter (notes 33–6).

[33] *Metaphysik L₁*, 28: 232.

[34] *Metaphysik Mongrovius*, 28: 585.

[35] *Metaphysik L₂*, 29: 882.

[36] *Metaphysik L₁*, 28: 232.

[37] *Critique of the Power of Judgment*, § 39, 5: 290.

38 Ibid., § 44, 5: 306. The point I am making is obscured by the Guyer-Matthews translation of this passage. They use 'mere sensation' not only to translate *bloßer Empfindung* but also to translate the occurrence of *Sinnenempfindung* in the final sentence. This departure from their standard translation of *Sinnenempfindung* as 'sensory sensation' is misleading. Pluhar's translation of this passage remains consistent with his general practice of using 'sensation proper.'

39 *Critique of the Power of Judgment*, § 21, 5: 239.

40 Hannah Ginsborg, 'Thinking the Particular as Contained under the Universal' defends this line of interpretation. This thought also underlies the contention that Kant's analysis of the judgment of taste represents the culmination of his 'Copernican Revolution' in Longuenesse, 'Kant's Leading Thread in the Analytic of the Beautiful' and 'Kant's Theory of Judgment, and Judgments of Taste.' Kant himself discusses the relation between objective and intersubjective validity in the *Prolegomena*, § 18.

41 Philosophers sympathetic to Kant (e.g., Strawson, *Individuals*, Chapters 1–2) and unsympathetic to Kant (e.g., Evans, *The Varieties of Reference*, especially Chapter 6) share the view that vision is cognitively privileged. But as the debate between Strawson, *Individuals*, Chapter 2, and Evans, 'Things without the Mind' makes clear, there is far more to be said about the relation between sound and representation of an objective world.

42 Stroud, *The Quest for Reality*, is a trenchant and interesting discussion of these issues, containing ample references to the relevant contemporary literature.

43 For instance, Stroud describes sounds as 'particulars with definite temporal position.' Ibid., p. 210.

44 This may indeed be tantamount to a rejection of a Kantian approach to matters of taste. In particular, I don't see why—unless one has already accepted the theoretical terms of Kant's aesthetic theory—one would (or should) think that one sensory modality is (or should be) privileged in matters of taste simply because it is privileged with respect to cognition. For example, I don't see why I should automatically take a judgment about the way something looks to be normative while automatically taking a judgment about the way something smells to be a case of 'to each his own.' But I am concerned here to investigate Kant's connection between the beautiful-agreeable distinction and the requirements of cognition, so I cannot subject the very idea of such a connection to serious questioning in this chapter.

45 *Critique of the Power of Judgment*, § 14, 5: 224.

46 Ibid.

47 Ibid.

48 Ibid.

49 The view I sketch concerning the role of the imagination in the production of unified representations is heavily influenced by the overarching argument of Longuenesse, *Kant and the Capacity to Judge*.

50 A full account of the role of synthesis in cognition would of course have to reckon with the role of *synthesis speciosa* in generating the *a priori* intuitions of space and time. This is well beyond the scope of my purposes here. For a trenchant account, see ibid., pp. 199–242.

51 *Critique of the Power of Judgment*, § 9, 5: 217–19.

[52] Ibid.

[53] Ibid., § 21, 5: 239.

[54] For an approving discussion of Euler's theory, see *Metaphysical Foundations of Natural Science*, 4: 520n. For Kant's attraction to an alternative view, see *Anthropology from a Pragmatic Point of View*, 7: 156. Matters are made more confusing by the parenthetical comment in § 14, about whether or not the mind 'perceives the regular play of the impressions . . ..' As Guyer and Matthews detail in footnote *b*, p. 109 of their translation of the third *Critique*, in the first two editions the parenthetical reads '*woran ich doch gar* **sehr** *zweifle*,' whereas in the third edition it reads '*woran ich doch gar* **nicht** *zweifle*' (my emphases). They further report in the 'Editor's Introduction' that we do not know who made the corrections for the third edition in 1799, but we do know that Kant himself made the corrections for the second edition in 1792 (pp. xlv–xlvi). Guyer and Matthews (p. 370, n. 30), Pluhar (p. 70, n. 40 of his translation), and Allison (*Kant's Theory of Taste*, p. 134) all seem to think that the evidence, though not decisive, favors the conclusion that Kant eventually accepted Euler's theory.

[55] Guyer, *Kant's Theory of Taste*, p. 131.

[56] *Critique of the Power of Judgment*, § 51, 5: 324.

[57] Ibid. The phrase 'a special sensation' [*einer besonderen . . . Empfindung*], which refers to the ability to recognize pitch, is question begging, since the point of the passage is that we *cannot tell* whether this ability 'has as its ground sense or reflection.' This slip in Kant's formulation of the question is yet more evidence of how much pull restrictive formalism, which conceives of tones as mere sensations, exerts on his thinking. That is, appealing to some such 'special sensation' might make some sense if one thinks that tone perception is a matter of perceiving the effects of vibrations of air on our sense organs. Tone-deaf people, as a matter of brute physiology, might simply fail to receive this 'special sensation'; their ears may just not be affected in this way. If, however, one thinks of tone perception as a matter of 'reflection' on a manifold of sensation, the gratuitous postulation of this 'special sensation' would explain absolutely nothing.

[58] Ibid., § 51, 5: 325.

[59] Ibid., § 51, 5: 324–5.

[60] *Critique of Pure Reason*, A99.

[61] *Critique of the Power of Judgment*, § 51, 5: 325.

[62] The following three paragraphs summarize the argument defended over the course of Chapter 6 of Guyer, *Kant and the Claims of Taste*. pp. 184–7 provide Guyer's own helpful overview of the argument.

[63] Ibid. See especially the section titled 'Form and Matter,' pp. 199–210.

[64] Ibid. See especially pp. 203–5.

[65] Ibid, p. 208.

[66] Ibid.

[67] *Critique of the Power of Judgment*, § 17, 5: 236.

[68] See Guyer, *Kant and the Claims of Taste*, Chapter 6. Allison, in Chapters 2, 6 of *Kant's Theory of Taste*, agrees that Kant is not committed to restrictive formalism and that Kant's identification of the 'form of purposiveness' with perceptual, or spatiotemporal, form is unwarranted. But Allison disagrees that the notion of a form of purposiveness is just an indeterminate placeholder for whatever happens

to occasion the free play; he therefore thinks that Kant does have an answer to the traditional aesthetic question and is committed to aesthetic formalism, but in a broader and more tolerant sense: only features that comprise an object's 'aesthetic form' can contribute to beauty and occasion the free play (p. 136). Aesthetic form, Allison says, 'is a form that one might term "schema-like" or, perhaps, as the "schema of a schema," since it presents itself as if it were structured in accordance with a certain rule, though no particular rule can be specified' (p. 49). This allows the imagination to 'simulate the exhibition of a concept' without any concept actually being exhibited (p. 50). These rather obscure remarks appear to mean that aesthetic form exhibits whatever underlies or is required for the exhibition of any schema, without any particular schema being fully and determinately exhibited. First, I doubt that provides enough determinate content to overcome Guyer's charge; at any rate, it is exceedingly opaque. Second, Allison never acknowledges that what underlies every schema—what makes it 'homogeneous' with both the sensible and the intellectual aspects of our representations, and thereby allows the category to be applied to the appearance—is the 'transcendental time-determination,' *Critique of Pure Reason*, A139/B178. Allison's account therefore dodges a central aspect of the apprehension that must be involved in aesthetic judgment. Finally, by maintaining that Kant's analysis of the free play clearly entails that a judgment of taste is based on form—but not in the strict sense of perceptual form—Allison can provide no explanation of why this latter notion appears ubiquitously in the third *Critique*, it must remain an unaccountable blunder.

[69] Guyer, *Kant and the Claims of Taste*, especially pp. 204–6.

[70] *Critique of the Power of Judgment*, 'First Introduction,' § VII, 5: 220–1. I have slightly modified the Guyer-Matthews translation.

[71] Meerbote, 'Reflection on Beauty,' offers an interpretation similar to mine. Meerbote argues that 'the object of a pure judgment of taste is the presence or absence of conformity of the apprehended features of a manifold to the *invariant* features of the understanding' (p. 72), which include both spatial and temporal 'orderliness' or 'orderability,' and 'lawfulness' or 'categorizability' (p. 80). On Meerbote's view, Kant argues, albeit indecisively, that colors and tones are 'regularities of other qualities,' which points toward taking 'lawfulness' or 'categorizability' as a 'co-equal candidate for aesthetic formhood' (p. 80). On my view, however, Kant's strategy is to investigate the prospects for arguing that our representations of colors and tones implicate precisely the 'invariant features' Meerbote has enumerated—spatial ordering (colors) and temporal ordering (tones)—and not to suggest any further putative candidates for the relevant 'invariant features.' More importantly, Meerbote fails to link what he rightly describes as Kant's wavering over the aesthetic status of colors to his broader wavering over their ontological and epistemological status.

[72] *Critique of Pure Reason*, A98–9. See also Longuenesse, *Kant and the Capacity to Judge*, Chapter 8, especially p. 214.

[73] Some may object: if the necessary condition for cognition manifested in the free play is taken to be an apprehension of a manifold in terms of spatiotemporal form, what happens in the free play will be *the same* as what happens in a cognitive judgment. Thus, I will not be able to account for the indeterminate or

nonconceptual status of the judgment of taste, and I will be faced with the so-called everything is beautiful problem.

First, on my view, no sense can be made of the idea that an apprehension of a manifold can occur without the actual application of concepts. See Strawson, 'Imagination and Perception,' for the reasons why. My view only requires that concepts are not *grounds* for the judgment of taste: the apprehension of a manifold in terms of spatiotemporal features, *irrespective* of whatever concepts are or can be applied, provides the material for aesthetic reflection. Aesthetic reflection simply requires the ability to apprehend a spatiotemporal form and to judge it in its own right, in terms of whether it is pleasing to behold, without judging it *as* the form of a this-or-that.

Second, my interpretation has no special difficulty with the so-called everything is beautiful problem. For not every spatiotemporal form is pleasing to behold, and I am not saying that one is pleased simply because the object (or rather, the manifold) has been apprehended as having *a* spatiotemporal form. Roughly: those forms are beautiful that 'animate' or 'enliven' the cognitive faculties in an open-ended and self-perpetuating way. *Critique of the Power of Judgment*, § 9, 5: 218–19. Some forms leave the cognitive faculties particularly stimulated, alert, and ready to undertake their standing aim of arriving at cognition, without being geared toward any particular achievement of cognition: aesthetic reflection is neither grounded on, nor itself produces, the application of any concept of its object. Not every apprehended form will be capable of underwriting this kind of open-ended activity of the faculties. The pleasure that results from beholding forms those that produce this open-ended and self-sustaining enlivening of the cognitive faculties has no *interest*, but does have a very general underlying cognitive *motive*. I am indebted to David Hills for discussion of this distinction. I sketch some more of this view in note 27 of Chapter 3.

[74] Guyer, *Kant and the Claims of Taste*, pp. 204–5.

[75] The same problem underlies Allison's distinction, in Chapter 6 of *Kant's Theory of Taste*, between 'perceptual' (or 'spatiotemporal') form and 'aesthetic' form. I employ a contrast between the strict and broad senses of spatiotemporal form, rather than a contrast between spatiotemporal and aesthetic form, because the latter contrast fails to appreciate that, on Kant's view, colors and tones can be elements of beauty only if our representations of them require an apprehension of spatiotemporal form.

[76] Guyer, *Kant and the Claims of Taste*, p. 204.

[77] Ibid.

[78] Allison, *Kant's Theory of Taste*, p. 136. Allison takes the point of § 14 to be that Euler's theory provides grounds for holding that color perception 'necessarily involves an element of reflection, in contrast to mere sensation.' But § 14 makes the more specific point that color perception and tonal perception involve not just any old manifold of sensation—and thus a need to unify it *somehow*—but rather the *spatiotemporal* unification of a manifold of sensation. I focus on Guyer's view, however, since, to my mind, it presents the underlying interpretive issues more sharply than does Allison's.

[79] Guyer's interpretation appears to be motivated by his own aesthetic view: it is a 'strained view,' he says, that 'the simple constituents of manifolds . . . are

themselves beautiful,' *Kant and the Claims of Taste*, p. 207. Compare my example of the tone of Pace de Lucia's guitar in Section 4 of Chapter 1. And on my reading, it makes sense for Kant to think that *if any* judgments about color or tone are to count as judgments of beauty, then it must be possible for judgments about a *single* color or tone to count as judgments of beauty. Kant's strategy is to look for an argument that colors and tones are not mere sensations but intuitions, which must involve the presence of a manifold. *Critique of Pure Reason*, A99. Guyer's characterization of colors and tones as 'simple' is therefore unavailing.

Now, the possibility of transposition in tonal music might be thought to fund a view like Guyer's: since it is possible to change the entire series of tones (in the sense of pitches) while preserving both the recognizability and the beauty of the piece—provided the harmonic and melodic *relations* stay constant—one might think that at least the *specific tones* the piece employs is irrelevant (or close to irrelevant); what is central to our experience of the music's beauty are rather formal or structural features. Without taking issue with this as an aesthetic claim, notice that these formal features cannot be captured within the framework of Guyer's proposal. To understand harmony and melody as 'proportionate dispositions,' as Kant does, we need more than the thought that they are the sparse temporal relations of simultaneity and succession, as Kant sometimes describes them. See, for example, *Critique of the Power of Judgment*, § 53, 5: 329. We need the further thought that individual tones—the relata of these relations—are themselves temporally organized. But that implies that *individual* tones can be beautiful, and Guyer's view thereby founders.

80   Ibid., p. 204.
81   Guyer's proposal is further motivated by his conception of aesthetic judgment (or more precisely, on Guyer's view, aesthetic response) as involving a 'synthesis without concepts,' that is, a synthesis that fails to follow through to the third stage of 'recognition in a concept.' I agree with Ginsborg that there are not three separate and temporally successive processes of synthesis, but rather three aspects of one single process of synthesis. See her 'On the Key to Kant's Critique of Taste,' p. 295. So I do not think that aesthetic judgment (or response) involves a 'synthesis without concepts' at all.
82   Of course, Guyer thinks that Kant's strategy for a 'deduction' of the normative claims of taste *is* a failure, and so he might not be terribly bothered by this criticism. See Guyer, *Kant and the Claims of Taste*, Chapters 8–9. I do not mean to suggest that I find the 'deduction' a philosophical success, but I do think that Guyer's proposal slams the door too quickly on Kant's attempt to bear out the alleged connection between taste and the possibility of cognition.
83   Quite the opposite: in § 14, Kant proposes that individual colors or tones might be beautiful, provided that they are 'pure.' Guyer objects to this dictum: not only is it a strained view, it leaves Kant unable to account for the beauty of the Albers paintings or for orchestration in music. While this latter claim is true, Guyer misses the point of the restriction: only if our incoming sensations of sound, for instance, are 'pure'—not interrupted, interfered with, or mixed with any others—would we be able to track the 'division of time' and therefore perceive pitch. This has two manifest problems: first, it is brute assertion; second, it presupposes the eliminativist view that underlies restrictive formalism. Thus, Kant need not be committed to it.

And happily so. Not only would it impoverish Kant's account in the way Guyer recognizes; Kant would also be unable to account for the beauty of *chords* if he cannot say that 'mixed' tones are beautiful—since many of Kant's discussions of tones, including those in §§ 14, 51, are really discussions of pitch rather than timbre (see note 27 in Chapter 1). This would throttle an aesthetic theory that privileges *harmony* as the locus of beauty in music. See, for example, *Anthropology*, § 53 (15.1: 276–7) (not available in translation); Gammon, 'Parerga and Pulchritudo Adhaerens.' On my reading, § 14's dictum is merely Kant's initial attempt to attenuate the scope of restrictive formalism, by allowing at least a subset of colors and tones to count as elements of beauty. Further inquiries in the third *Critique* supersede this initial proposal.

[84] Hannah Ginsborg pressed this objection against my interpretation and against my criticism of Guyer. It should not be imputed to Guyer.

[85] Kant argues for this claim in the 'Metaphysical Exposition' of the 'Transcendental Aesthetic,' *Critique of Pure Reason*, A22/B37–A25/B41.

[86] *Critique of the Power of Judgment*, 'Introduction,' § VII, 5: 189–90.

[87] Ibid.

[88] Ibid., 'Introduction,' § VII, 5: 190. I have slightly modified the Guyer-Matthews translation.

[89] Ibid.

[90] Ibid.

[91] Ibid., 'Introduction,' § VII, 5: 191.

[92] Ibid., 'Introduction,' § VII, 5: 192.

[93] For a useful discussion of this important Kantian theme, see the 'Introduction' to Longuenesse, *Kant and the Capacity to Judge*.

[94] This is a quite general interpretive difficulty, not an artifact of my own view, and I know of no interpretation that offers a convincing account. For now, I make only the minimal claim that the constraints on which pleasurable mental states one can take to be communicable is tied to Kant's conception of the (sensible) conditions for the possibility of cognition. Thus, on Kant's view, I must be entitled to take some pleasurable experiences of my mental states to be valid for all, and this entitlement cannot extend to any mental state that does not involve an apprehension of spatiotemporal form. Clearly, not every apprehension of spatiotemporal form will be pleasurable, and not everyone will take pleasure in the apprehension of the same spatiotemporal forms. Kant's view therefore operates as a constraint on substantive aesthetic criticism and allows for the possibility of genuine disagreement.

Compare the views of Ginsborg, who attempts to skirt the general interpretive difficulty altogether. For Ginsborg, the judgment of taste reveals a condition for the possibility of cognition in the sense that I must be able to make what she calls a 'primitive recognition' of the normativity of my mental states. Taking a pleasure to be communicable is but one example of this; thus, on her view, there is no need to connect pleasure per se to the conditions for the possibility of cognition. I discuss Ginsborg's views at length in Chapter 4.

[95] One would think that the application of the notion of an intuition, which is part of the very core of Kant's theory of mind, should be fixed independently of Euler's (or anyone's) empirical-scientific investigations, and that transcendental philosophy should, by its own lights, be able to provide a characterization of our

cognitive faculties that doesn't depend on any particular theory of light or sound. It therefore seems to me that it would be unavailing to protest that Kant's uncertainty about the aesthetic status of colors and tones reflects a desire to wait until the full results of Euler's theory came in.

3. Sensations and Interests

1. Allison, *Kant's Theory of Taste*, p. 94. Allison's main concern is with Kant's strategy for distinguishing the judgment of taste from moral judgments, and he suggests that the requirement of disinterestedness is primarily in the service of that distinction (see especially pp. 94–7). But the requirement of disinterestedness, in addition to serving that distinction, is also clearly meant to help distinguish the beautiful from the agreeable. On this issue, Allison has little to say by way of substantiating his charges against Kant.

2. I generally leave aside questions about the distinction between aesthetic and moral judgments, and hence from issues relating to the interests that arise in the context of rational or nonsensuous desires. Kant construes moral judgments as connected to the fulfillment of interests as well, yet the interests in question are not *sensuous* interests. It seems to me that Kant introduces an unnecessary complication at this point, which is most explicit in § II of the 'Introduction' to *The Metaphysics of Morals* (6: 211–12) (available in *Practical Philosophy*). Kant argues that interests can be of two sorts, depending on whether the pleasure precedes the desire or the desire precedes the pleasure. The former is the agreeable, the latter interested moral judgments. But we needn't insist that the pleasure precedes the desire in cases of the agreeable. Kant seems to have in mind the idea that the pleasures of the agreeable give rise to *further* desires for objects of the same kind: having tasted the lamb and enjoyed it, I desire more. But this formulation obscures that fact that a pleasure in the agreeable is still a satisfaction or gratification of a (sensuous) desire, a point which becomes difficult to make out if we insist that the pleasure is literally and temporally *antecedent* to the desire. Hence I will not follow this formulation. For helpful discussion, see Allison, *Kant's Theory of Taste*, pp. 91–2.

3. I am grateful to David Hills for these formulations of the desire conception. I want to note two points. *First*, the pleasures of the agreeable are generally not pleasures that require *this* particular object, but rather any old object of a particular kind. There is a substitutability of objects of desire that marks a clear difference between the agreeable and the irreducible singularity of the pure judgment of taste. *Second*, the idea of 'doing something *to*' the object of desire needs to be interpreted in a broad sense that would include, for instance, acting upon Y as a means of acquiring X (where X is the object I actually desire). Or one might, as Daniel Warren has suggested to me, describe the general notion of an object of desire as something that satisfies a *lack*, that is, something that I don't have but want. Wants or lacks in the bodily sense of the agreeable cannot, in general, be satisfied through contemplation alone: their satisfaction demands that I *act*, even if my action affects the object of my desire in an indirect way.

⁴ For helpful discussion of Kant's conception of pleasure and its relation to desire, see Zuckert, 'A New Look at Kant's Theory of Pleasure.'

⁵ See, for example, the discussions in *Critique of the Power of Judgment*, §§ 7, 14.

⁶ See ibid., §§ 4–5.

⁷ See ibid., § 7, 5: 212; § 14, 5: 224–6.

⁸ Ibid., § 4; 5: 207; § 5, 5: 209.

⁹ Ibid., § 12, 5: 222.

¹⁰ Ibid., § 2, 5: 204–5.

¹¹ I thank Daniel Warren for urging objections along these lines.

¹² See *Critique of the Power of Judgment*, § 12, 5: 222. I do not mean to suggest that Kant himself is confused here, or that his texts cannot be read as describing pleasure in the way I claim it should be described. Zuckert, 'A New Look at Kant's Theory of Pleasure,' defends the view that pleasure is 'motivational,' which I take to be compatible with my suggestion that pleasures are states that provide us with reasons for maintaining them. Zuckert's quotation of a passage from *Anthropology from a Pragmatic Point of View* is particularly useful in this connection: 'What directly (by the senses) prompts me to *leave* my state (to go out of it) is disagreeable to me—it pains me. What directly prompts me to *maintain* my state (to remain in it) is agreeable to me—it delights me' (p. 230).

¹³ In *Values of Beauty*, Guyer considers the question whether 'the contemplation of the beautiful should be understood as a state of mind that is sometimes *protracted* rather than instantaneous' (p. 93). Guyer suggests that while Kant's descriptions of pleasure sometimes suggest that it should be, these descriptions of pleasure are the *only* theoretical description of pleasure that one could ever provide, and therefore nothing ought to be inferred from them about the pleasurable contemplation of the beautiful. Moreover, Guyer suggests, Kant does seem to view aesthetic contemplation as at least sometimes an instantaneous rather than protracted pleasure. Guyer deploys this view against the proposal in Rush, 'The Harmony of the Faculties,' that the free play be understood as a temporally extended entertaining of 'proleptic unities.' I agree with Guyer that the pleasures of aesthetic contemplation *could* be more or less instantaneous, or at least pleasurable right from the get-go (i.e., not requiring temporal protraction in order to first become pleasurable), but I want to stress that contemplative pleasures are typically states that we actively seek to *extend* by continued or renewed engagement with the beautiful object. Rarely, in fact, do we not. This requires that the object of contemplation stick around, as real objects are known to do more reliably than anything else.

¹⁴ See Zuckert's discussion of the 'motivational' view of pleasure in 'A New Look at Kant's Theory of Pleasure.' While Zuckert's rhetoric does not stress the idea of the reason-giving force of pleasure—stressing instead its motivational force—I do not see that there is a substantive disagreement between her view and mine on this point.

¹⁵ I am grateful to Hannah Ginsborg for alerting me to this objection and for discussion of various replies.

¹⁶ This is oversimplified. Of course, aesthetic theorists from Hutcheson to Schiller did not all formulate the notion of disinterestedness in the same way. I intend only the more modest point that Kant is part of an ongoing and complex debate

in which nearly all theorists advance some conception of the desire independence of aesthetic pleasure—including those, like Gerard and Kames, who explicitly attack the notion of aesthetic detachment found in Hutcheson. For a useful and detailed discussion of the development of the notion of aesthetic disinterestedness from Hutcheson to Schiller, see Guyer, *Kant and Experience of Freedom*, Chapters 2, 3, and Guyer, *Values of Beauty*, Chapters 1, 4.

[17] For Kant's definition of 'gratification' [*Vergnügen*], see *Anthropology from a Pragmatic Point of View*, § 60: 'Gratification is a pleasure of sensation.' I leave aside Kant's cryptic characterization of gratification as a 'feeling of the advancement of life.'

Note that the conclusion of this argument can be paraphrased as the conditional 'if x is a pleasure in the agreeable, then x involves an interest in something's real existence.' The converse does not hold, but a closely related claim does: 'if x is a pleasure that involves an interest in something's real existence, then x is either a pleasure in the agreeable or in the good.' I assume throughout that the examples I discuss do not bear on questions of the good; they are all straightforward examples of aesthetic pleasures. Since the agreeable and the good jointly exhaust the options, one can take the converse of this conditional to hold, as far as our purposes here are concerned. I thank Berislav Marušić for pointed questioning of this argument.

[18] *Critique of Pure Reason*, A19/B33–A20/B34.

[19] In this connection, see Kant's discussion of 'the real of the sensation' in the 'Anticipations of Perception' of the *Critique of Pure Reason*, especially A165/B207–A166/B208. I have been aided in understanding this section by Guyer, *Kant and the Claims of Knowledge*, pp. 185–8, and Bennett, *Kant's Analytic*, pp. 170–6. See also *Critique of the Power of Judgment*, § 39, 5: 291, where Kant describes sensation as 'the real in perception.'

[20] Hannah Ginsborg has urged on me the usefulness of distinguishing 'sensory pleasures' from 'pleasures that depend on the existence of an object.' I think she is correct; my point is precisely that the latter notion has a wider applicability than the former, that is, that an existence conception inevitably encompasses more than just sensory pleasures—unless an existence conception is constrained by a more fundamental desire conception.

In conversation, Ginsborg offered this distinction in the context of a discussion of her own view, on which the pleasure associated with a judgment of taste is not a sensory pleasure—since it is a pleasure taken in the judging itself—but is nevertheless a pleasure that depends on the existence of an object. An unconstrained version of the existence conception would therefore preclude Ginsborg's conception of the judgment of taste from counting as disinterested. But that is not meant as an objection to Ginsborg's view; rather, it is just to say that, given her conception of the judgment of taste, Ginsborg must take the applicability of the existence conception to be constrained by a more fundamental desire conception.

[21] See *Critique of Pure Reason*, A20/B34–A21/B35 ('Transcendental Aesthetic'), and A165/B207–A166/B208 ('Anticipations of Perception') for instances of the claim that we do not sense space and time.

[22] *Critique of the Power of Judgment*, § 14, 5: 224.

[23] Ibid., § 3, 5: 207.

[24] Daniel Warren has objected that the notion of *corporeality* rather than desire per se generates the natural connection to noncommunicability here. If that is so, one might wonder whether an existence conception could be supplemented by a notion of corporeality to yield the same connection. I do not think so. I acknowledge that, on my view, it is the notion of desire in conjunction with corporeality that yields such a natural and intuitive connection to noncommunicability. But that is because the key notion here is the noncommunicability of an *appetite*. An existence conception—independently of the desire conception—will never yield a natural and unforced notion of an appetite. To do so, it would have to be an existence conception in the limited or constrained sense, in which an 'interest' in existence is taken to arise *because* and *to the extent that* a more fundamental desire—a bodily appetite—is present. But then the desire conception is actually generating the connection to noncommunicability.

[25] I rely here on the double abstraction procedure, which Kant outlines at the start of the 'Transcendental Aesthetic' in *Critique of Pure Reason*, A20/B34–A21/B35. By means of this procedure, Kant thinks we can isolate the contributions of the 'pure form of sensible intuition,' that is, spatiotemporality. As Kant is quite explicit about, space and time are the *only* contributions that can be imputed to this form; they are all that is left when one abstracts away all conceptual content and all sensation from one's representations. Hence space and time are the only aspects of our intuitive representations that are not indicators of something's real or material existence. Clearly, this double abstraction procedure leaves nothing that could reasonably be called a representation of a color or a tone.

[26] I record here a dissatisfaction prompted by criticism from Daniel Warren. It mirrors a general interpretive problem concerning Kant's own formalist rhetoric. Kant often describes a pure judgment of taste, that is, one based on a pleasure taken in the formal features of object, as one in which sensation does not figure as part of its 'determining ground.' But one might object that when I take pleasure in, say, something's figure (*i.e.*, shape), my pleasure *is*, to some extent, based on sensations I have received. For a representation of a thing with a particular shape is also an empirical intuition, a complex of sensation and pure intuition. Pure intuition alone provides only the representation of spatiality, not the representation of a thing of a particular shape. And so my way of framing the problem with counting pleasures taken in colors and tones on the existence conception would arise for pleasures taken in formal features as well.

I think there is the threat of a problem here both for my own account as well as for Kant's formalist rhetoric, but I want to indicate the ways in which such problems could begin to be addressed. While it is true that when I take pleasure in a particular thing's shape I am de facto receiving sensations from that thing, sensation is not *essential* to the representation of this particular shape. For the representation of a particular shape is constructible in pure intuition, by the introduction of boundaries to the *a priori* representation of space itself. That is the only functional role that sensations play in this case, a functional role for which they are not essential on Kant's view. It is important to note that it is *shape itself* and not the presence of a thing with a particular shape that is supposed to be the basis of a pure judgment of taste: whether I introduce boundaries to the representation of space in pure intuition or I have an actual drawing do it for me should be inconsequential for a strict Kantian formalist. In fact, I believe this is what ultimately underlies Kant's claim that I am, or should be, indifferent between the presence of a real object and a mere representation when it comes to pleasures I take in the formal properties of things (or in my representations of them).

In contrast, it would be wholly unreasonable to think of representations of colors or tones as constructible in pure intuition. These are representations for which sensation seems essential; even a representation of the (reproductive) imagination will be derivative from sensations in these cases. In other words, pure intuition can produce representations that have the requisite purely formal features to ground a judgment of taste, whereas representations of colors and tones are ineliminably tied to the presence of material objects. They require more than just the introduction of boundaries to *a priori* representations; they require sensations with intensive magnitudes. Hence they will never be able to count as disinterested on the existence conception.

[27] Conspicuously absent from this list is the notion of as-if purposiveness, which raises issues far beyond the scope of this chapter. But I want to briefly note how this further aspect of the beautiful figures in my interpretation. The principal connection is between as-if purposiveness and formality: only a judgment made on the basis of formal features exhibits the as-if purposiveness associated with the pure judgment of taste. As Guyer has helpfully detailed, Kant's *Anthropology* lectures reveal that he long believed aesthetic properties associated with shape— in particular, the notions of spatial symmetry and proportionality—facilitate the mind's comprehension of an object. See Guyer, *Values of Beauty*, Chapter 6. The focus on notions like symmetry and proportionality places Kant within the tradition of classical conceptions of beauty, and allows him to connect these traditional elements of beauty to his conception of the pure judgment of taste as manifesting a condition for the possibility of cognition. This connection is also visible at the start of the 'Deduction of Pure Aesthetic Judgments,' where Kant claims that the beautiful forms in nature are as-if purposive because of their *shape*: it is in virtue of their shape that the beautiful forms in nature 'show [themselves] in the mind to be suitable to the **faculty** both of concepts and of the presentation of them,' *Critique of the Power of Judgment*, § 30, 5: 279. The passages Guyer cites from the *Anthropology* lectures, along with a number of passages from the *Metaphysics* lectures (see, for example, *Metaphysik L$_2$*, 28: 586 for a characteristic example) describe beauty as that which pleases 'according to universal laws of sensibility.' In none of these passages does Kant clearly explicate the intended reference of this phrase, but it is given a natural reading on the interpretation I have proposed: these universal laws of sensibility range over the properties associated with the features of our representations provided by the *a priori* forms of sensibility. A fuller investigation of this line of thought would be needed to bear out the claims I make in note 22 of Chapter 2. In general, Kant's characterization of beauty as 'enlivening' or 'stimulating' or 'animating' the cognitive faculties in the free play should be understood as follows: certain features of an object's form—insofar as they facilitate the apprehension and comprehension of the object—'enliven' or 'stimulate' or 'animate' the cognitive faculties in the sense of bearing out

reflective judgment's presumption that nature is as if made to the measure of our cognitive faculties. For Kant, beauty—as the notions of symmetry and proportionality themselves suggest—is a kind of *coherence*, a limiting case of our capacity to order and comprehend the sensible world, and it is precisely the presumption of this capacity that reflective judgment's principle of purposiveness encapsulates. These highly metaphorical descriptions of the free play should, on my reading, be understood as gesturing at the way in which the experience of beauty tends to confirm this presumption, thereby providing renewed strength and encouragement to our cognitive faculties for their overall task of ordering and comprehending the sensible world. See note 73 in Chapter 2.

[28] David Hills once claimed in conversation that on his view, Kant's aesthetic theory could drop the disinterestedness requirement altogether and keep the overall logic of its position intact. I do not know precisely what he had in mind, and I do not impute any aspect of the view I defend to him. In any event, I am grateful for the stimulating comment, which first prompted me to think more seriously about the role of transcendental idealism—rather than disinterestedness—in framing the overall logic of Kant's aesthetic theory.

[29] *Critique of the Power of Judgment*, § 58, 5: 346.

[30] The reference, of course, is to one aspect of the empiricist conception of the mind that Wilfred Sellars famously called 'The Myth of the Given.' For a sense of which aspects of Sellars' picture of empiricism are relevant to the Kantian themes I discuss here, the 'Introduction' to McDowell, *Mind and World*, is especially helpful. See also Sellars, 'Empiricism and the Philosophy of Mind.'

[31] Locke, *Essay Concerning Human Understanding*, Book II, Chapter i, § 3.

[32] *Prolegomena to Any Future Metaphysics*, 4: 299.

[33] Commentators have long been puzzled by Kant's choice of examples in this passage, particularly his use of the example 'the room is warm' as an instance of a judgment of perception that cannot become a judgment of experience. Part of the puzzlement certainly results from a lack of clarity concerning the contrast between these examples and examples such as 'the tower is red' from the *Jäsche Logik* (§ 40) (available in *Lectures on Logic*) that Kant thinks *can* become judgments of experience. See also the example of the 'green color of the meadow' in *Critique of the Power of Judgment*, § 3, 5: 206. The epistemological issues raised by an attempt to square these various discussions in a fully satisfactory way are inordinately complex, and I do not pretend to settle them here. For a very helpful account of the difficulties, and a maximally charitable attempt to resolve them, see Longuenesse, *Kant and the Capacity to Judge*, Chapter 7, especially pp. 188–95.

[34] *Critique of the Power of Judgment*, § 5, 5: 210.

[35] Ibid.

[36] To forestall a potential misunderstanding, I note that this line of thought should not be taken to imply that other animals cannot have any awareness of colors or tones. If *our* representations of colors or tones have or require intuitive form, then Kant's view will entail that other animals don't have the same representations of colors or tones that we do. His view will not, however, preclude the thought that, by means of mere sensation, animals can respond differentially to color stimuli or tone stimuli, and in that limited sense be said to 'perceive' them. Whether this should be counted as a form of genuine perception is a highly

contested issue in contemporary philosophy, about which I remain neutral for present purposes. However, I am both philosophically and interpretively sympathetic to the view of this issue presented in Young, 'Kant's View of Imagination,' pp. 149–50.

37 See note 27 in this chapter for citations in which Kant uses the phrase 'universal laws of sensibility' in connection with judgments of beauty.

38 For a helpful survey of the landscape of this debate, and a defense of a nonconceptualist reading, see Hanna, 'Kant and Non-Conceptual Content.' For a defense of conceptualism, see Ginsborg, 'Empirical Concepts and the Content of Experience' and 'Was Kant a Nonconceptualist?'

39 McDowell, *Mind and World*, pp. 46–7, famously claims that 'experience has its content by virtue of the drawing into operation, in sensibility, of capacities that are genuinely elements in a faculty of spontaneity.' It is clear that McDowell uses 'sensibility' to refer to *intuition*, not to mere sensation. Thus, McDowell's claim exemplifies the kind of 'conceptualist' reading that I find correct yet in danger of potentially overstating its point. I would emphasize that McDowell's claim should be read in a way that allows its construal of 'sensibility' to remain consistent with the distinction between the beautiful and the agreeable. Indeed, if the pleasures of the agreeable are those pleasures we can take in what is simply presented to us in sense experience, independently of any discursive mental activities, then the pleasures of beauty are those pleasures we can take in mental states that are *not* simply presented to us in sense experience, but rather require 'the drawing into operation, in sensibility, of capacities that are genuinely elements in a faculty of spontaneity.' In other words, a mental state can ground a judgment of beauty only if it is part of the judgeable content of experience in McDowell's sense. On my view, therefore, Kant's conception of beauty is precisely *not* evidence of any nonconceptual content. Compare the argument of Hanna, 'Kant and Non-Conceptual Content.'

I want to stress that my aim here is interpretive, and that I want to remain as philosophically neutral as possible on the contentious issues of these contemporary debates. In particular, I don't wish to enter the debate whether 'nonconceptual content' is rightfully called *content* in the first place. I wish only to make the point that some of our representations, or our awareness of some sensible qualities—those that figure in the paradigmatic cases of the agreeable—are given to us in sensation, independently of any discursive mental activity; others, however, are not. I do not mean to prejudge the debate about the philosophically correct language to use in describing any of these forms of awareness.

40 Stroud, *The Quest for Reality*, is helpful on this point. Stroud's discussion reflects the focus in contemporary philosophy on the case of color, but Stroud is quite careful to resist any attempt to generalize from color to any other so-called secondary qualities (p. 210). Stroud is acutely aware—more so than most contemporary philosophers—of the effects of a craving for generality in philosophical explanation. Indeed, Stroud points out a number of differences between color and sound that call for distinct treatments of these two cases (p. 210). In the Kantian context, however, the relevant question—for better or worse—is simply whether a representation (of a color or a tone) requires intuitive form in Kant's

technical sense or is properly construed as mere sensation. Thus, I prescind from the differences brought in by the contrast between spatiality and temporality in the two cases, but I do not mean to imply that a completely univocal account can or should be given.

[41] Of course, this presupposes that the source of norms for aesthetic claims is ultimately the same as the source of norms for cognitive claims, a view about which I have some reservations. Put differently, it requires that we construe the beautiful as pertaining, necessarily, only to that which can be a judgeable content of experience in something like McDowell's sense of this idea. This conception of the overall structure of a philosophical aesthetics is a core piece of what I call a 'broadly Kantian view,' and links it to the more general project of providing a nonnaturalistic account of our capacity to represent and make judgments about sensible qualities—an account of how we 'take up sensible data into . . . the space of reasons.' See Longuenesse, *Kant and the Capacity to Judge*, p. 398.

4. Some Varieties of Normativity

[1] See especially § 242 of Wittgenstein, *Philosophical Investigations* for Wittgenstein's use of this phrase. Details of the relevant secondary literature from these commentators can be found in the bibliography. Bell, 'The Art of Judgment,' presents a different understanding of how Wittgenstein's thought might bear on Kant's conception of aesthetic judgment. While I find Bell's paper stimulating, I have serious reservations about his interpretation of Wittgenstein.

[2] Stroud, 'Wittgenstein on Meaning, Understanding and Community,' p. 83.

[3] My discussion of Ginsborg's position in this section is based on §§ 2–3 of her 'Lawfulness without a Law.'

[4] The term 'precondition,' as I will use it, originally comes from Wittgenstein's phrase 'pre-condition of our language-game.' Stroud quotes it in the passage I cite in note 21 of this chapter. Stroud's citation—Wittgenstein, *Remarks on the Foundations of Mathematics*, § V; 7—is incorrect; the quotation comes from § VII; 9 of that work.

[5] To forestall a potential misunderstanding, I note that references to '*following* a rule,' from Wittgenstein or any of the commentators listed in note 1 of this chapter, should not be taken as confined to what Ginsborg calls being 'rule *guided*.' The notion of 'following a rule' can apply to either half of Ginsborg's distinction.

[6] Ginsborg, 'Lawfulness without a Law,' p. 60.

[7] Ibid.

[8] Ibid.

[9] Ibid.

[10] The terminology is from the *Jäsche Logik*, § 1 (available in *Lectures on Logic*).

[11] Ginsborg, 'Lawfulness without a Law,' p. 64.

[12] This theme appears ubiquitously in Wittgenstein's later writings but the following passages of *Philosophical Investigations* are of particular interest: §§ 224, 225, 227, 242, 569, 570; Part II, § xii.

13 A primitive recognition is not confined to human activities only; it also applies to natural things, specifically, to judgments about organisms made in normative terms. See Ginsborg, 'Lawfulness without a Law,' p. 62. I will not be concerned with this aspect of Ginsborg's argument, but I note that, for the kinds of normative judgments about organisms she discusses to make sense, there must be a way that such and such a kind of organism *generally* is. There is a notion of regularity required here that is analogous to the notion of agreement I explore in this chapter. In this connection, note further that the idea of constancy or regularity is part of the etymology of the word 'norm.' It derives from the Latin word *norma*, the original meaning of which was a carpenter's rule or T-square.

14 I find Ginsborg's claim that something that exemplifies rules 'constitute[s]' the standards for how it ought to be potentially misleading, in that it might suggest to one a reductive account of those standards. See Ginsborg, 'Lawfulness without a Law,' p. 63. I do not think that Ginsborg herself is misled; clearly, she takes normativity to involve more than *just* the presence of regularities. But I will systematically avoid this phrasing and will continue to speak of a practice as a precondition for its own normative standards, rather than as constitutive of them.

15 Guyer, *Kant and the Claims of Taste*, p. 146.

16 Ibid., pp. 146–7.

17 *Kritik der Urteilskraft*, § 22: 239. Guyer and Matthews translate this passage as follows: 'it does not say that everyone **will** concur with our judgment but that everyone **should** agree with it.' *Critique of the Power of Judgment*, p. 123 of their translation.

18 See Ginsborg, 'On the Key to Kant's Critique of Taste,' § 1, for Ginsborg's criticisms of Guyer. Guyer discusses this passage several times throughout *Kant and the Claims of Taste*, Chapter 4, and in *Kant and the Experience of Freedom*, p. 288. Whereas Guyer uses 'should' to translate *solle*, Ginsborg prefers the more unambiguously normative 'ought.' As should be clear, I believe Ginsborg's translation better captures Kant's meaning.

19 I am inclined to find the distinction between applying a concept and using a word somewhat artificial, as I am not inclined to think of the application of a concept in non- or extra-linguistic terms. Ginsborg, however, treats linguistic rules as distinct from rules for concept formation and use, and this distinction will be crucial in ways that emerge in Section 4 of this chapter.

20 Ginsborg, 'Lawfulness without a Law,' p. 51.

21 Stroud, 'Wittgenstein on Meaning, Understanding and Community,' p. 86.

22 Ginsborg formulated and pressed this example on me in a slightly different context, but I think it is very apt for present purposes.

23 For more on the issue of concept projection that has arisen in this section, see my 'Kantian Reflection and Ordinary Reflection' (unpublished manuscript), where I argue that the activity of projecting concepts into novel applications is one of the cognitive tasks that Kant assigns to the power of 'reflecting' or 'reflective' judgment [*reflektierende Urteilskraft*]. In the present context, the same issue arises in terms of discerning *how* normative standards that are set by the grasp of a concept one has already achieved are to be extended into difficult or unprecedented cases. I am equally happy to accept that as a characterization of one of reflecting judgment's tasks.

[24] Ginsborg, 'Lawfulness without a Law,' pp. 73–4.

[25] Ibid., p. 62.

[26] This requires qualification. In particular, the act of synthesis through which an empirical concept is first acquired will not be an act that conforms to any *antecedent* standard, as it is *through* that act of synthesis that the concept is acquired. Hence it is not available antecedently. However, any particular *application* of a concept that one already possesses will be such an act, and the act of acquiring an empirical concept still conforms to some *determinate* standard, even if it is not available antecedently. Thus, it still counts as a recognition of normativity in the derivative sense. See ibid., p. 69.

[27] Ibid., p. 63.

[28] Ibid. There are further features of the contrast between a primitive and derivative recognition. For instance, the rules that an activity exemplifies are in a certain sense arbitrary: English would be no less effective if the word 'knife' was used to mean what we mean by 'spoon.' See ibid, p. 61. I will not be concerned with all of the features of this contrast.

[29] Ibid., p. 63.

[30] Ibid., p. 73.

[31] See Ginsborg, 'Thinking the Particular as Contained under the Universal,' where she uses this terminology ubiquitously.

[32] Ibid., p. 73.

[33] Ginsborg, 'Lawfulness without a Law,' p. 66.

[34] Ibid.

[35] Ibid.

[36] Ibid., p. 64.

[37] But see the passage from 'Lawfulness without a Law,' p. 64, cited in note 11 of this chapter, for a formulation that employs the first-person plural. The plural phrase 'our imagination' could be meant to express the idea of imaginative activity manifesting shared, natural dispositions—an idea of Ginsborg's that I will soon explore. But it is impossible to say for sure. Indeed, that's part of the problem: it isn't clear whether Ginsborg intends the fact of agreement to function in her argument about cognitive norms as it does in her argument about linguistic norms.

[38] The particular way of articulating the suggestion I am about to give derives from Ginsborg's comments on a previous draft of my argument, although we'll see that the elements of the objection are present in her published work—and in deep tension with other aspects of her published views. So I do not ascribe any settled view to her.

[39] Ginsborg, 'Thinking the Particular as Contained under the Universal,' p. 51 (my emphasis).

[40] Ibid.

[41] Wittgenstein, *Philosophical Investigations*, § 202.

[42] Ibid., § 198.

[43] Ginsborg, 'Thinking the Particular as Contained under the Universal,' p. 55. See also pp. 48–9, where Ginsborg 'amends' the idea that we are simply aware of 'actual psychological processes and tendencies in [ourselves]' to include the idea that one *takes* these processes and tendencies to be appropriate.

44 I take this to be the point of Ginsborg's central thesis that the capacity to take one's representations to be intersubjectively valid is presupposed by the capacity to form empirical concepts, which are, after all, ways of characterizing *objective* features of things, not subjective features of representations. See ibid., especially § 1; Ginsborg, 'Reflective Judgment and Taste,' § 2; Ginsborg, 'Lawfulness without a Law,' § 2.

45 Strictly speaking, the proposal under scrutiny doesn't even require this much. But it would be totally implausible to take the idea of normativity to be applicable in its absence: if people's cognitive dispositions or performances changed from moment to moment, it would be irremediably unclear how any normative notions were supposed to apply. So I impute this minimal requirement to Ginsborg mainly on the basis of interpretive charity.

46 *Critique of the Power of Judgment,* § 6, 5: 211.

47 Ginsborg, 'Thinking the Particular as Contained under the Universal,' p. 59. It is clear, moreover, that Ginsborg does not offer this merely as a reading of Kant.

48 I opt to describe these as 'features of my own personal psychological constitution' rather than as 'contingent features of my psychology' because *all* the features of my psychology—including any that I might share with all human beings—are of course contingent. It isn't necessary that human beings have any of the particular psychological features that they, in general, happen to have.

49 Compare Ginsborg, 'Thinking the Particular as Contained under the Universal,' § IV, especially pp. 57–8: 'The fact of our shared natural dispositions enables us to agree . . . on a shared set of concepts.'

50 This claim, and the discussion of it to follow in Section 5, is heavily indebted to Diamond, 'Rules: Looking in the Right Place.' In discussing the literature on Wittgenstein's notion of 'following a rule,' Diamond complains that the literature is in general confused, and that 'such confusion is fed by the abstracting of "agreement" from the life into which it is woven' (p. 33). Consequently, we characteristically ask 'What does enable us to talk about right?' rather than 'What is it like for there to be talk about right, what does that talk look like in human life?' (p. 27). Diamond argues that asking after the necessary conditions for the possibility of rules is the wrong inquiry. What we should do is rather *describe* what our life-with-rules is actually like. That is what I shall be attempting to do in the next section, by a kind of reverse projection. I agree with Diamond that an account of necessary and/or sufficient conditions for normative rules is the wrong kind of question to ask. So the idea of a 'precondition' that I have been employing needs to be understood in a very particular sense, namely, that agreement is a part of the surroundings within which our conception of normative rules functions, and within which it makes the sense that it does. I believe that is the sense in which Wittgenstein uses it as well.

The difference between taking agreement to be *part of* our life-with-normativity, as it were, and to be a *logically necessary condition* for something—precisely the confusion Diamond wants to reject—is indeed widespread, and a version of this confusion is even codified in Anscombe's mistranslation of § 242 of the *Philosophical Investigations*. Wittgenstein says there, 'Zur Verständigung durch die Sprache gehört nicht nur eine Übereinstimmung in den Definitionen, sondern (so seltsam dies klingen mag) eine Übereinstimmung in den Urteilen.' Anscombe translates Wittgenstein's use of *gehören zu* as 'must,' when its meaning is 'to belong to,' in the sense of something being a part of something. That is *not* to say that something is a logically necessary condition. Furthermore, astute readers will have noticed that the objection I have formulated against Ginsborg's proposal is a version of the famous paradox of § 198. I do not mean to imply that positing agreement 'solves' the paradox by providing a needed 'condition' for the possibility of correctness and incorrectness. Rather, my point is that it is only when we attempt to disengage the notion of 'following a rule' from the notion of 'agreement' that we land in the predicament of § 198, because we are attempting to treat the former notion in abstraction from one of its constituent parts, abstracting it from the surroundings within which it functions. When we stop doing so, the so-called paradox reveals itself to be a specious appearance of a problem.

⁵¹ The phrase 'characteristic surroundings,' of course, comes from Wittgenstein, *Remarks on the Foundations of Mathematics*, § VI; 21. In Wittgenstein's passage, the phrase refers to the 'peaceful agreement' that surrounds 'the use of the word "same."' It is precisely some salient aspects of this 'peaceful agreement' that I describe in this section.

⁵² Wittgenstein, *Philosophical Investigations*, § 185.

⁵³ The argument of this paragraph is especially indebted to Diamond, 'Rules: Looking in the Right Place,' § III, especially pp. 16–17.

⁵⁴ The distinction drawn in this paragraph comes from Wittgenstein, *Philosophical Investigations*, Part II, § xii.

⁵⁵ See ibid, Part II, § xi, where Wittgenstein draws a distinction between imagining the practices of beings quite different from us, and being able to adopt and engage those practices as our own. It is the latter that he claims we are sometimes unable to do. Commenting on some aspects of what we can imagine [*sich denken*] about the beings of our philosophical thought experiments, Wittgenstein says, 'Wir können uns nicht in sie finden.' The same point applies to the Sorters, with respect to *our* conception of universally valid normative rules. In this connection, see also Diamond, 'Rules: Looking in the Right Place'; Cavell, *The Claim of Reason*, Chapter V; Stroud, 'Wittgenstein and Logical Necessity,' especially pp. 6–15; Stroud, 'The Allure of Idealism,' especially pp. 93–5.

⁵⁶ I owe the phrase 'normative being,' and this rough characterization of its meaning, to a discussion with Cora Diamond.

⁵⁷ See Wittgenstein, *Philosophical Investigations*, Part II, § xii.

⁵⁸ *Critique of the Power of Judgment*, § 6, 5: 211.

⁵⁹ I am grateful to David Hills for pointing out the significance of the pleasures of involuntary memory in this context. He also suggested—and I think he is correct—that the pleasures of involuntary memory drive a conceptual wedge between the notions of disinterestedness and freedom from idiosyncrasy. The Taste of the Madeline, or some such pleasure, is of course disinterested, yet it is also as idiosyncratic as pleasures get.

⁶⁰ *Critique of the Power of Judgment*, § 6, 5: 211.

⁶¹ A full elaboration of this point would require a detailed examination of Kant's idea of taste as a 'common sense' [*Gemeinsinn*]. It is clear that Kant does think the (pure) judgment of taste is based on conditions common to human beings in general. In describing this kind of judgment, he writes, 'One solicits assent from

everybody else because one has a ground for it that is common to all; one could even count on this assent if only one were always sure that the case were correctly subsumed under that ground as the rule of approval,' *Critique of the Power of Judgment*, § 19, 5: 237. And in § 21 Kant argues that a common sense 'must be able to be assumed with good reason, and indeed without appeal to psychological observations, but rather as the necessary condition of the universal communicability of our cognition, which is assumed in every logic and every principle of cognitions that is not skeptical,' Ibid, § 21, 5: 239. Kant's discussion makes clear that there could only be normative claims of taste on the presupposition that there are conditions common to us all in virtue of which we take pleasure in the experience of certain objects, and that those conditions are the same conditions in virtue of which we are capable of empirical cognition.

It is unclear to me how Ginsborg's account of natural dispositions and the primitive appreciation of their appropriateness avoids the kinds of 'psychological observations' that Kant disallows in § 21. However, Ginsborg elsewhere makes clear that she does not think that the sense in which the judgment of taste is based on conditions common to all is one that can be ascertained or supported by any appeal psychological or empirical observations. See her criticisms of Guyer's 'two-acts view' in 'On the Key to Kant's Critique of Taste,' pp. 292–7. I think a two-acts view that did not count an empirical or predictive claim as part of the *content* of a judgment of taste could evade many of Ginsborg's criticisms, for the reasons discussed in § 2 of this chapter. One could call it a 'two-acts view with normativity,' and that is the view toward which I am most inclined.

Remarks like the one from § 19 also suggest to me that something like Guyer's ideal prediction model is (interpretively) correct—but for various forms of opacity in our mental lives, we would achieve general agreement in matters of taste. That is not to say that Guyer is correct to include this ideal prediction within the content of a judgment of taste. But an account of opacity can helpfully function as part of an explanation of why—given that the judgment of taste is based on conditions common to us all, as cognizers, so to speak—we find so much less agreement in particular questions of taste than we find in ordinary cognitive or matter-of-fact questions. Thus, I agree with Guyer's account of opacity, and with the idea of an ideal prediction, minus the placement of that prediction within the content of the judgment of taste, which I follow Ginsborg in taking to be a normative claim.

For Guyer's discussion of the idea of opacity, see *Kant and the Claims of Taste*, pp. 103–5. For dissenting views, on which our pleasures are not opaque but rather transparent to us, or 'intentional,' see Ginsborg, 'On the Key to Kant's Critique of Taste,' especially pp. 300–3, and 'Aesthetic Judging and the Intentionality of Pleasure'; Allison, *Kant's Theory of Taste*, especially pp. 53–4, and 'Reply to Comments of Longuenesse and Ginsborg.'

[62] Ginsborg, 'Lawfulness without a Law,' p. 72.

[63] Ibid, p. 70. When discussing the imaginative activity involved in a judgment of taste, Ginsborg's formulations do not shift between singular and plural first-person formulations, as they do when discussing the imaginative activity involved in empirical cognition (see notes 12 and 38 of this chapter). This is some evidence—though by no means conclusive—that Ginsborg does not intend agreement to be taken as a part or precondition of the idea of norms for taste.

64 Ibid., p. 74.
65 Ibid.
66 Ibid.
67 Ibid.
68 I think we would do well to heed Hume's warning that language may well mislead
    us when we ask how much agreement there is in matters of taste:

> As this variety of taste is obvious to the most careless inquirer; so will it be
> found, on examination, to be still greater in reality than in appearance. The
> sentiments of men often differ with regard to beauty and deformity of
> all kinds, even while their general discourse is the same. (Hume, 'Of the
> Standard of Taste,' p. 2)

Indeed, the question of how much agreement there is in matters of taste is
more complicated to answer than one might initially think, and we should not be
too hasty to find commonality or consensus among us in matters of taste; a cursory survey of responses from people as to whether or not some particular object
is beautiful is apt to give the appearance of more consensus than there genuinely
is. For instance, if you ask whether a particular flower is beautiful (to take one of
Kant's favorite examples), some people who answer 'yes' may well mean that it is
has a beautiful *color*; others may mean that it has a beautiful *shape*; there are
undoubtedly further possibilities as well. The word 'beautiful' does not have a
fixed and settled meaning in our ordinary discourse; an object that one is willing
to call beautiful may, for that person, be beautiful in any number of different
aspects, and we cannot presume that there is some particular aspect—say the
thing's shape or 'form'—that one is responding to. The word 'beautiful' routinely means different things coming from the mouths of different people, or
even the same person at different times. But to say that something has a beautiful
color is obviously not the same as to say that it has a beautiful shape, and it is
therefore unjustified to take these people to agree simply because they both say
that the flower is beautiful.

69 An individualistic approach to cognitive norms may well be the result of thinking
    of concept formation and use on a non- or extra-linguistic model (see note 20 in
    this chapter). But this question is beyond the scope of the present chapter.
70 On the issue of the attunement of our cognitive faculties, and the importance of this
    fact for the efficacy of our attempts to communicate with one another, see Cavell,
    The Claim of Reason, Chapters V and VII, and 'The Availability of Wittgenstein's
    Later Philosophy,' especially pp. 51–2.
71 See Diamond, 'Rules: Looking in the Right Place.' On the differences between
    this style of approach, which one might call Wittgensteinian, and a Kantian
    transcendental approach, which takes as central a question of what justifies
    or legitimates a certain kind of claim, see Stroud, 'The Allure of Idealism,'
    pp. 83–98.
72 See especially the arguments of *Critique of the Power of Judgment*, §§ 9, 21.
73 It is probably the case that Kant himself thinks of cognitive norms on what I have
    called the individualistic model. Alternatively, this point can be put by saying that

agreement in the thin intersubjective sense may be all that Kant requires for nor-mativity in the cognitive realm. That would be consistent with Kant thinking of empirical concepts and cognition on a non- or extra-linguistic model. If that is true, it would speak in favor of adopting Ginsborg's 'proposal' rather than her 'suggestion.' That would indeed bring the cognitive and aesthetic applications of the primitive-recognition model into line, but at the price of disengaging them both from the analogy to natural languages. More importantly, though, I think it will misconstrue the role that normative claims play within the cognitive affairs of human life.

[74] See Wittgenstein, *Philosophical Investigations*, Part II, § xii.

[75] This approach to understanding the significance of judgments of taste, and the reinterpretation of their normative dimension it requires, is radically different from Kant's own approach. I have sketched the beginnings of such an approach, programmatically but less so than here, in my 'Taste and Human Attunement' (unpublished manuscript). I am indebted to the writings of Stanley Cavell for provocation in this line of thought, especially his 'Aesthetic Problems of Modern Philosophy.' I am also indebted to the global summary of Cavell's views on aesthetics sketched concisely in Chapter 1 of Mulhall, *Stanley Cavell.* Pippin, 'The Significance of Taste: Kant, Aesthetic and Reflective Judgment' has been particu-larly useful in helping me place my own conception of the normative dimension of taste with respect to Kant's. Chapter 1 of Bernstein, *The Fate of Art,* argues for a conception of the normative dimension of taste that has some affinities with my own as well as with Cavell's. I have many reservations about his analysis, but have found it very thought provoking.

Bibliography

Allison, Henry E. *Kant's Theory of Taste: A Reading of the Critique of Aesthetic Judgment.* Cambridge: Cambridge University Press, 2001.

—. 'Reply to the Comments of Longuenesse and Ginsborg.' *Inquiry* 46 (2003): 182–94.

Bell, David. 'The Art of Judgment.' *Mind* 96 (1987): 221–44.

Bennett, Jonathan. *Kant's Analytic.* Cambridge: Cambridge University Press, 1966.

Berger, David. 'Kantian Reflection and Ordinary Reflection' (unpublished manuscript).

—. 'Taste and Human Attunement' (unpublished manuscript).

Bernstein, J. M. *The Fate of Art: Aesthetic Alienation from Kant to Derrida and Adorno.* University Park: Pennsylvania State University Press, 1992.

Cavell, Stanley. 'Aesthetic Problems of Modern Philosophy.' In *Must We Mean What We Say? A Book of Essays.* Cambridge: Cambridge University Press, 1976.

—. 'The Availability of Wittgenstein's Later Philosophy.' In *Must We Mean What We Say? A Book of Essays.* Cambridge: Cambridge University Press, 1976.

—. *The Claim of Reason: Wittgenstein, Skepticism, Morality, and Tragedy.* Oxford: Oxford University Press, 1979.

—. *A Pitch of Philosophy: Autobiographical Exercises.* Cambridge: Harvard University Press, 1994.

Diamond, Cora. 'Rules: Looking in the Right Place.' In *Wittgenstein: Attention to Particulars*, edited by D. Z. Phillips and Peter Winch, 12–34. New York: St. Martin's Press, 1989.

Evans, Gareth. 'Things without the Mind.' In *Philosophical Subjects: Essays Presented to P. F. Strawson*, edited by Zak van Staaten, 76–116. Oxford: Clarendon Press, 1980.

—. *The Varieties of Reference.* Edited by John McDowell. Oxford: Oxford University Press, 1982.

Gammon, Martin. '*Parerga and Pulchritudo Adhaerens*: A Reading of the Third Moment of the "Analytic of the Beautiful."' *Kant-Studien* 90 (1999): 148–67.

Ginsborg, Hannah. 'Aesthetic Judging and the Intentionality of Pleasure.' *Inquiry* 46 (2003): 164–81.

—. 'Empirical Concepts and the Content of Experience.' *European Journal of Philosophy* 14 (2006): 349–72.

—. 'Lawfulness without a Law: Kant on the Free Play of Imagination and Understanding.' *Philosophical Topics* 25 (1997): 37–81.

—. 'On the Key to Kant's Critique of Taste.' *Pacific Philosophical Quarterly* 72 (1991): 290–313.

—. 'Reflective Judgment and Taste.' *Noûs* 24 (1990): 63–78.

—. 'Thinking the Particular as Contained under the Universal.' In *Aesthetics and Cognition in Kant's Critical Philosophy*, edited by Rebecca Kukla, 35–60. Cambridge: Cambridge University Press, 2006.

—. 'Was Kant a Non-Conceptualist?' *Philosophical Studies* 137 (2008): 65–77.

Guyer, Paul. *Kant and Claims of Knowledge*. Cambridge: Cambridge University Press, 1987.

—. *Kant and the Claims of Taste*. Second Edition. Cambridge: Cambridge University Press, 1997.

—. *Kant and the Experience of Freedom: Essays on Aesthetics and Morality*. Cambridge: Cambridge University Press, 1993.

—. *Values of Beauty: Historical Essays in Aesthetics*. Cambridge: Cambridge University Press, 2005.

Hanna, Robert. 'Kant and Non-Conceptual Content.' *European Journal of Philosophy* 13 (2005): 247–90.

Hume, David. 'Of the Standard of Taste.' In *Of the Standard of Taste and Other Essays*, edited with an Introduction by John W. Lenz. Indianapolis: Library of Liberal Arts, 1965.

Kant, Immanuel. *Anthropology from a Pragmatic Point of View*. Translated by Victor Lyle Dowdell. Carbondale: Southern Illinois University Press, 1978.

—. *Critique of Judgment*. Translated by Werner S. Pluhar. Indianapolis and Cambridge: Hackett, 1987.

—. *Critique of the Power of Judgment*. Edited by Paul Guyer, translated by Paul Guyer and Eric Matthews. Cambridge: Cambridge University Press, 2000.

—. *Critique of Pure Reason*. Translated and edited by Paul Guyer and Allen W. Wood. Cambridge: Cambridge University Press, 1998.

—. *Kants Gesammelte Schriften*. Herausgegeben von der Deutschen (formerly: Königlichen Preussischen) Akademie der Wissenschaften, 29 volumes. Berlin: Walter de Gruyter, 1902—.

—. *Lectures on Logic*. Translated and edited by J. Michael Young. Cambridge: Cambridge University Press, 1992.

—. *Lectures on Metaphysics*. Translated and edited by Karl Ameriks and Steve Naragon. Cambridge: Cambridge University Press, 1997.

—. *Metaphysical Foundations of Natural Science*. Translated and edited by Michael Friedman. Cambridge: Cambridge University Press, 2004.

—. *Practical Philosophy*. Translated and edited by Mary J. Gregor. Cambridge: Cambridge University Press, 1996.

—. *Prolegomena to Any Future Metaphysics*. Translated and edited by Gary Hatfield. Cambridge: Cambridge University Press, 1997.

Locke, John. *An Essay Concerning Human Understanding*. Edited with an Introduction by Peter H. Nidditch. Oxford: Clarendon Press, 1975.

Longuenesse, Béatrice. *Kant and the Capacity to Judge: Sensibility and Discursivity in the Transcendental Analytic of the Critique of Pure Reason*. Translated by Charles T. Wolfe. Princeton: Princeton University Press, 1998.

—. 'Kant's Leading Thread in the Analytic of the Beautiful.' In *Aesthetics and Cognition in Kant's Critical Philosophy*, edited by Rebecca Kukla, 35–60. Cambridge: Cambridge University Press, 2006.

—. 'Kant's Theory of Judgment, and Judgments of Taste.' *Inquiry* 46 (2003): 143–63.

McDowell, John. *Mind and World.* Cambridge: Harvard University Press, 1994.

Meerbote, Ralph. 'Reflection on Beauty.' In *Essays in Kant's Aesthetics*, edited by Ted Cohen and Paul Guyer, 21–54. Chicago: University of Chicago Press, 1982.

Minar, Edward. 'Paradox and Privacy: On §§ 201–202 of Wittgenstein's *Philosophical Investigations.*' *Philosophy and Phenomenological Research* 54 (1994): 43–75.

—. 'Wittgenstein and the "Contingency" of Community.' *Pacific Philosophical Quarterly* 72 (1991): 203–34.

Mulhall, Stephen. *Stanley Cavell: Philosophy's Recounting of the Ordinary.* Oxford: Clarendon Press, 1994.

Nietzsche, Friedrich. *On the Genealogy of Morals and Ecce Homo.* Translated by Walter Kaufmann and R. J. Hollingdale; edited, with commentary, by Walter Kaufmann. New York: Random House, 1967.

Pippin, Robert B. 'The Significance of Taste: Kant, Aesthetic and Reflective Judgment.' *Journal of the History of Philosophy* 34 (1996): 549–69.

Randel, Dan, ed. *The New Harvard Dictionary of Music.* Cambridge: Harvard University Press, 1986.

Rush, Fred L., Jr. 'The Harmony of the Faculties.' *Kant-Studien* 92 (2001): 38–61.

Schaper, Eva. 'The Pleasures of Taste.' In *Pleasure, Preference and Value: Studies in Philosophical Aesthetics*, edited by Eva Schaper, 39–56. Cambridge: Cambridge University Press, 1983.

Sellars, Wilfred. 'Empiricism and the Philosophy of Mind.' In *Minnesota Studies in the Philosophy of Science*, vol. 1, edited by Herbert Feigl and Michael Scriven, 253–329. Minneapolis: University of Minnesota Press, 1956.

Strawson, P. F. *The Bounds of Sense.* London: Methuen, 1966.

—. 'Imagination and Perception.' In *Freedom and Resentment and Other Essays*, 45–65. London: Methuen, 1974.

—. *Individuals: An Essay in Descriptive Metaphysics.* London: Routledge, 1959.

Stroud, Barry. 'The Allure of Idealism.' In *Understanding Human Knowledge: Philosophical Essays*, 83–98. Oxford: Oxford University Press, 2000.

—. *The Quest for Reality: Subjectivism and the Metaphysics of Colour.* Oxford: Oxford University Press, 2000.

—. 'Wittgenstein and Logical Necessity.' In *Meaning, Understanding, and Practice: Philosophical Essays*, 1–16. Oxford: Oxford University Press, 2000.

—. 'Wittgenstein on Meaning, Understanding, and Community.' In *Meaning, Understanding, and Practice: Philosophical Essays*, 80–94. Oxford: Oxford University Press, 2000.

Wittgenstein, Ludwig. *Philosophical Investigations.* Second Edition. Edited and Translated by G. E. M. Anscombe. New York: Macmillan, 1958.

—. *Remarks on the Foundations of Mathematics.* Revised Edition. Edited by G. H. von Wright, R. Rhees and G. E. M. Anscombe; translated by G. E. M. Anscombe. Cambridge, MA: MIT Press, 1978.

Yiddish Radio Project. 'Bei Mir Bist Du Schoen.' Yiddish Radio Project.www.yiddishradioproject.org/exhibits/ymis/ymis.php?pg=2 (accessed October 20, 2008).

Young, J. Michael. 'Kant's View of Imagination.' *Kant-Studien* 79 (1988): 140–64.

Zuckert, Rachel. 'A New Look at Kant's Theory of Pleasure.' *The Journal of Aesthetics and Art Criticism* 60 (2002): 239–52.

Index